CHANGING
PLACES

TRAVELS IN A VANISHING WORLD

JEFF APPELQUIST

AWARD-WINNING AUTHOR OF
SACRED GROUND

ISBN-13: 978-1-63489-233-9

Cover and interior design by Emily Rodvold

Printed in the United States of America
First Printing: 2019

23   22   21   20   19   5   4   3   2   1

WISE *Ink*
CREATIVE ★ PUBLISHING

Wise Ink Creative Publishing
807 Broadway St. NE, Suite 46
Minneapolis, MN 55413
www.wiseink.com

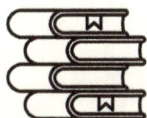

ALSO BY JEFF APPELQUIST

NONFICTION

Sacred Ground: Leadership Lessons from Gettysburg & the Little Bighorn

Wisdom Is Not Enough: Reflections on Leadership & Teams

Legacy of Excellence: A Centennial History of the Toro Company

FICTION

The Great Wild West: An American Journey

**TO MY WIFE, BEST FRIEND AND
ALL-TIME TRAVEL BUDDY:
FAITH**

"It's just you and me, kid..."

"One generation passeth away, and another generation cometh: but the earth abideth forever."

— ECCLESIASTES 1:4 —

"The environment, after all, is where we all meet, where we all have a mutual interest. It is one thing that all of us share. It is not only a mirror of ourselves, but a focusing lens on what we can become."

— LADY BIRD JOHNSON —

"One of the gladdest moments in life, methinks is the departure upon a distant journey into unknown lands. Shaking off with one mighty effort the fetters of habit, the leaden weight of routine, the cloak of many cares and the slavery of home, man feels once more happy... The blood flows with the fast circulation of childhood... afresh dawns the morn of life."

— SIR RICHARD FRANCIS BURTON —

"Adventure is worthwhile."

— AESOP —

"Adventure is just bad planning."

— ROALD AMUNDSON —

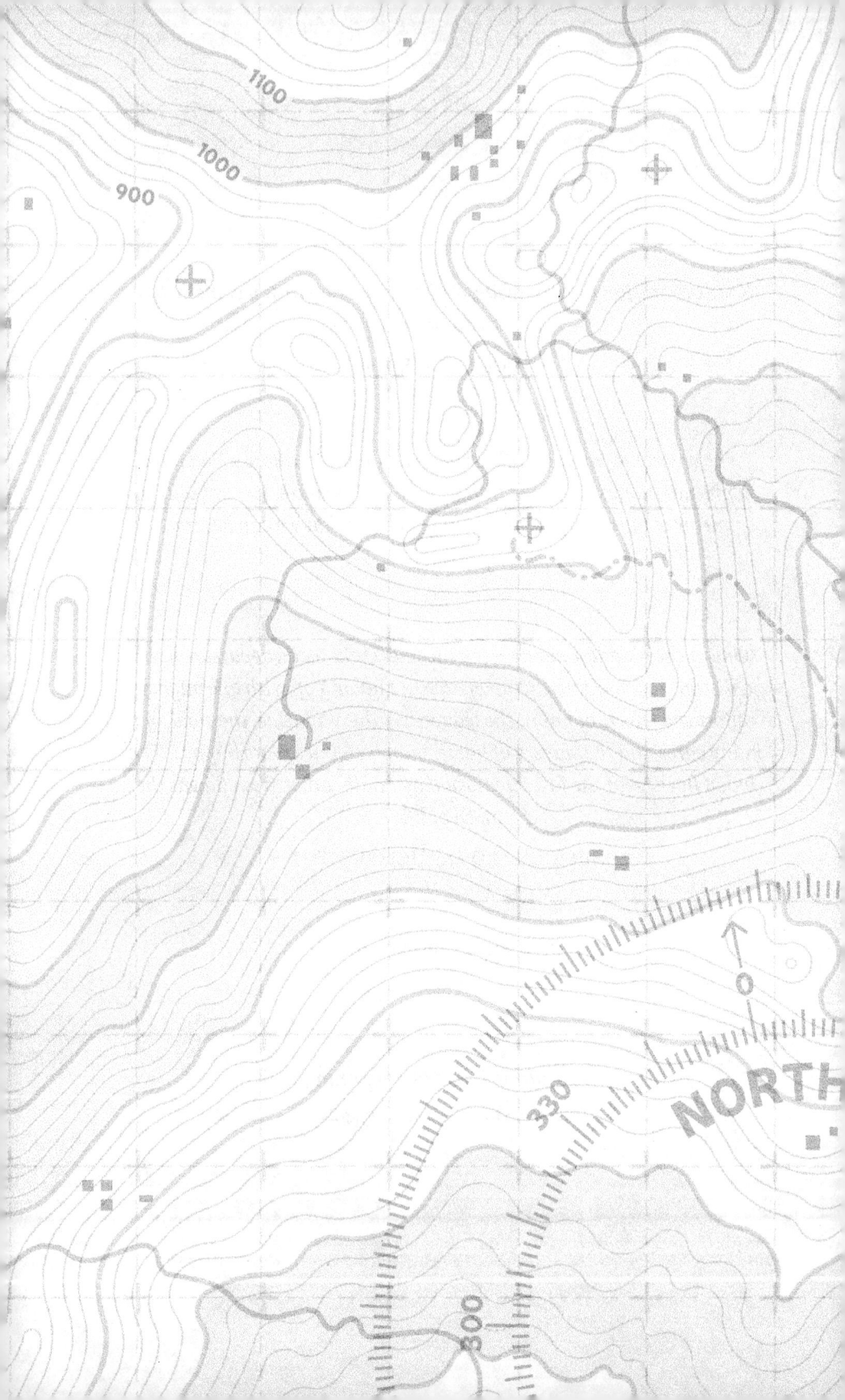

TABLE OF CONTENTS

Introduction 1

MOTHER GREEN THE KILLING MACHINE 4

THE ROOF OF AFRICA 17

A NIGHT AT THE OPERA 39

DÉJÀ VU ALL OVER AGAIN 51

BOTTLED POETRY 60

OCEAN QUEST 73

HUNT 'EM UP! 79

DOWN UNDER 92

SACRED GROUND 112

LAND OF FIRE & ICE 127

PARADISE OF THE PACIFIC 150

AWE 180

COWS, COLLEGES & CONTENTMENT 187

CAYO HUEUSA 197

THE INCA TRAIL 206

THE LAST BEST PLACE 225

HIGH COTTON 241

QUATTOUR AMICUS 264

Conclusion 273

Acknowledgments 285

Photo Credits, Et Cetera 286

INTRODUCTION

"We are on the side of science, on the side of facts, and on the side of the planet."

— NATIONAL GEOGRAPHIC VISION STATEMENT —

I am a truly lucky man who has had the opportunity to travel all over America and the world in my six-plus decades of life. Augustine of Hippo (whoever the heck that guy was) is supposed to have said, "The world is a book and those who do not travel read only one page." And Annie Dillard says, "The point of going somewhere like the Napo River in Ecuador is not to see the most spectacular anything. It is simply to see what is there. We are here on the planet only once, and might as well get a feel for the place." I agree.

In several instances described in this book, I have had death-defying experiences. But for the most part, the travel stories contained herein represent pretty standard stuff. Most of the time, like most travelers, I am just a regular tourist, trying to see the sights, be respectful, learn from other cultures and, hopefully, not acting like an "Ugly American." The talented and extremely funny travel writer Mark Adams identifies a certain type of person whom he has encountered in his journeys. He has contempt for and makes fun of this person. He calls this person, "Mr. Super Deluxe Travel Guy." This guy buys all the most expensive gear, takes the easiest, least hazardous, and most luxurious route on every trip, never interacting with the locals while being majorly stressed-out and refusing to untether from his phone, his laptop, and corporate headquarters back home. Gosh, I hope I am not that guy, because that guy is clearly an asshole.

On the other hand, Hiram Bingham, the Yale history professor who "discovered" Machu Picchu in 1911 (he was guided to the site by local Peruvians, for crying out loud, and there were people living there when he showed up with his camera) has been described by some as a "Martini Explorer." Now this is the guy who has done his research and is willing to work and pay close attention during the day while he travels – he might even be willing to take a risk or two; but he also likes to unwind with a cocktail(s) and a nice meal in comfortable accommodations when the day is done. Okay, okay, I admit it: I might be that guy. But I mean well.

Speaking of food and wine, you will notice my keen interest throughout the book in food and wine. Generally, I prefer good food and wine, but I am willing to try just about anything once. In the course of my travels I have eaten squirrel, bear, cat, octopus, whale, wild boar, kangaroo, crocodile, goat, alpaca (cousin of llama), cuy (guinea pig) and lots of kimchi. I drank a beer in Iceland containing "essence of whale testicles." Who knew? This pursuit of new flavors has been really interesting, edifying and, occasionally, gastrointestinally disruptive.

The other, more serious focus of the book is on climate change and, specifically, the existential crisis that is global warming. I am no climate scientist. All of my formal academic training is in the humanities (political science, public policy and administration, law). But like the vast majority of Americans, I am a thinking, caring citizen. I know what I read about scientific consensus, and what I have seen with my own eyes in my journeys around the world. I readily acknowledge that climate science is complicated - but I am also certain that climate change is real, it is upon us, and we human beings bear significant responsibility. It will be up to us to fix it, but there is no time to lose. I try in these chapters not to plead or be annoyingly preachy, but we've got a big problem folks, and we need to face it head on.

Some who read this book may assume that I don't like Republicans. Nothing could be further from the truth. I am myself a political independent who generally toggles somewhere in the middle, leaning right on some issues and left on others. I have voted for Republicans, Democrats and Independents. Some of my best friends are staunch Republicans (really). So, some will say I just don't like Trump supporters. Again, untrue. This is America, and we are all entitled to vote for any candidate we choose. That's one of the multitude of reasons why it's a great country – and always has been. If I didn't get along with Trump supporters, I would never have lasted as long as I have in business. I know some really smart Trump supporters. A few of them may even be stable geniuses.

INTRODUCTION

The people that I struggle with, regardless of political affiliation, are those who deny the reality of global warming, who think that it is somehow a hoax, and who either don't care or, even worse, actively undertake to reverse whatever progress we've made in our battle to save the earth. Those are the folks that give me heartburn.

This book was written between 2016 and early 2019, and describes travel experiences going back as far as my Marine Corps days in the early 1980s. The chapters were neither written nor are they presented in any particular chronological order. Every chapter represents a point in time and has not been subsequently updated; whatever was happening in the world or was on my mind at the time I wrote that chapter, well, that's what you get dear reader. The stories in this book reflect my best recollection of events. Some names, locations, and identifying characteristics have been changed to protect the privacy of those depicted. Dialogue has been re-created, as best I could do it, from my journal notes or from memory.

This book is intended primarily as an engaging and, hopefully, educational travel romp. There is also a healthy dose of history – my favorite subject - in each chapter. I hope it will resonate with any person who possesses a spirit of adventure and curiosity about the world. But just as importantly, it also represents my best effort as an earnest statement – from a regular citizen's point of view - about the dire and imminent danger presented by climate change. My hope is that the book will inspire people to strive to be on the side of science, on the side of facts, and on the side of the planet. My hope is that the book will be a call to action for anyone who cares about the future of Mother Earth. Finally, my hope is that people, communities and nations will strive to do whatever it is that they can do, individually and collectively, to help us save the planet for our children and all succeeding generations. Let's not all of us commit suicide together, okay? Can we do it? I don't know, but I sure hope so. Let the journey begin.

Jeff Appelquist
Minneapolis, Minnesota
March 2019

CHAPTER ONE

MOTHER GREEN THE KILLING MACHINE

DIEGO GARCIA, INDIAN OCEAN

"From the Halls of Montezuma
To the shores of Tripoli;
We fight our country's battles
In the air, on land, and sea..."

— FROM THE "MARINE CORPS HYMN" —

*T*here we was. Diego Garcia. Southeast Asia Theater. India Company, Third Battalion, Ninth Marines, First Mar Div. Spring of '83. All kinda maritime prepositioned war gear, just sittin' on ships in the lagoon. Smack dab in the middle of the vasty reaches of the Indian Ocean. But undefended...

Every Marine knows that all great sea stories begin with the words, "There we was..." Grammatically incorrect, yes, but that doesn't matter. What's important is that the phrase is uttered in a soft, conspiratorial way with a kind of slow, guttural "grrrrr," like the guy telling the story is a crusty old one-eyed pirate or something. And he's letting you in on a special secret. Every Marine knows this. When those words are spoken every Marine smiles, takes a sip of cold beer, and settles in to hear a story.

$\longleftrightarrow$

When I was a young man, I had the opportunity and high honor to serve America as a Marine Corps infantry officer. I gave three years of my life in the early 1980s. Like perhaps most males in their early 20s, I was supremely sure that I was both indestructible and immortal. I could not be destroyed and, therefore, would never die - this is precisely why old men, who know better, send young men off to war. Only a few years removed from our disaster in Vietnam, the most challenging job in the toughest branch of service would suit me just fine, thank you very much. People thought I was batshit crazy for volunteering - this was during an era when "thank you for your service" was not in the national lexicon - and maybe I was. What I do know for certain is that I was a dumbass. But I was also lucky. I survived.

Training consisted of six weeks of Officer Candidate School in Quantico, Virginia, during each of the summers after my sophomore and junior years in college. I was commissioned a second lieutenant upon graduation, then entered The Basic School, also in Quantico, for the (then) 21-week overview course through which the Marine Corps sends all its new officers. Every Marine lieutenant is trained first as an infantryman.

I selected infantry as my military occupational specialty - designated MOS 0302, a ground pounder I would be - and went through eight weeks of additional training called the Infantry Officers' Course. At long last, after all of this, the U.S. government, probably still reluctantly, was finally willing to let me be near an enlisted Marine.

I received my assignment to the Fleet Marine Force as a rifle platoon leader with Lima Company of the Third Battalion, Ninth Regiment (we were known as "Striking 3/9") of the First Marine Division. I drove my 1981 Ford Mustang – with every worldly possession smashed into the back seat and the trunk - cross country to my new duty station at Camp Pendleton in sunlit, hardscrabble southern California.

While in truth it took me fully two years of struggle to mature and get on track as a military officer, I enjoyed the entire experience thoroughly - the challenge, camaraderie and adventure of it. I had no illusions as to what we did for a living. We were in the business of organized murder on a very large and sophisticated scale. We were the men of the USMC, Uncle Sam's Misguided Children; we were the warriors who comprised the greatest fighting force the world has ever seen: Mother Green the Killing Machine.

I never saw combat, but served with many men who did. The older Marines were virtually all Vietnam vets. I sat riveted for hours listening to their (mostly true, I think) war stories. *There we was. Tet Offensive. February '68. Fightin' and dyin' for Hue City...* And the guys who stayed in after me, many of them, also became combat veterans. Several friends were killed or injured when a truck bomb decimated Marine headquarters in Beirut, Lebanon in the fall of 1983, only a couple of months after I got out. There were 241 fatalities. I had just started my first year of law school when a friend called me with the sad and tragic news. I felt the whisper of mortality. Many other former colleagues continued to serve in all the long, unfortunate wars that have transpired since then.

As I said, I was lucky. A concussion, broken teeth, a dislocated finger and a sprained ankle - all sustained in training accidents - represented the extent of the physical pain I knew as a Marine. I heard countless gunshots and explosions over three years without adequate hearing protection, and now I am blessed with the incredibly annoying condition called tinnitus, in my left ear. I am reminded 24/7 by a low-grade ringing in the cranium of my time in service. But that's it. Not much to complain about.

In the spirit of luckiness, one time, before we deployed overseas, some lieutenant buddies asked me if I wanted to accompany them on a weekend jaunt south of the border to Tijuana. To this day, I cannot recall the reason I declined because I was normally first in line for such hijinks. But I said no. They got good and roaring drunk, hopped into someone's van, and had an altercation with another vehicle on a roadway near San Diego. Never even made it to Tijuana. They stopped the van and piled out one-by-one, ready for a fistfight. But there wasn't gonna be no fistfight. As the Marines disembarked - just as if they were hitting the beach at Iwo Jima - the passenger in the other vehicle calmly got out, went to the trunk, pulled out what was fortunately a small-caliber, non-automatic rifle, and started shooting. One lieutenant was hit in the thigh. Another, a good friend of mine, received a round that tore through his lower abdomen and lodged in his side. He was seriously injured and spent many weeks at the Balboa Naval Hospital in San Diego, shitting in a colostomy bag, waiting until his intestines could be surgically rerouted.

Thankfully, he fully recovered over time.

In looking back, I can only imagine that I would have been one of the first to jump out ready to rumble. I now believe that at least figuratively and almost literally, in missing this event, I had "dodged a bullet."

I also experienced two earthquakes, one while acting as the range safety officer for a mortar shoot at the far reaches of Pendleton. I thought the ground shaking was just the result of good solid mortar fire and did not learn until later that there had been an earthquake. The second took place as I sat one evening with another lieutenant at the Officer's Club at Camp Hansen in Okinawa, Japan. Felt like a bunch of B52s flying low overhead. We looked around, realized what had happened and that everything was mostly still in place, shrugged, then continued to drink beer and eat potato chips. And so the theme that 'it is better to be lucky than to be smart' continued for me.

I and my mates spent time in Okinawa, South Korea, Singapore and the Philippines. While in the Philippines I unknowingly ate a barbecued cat, a common delicacy there; it tasted like chicken; I also ate lots of octopus in Asia – salty and chewy. The Far East was fascinating, but by a good margin the most exotic place I had the opportunity to see was a little U-shaped atoll in the middle of the Indian Ocean. It was supposedly named for the Portuguese explorer who discovered it, and it was called Diego Garcia.

———————

The Chagos Archipelago comprises nearly 60 islands, all contained within the British Indian Ocean Territory (BIOT). Diego Garcia is the largest island, a flat, heavily vegetated coral atoll; it looks like a giant, off-kilter wishbone on the map, with a big lagoon in the middle. Land mass contains 6,700 acres and the island perimeter runs about 40 miles. The highest elevation is 22 feet above sea level. Temperatures average 85 degrees Fahrenheit. There are coconut trees everywhere. The massive lagoon, averaging 30 to 100 feet deep, runs five-and-one-half miles wide by 13 miles long.

Diego Garcia is the only inhabited island in the Chagos. It is located approximately seven degrees south of the equator, and a good long way from the nearest land mass. India is about 1,200 miles away. The Maldives sit 400 miles north, the Seychelles are located 1,000 miles to the west, and Mauritius lies 1,200 miles southwest. Diego Garcia is situated almost perfectly in the center of the Indian Ocean. The writer Alan Thompson said of Diego Garcia, and all of the islands of the Chagos, that they are "utterly lost in the great water wastes: star land in sea space."

Prior to our deployment in the early months of 1983, we were told Diego Garcia was named for the famous Portuguese explorer who discovered the island. Many of the books one might read on the subject today say the same thing. Turns out that's probably not accurate, primarily because there was no Portuguese explorer named Diego Garcia. It is possible that early Indonesian, Arab, and/or Chinese explorers knew of the Chagos, but there is no definitive record. It is a certainty that the Portuguese discovered the islands in the early 1500s, in an expedition most likely led by Pedro Mascarenhas. In 1509 and 1512, two Portuguese navigators named Diego Lopes and Garcia de Naronha led separate fleets into the Indian Ocean. Is that how the name came about? Who knows? Some accounts assert that there was indeed a Spanish explorer named Diego Garcia who set foot on the island in 1532, but that might be mere legend as well. We know for sure only that the existing name came into common use in the late 1700s. This is why history is fascinating and a great mystery, sometimes. What is fact and what is fiction?

I was at that time the Executive Officer (second-in-command) of a rifle company - about 150 Marines - which was India Company, Third Battalion, Ninth Marines. While we were deployed to Okinawa we were informed that we had a new mission. Diego Garcia needed our rifles. Inside the lagoon sat vast stores of maritime pre-positioned weaponry and equipment, rolling around on massive ships, ready to be sent quickly and in bulk to allow American forces to deal with any contingency that might arise in that part of the world, particularly Southeast Asia. There was enough equipment to sustain a fight for 30 days. Some genius in Washington D.C. determined that our stores might be targeted by terrorists and so, gee whiz, let's provide some protection. It was surely a more innocent time. We were only the second rifle company to serve in this mission, which would last six weeks.

We were airlifted in. First impressions of the island: one of the most wondrous places I had ever laid eyes on; it was tropical, there was dense vegetation, there were donkeys everywhere, it rained like hell every day for about half-an-hour, and there were no women. At least none that I ever saw.

There were, however, British naval and marine personnel, plus one Australian officer, and we had an absolute gas getting to know those guys. We really had fun together, servicemen far from home from three nations separated by a common language. The Aussie was a somewhat cherubic, bearded navy Sub-lieutenant (pronounced 'leftenant') named Jake Burns. He and I became fast friends when upon meeting him I demonstrated that I knew the name of his country's prime minister - I had recently read an article about Robert Hawke, who had just come into power, in *Time* magazine.

Jake Burns and I got to know each other well, teased each other mercilessly, laughed uproariously, ate too much greasy food, and drank a lot of beer. One day, after a bit of a bender the night before, he called me up in the early afternoon on the land line in our little headquarters Quonset hut.

"India Company 3/9, Lieutenant Appelquist speaking."

"Hello, Ex [he called me 'Ex' because I was my company's Executive Officer], Jake Burns here." (As if I wouldn't know who it was with the jaunty, one-of-a-kind accent, and the fact that he was the only person in God's creation who called me Ex. He was also, as I mentioned, the only man from Down Under on the entire island. Who else could it be?)

"What do you want you fuckin' Australian?"

(Jake Burns, undeterred) "Well Ex, here's the thing, what say we go over to the O [Officers] Club a bit later and knock back a few?"

"Jake, that's what we did yesterday, and the day before..."

(Jake Burns, indignant) "Come on Ex, where's your spirit?!"

Pause.

(Jake Burns, dogged) "Ex? Come on Mate. What say?"

"Oh alright alright! God, you're a nag."

(Jake Burns, triumphant) "Good good then Ex! See you at the O Club, what say we rendezvous around 1700 hours [5 pm]? Stay chipper Old Mate."

Over just six short weeks I came to love Jake Burns like my own brother. When we finally parted ways he gave me a t-shirt displaying the Australian national flag, Southern Cross and all. I wore it with pride and to tatters over the next two decades and thought of him whenever I put it on. Jake invited me to visit him in Australia any time. I never did. As so often happens in life, we lose track of our friends. It causes a pang of guilt and longing every time it happens, but it still happens all the time. Over the years I have often wondered: Whatever became of my Old Mate and comrade-in-arms, Jake Burns?

◄──────►

The history of Diego Garcia has been shaped by nations desiring to exert their naval power and expand maritime ambitions. The British made the first organized effort to colonize the island when, in 1786, the East India Company established a base there to provide food and supplies to passing ships. The French nominally controlled the Indian Ocean and became concerned with British incursions, but nevertheless formally ceded the Chagos Archipelago and other regions to the British by treaty in 1814. The British have owned the Chagos ever since.

By the time of the formal transfer of power, a plantation society based on the harvesting of coconuts for their oil – and slave labor - had become well established on Diego Garcia. Slaving to and from the island continued to be a problem even after the abolition of the slave trade in the British Empire in 1807, and despite the best efforts of the Royal Navy to thwart the practice. The institution of slavery was abolished entirely throughout the Empire in 1834. On Diego Garcia, the British attempted to supervise the emancipation of former slaves, but it was not until 1840 that those people, now free laborers, succeeded in making contracts with their former owners for wages. Conditions for workers on the island, however, remained much the same as before: difficult. The island was essentially run as a network of private estates, built upon the backs of poor laborers, for the benefit of affluent landowners.

With the onset of the Second World War, military interest in Diego Garcia had become keen. British Royal Marines installed a pair of six-inch naval guns to command the north entrance to the lagoon. The guns were never fired in anger, but they still sit as if poised for action at the spot known as Cannon Point. The Seychelles, Mauritius and Diego Garcia – code-named Port 2Y – served as minor maritime reconnaissance and refueling bases during the war, manned by British, Mauritian and Indian troops.

With the end of the war and the emergence of the United States as a world superpower, the U.S. Navy began to take an interest in the idea of base rights in certain key strategic locations. In 1964, a joint British and American survey team visited Diego Garcia, and soon thereafter the British Indian Ocean Territory came into being. The U.S. and Great Britain signed an agreement in 1966 which ensured that BIOT would strive to meet the defense needs of both nations, essentially indefinitely. American Seabees (naval combat engineers) arrived in 1971, and in cooperation with the British the long, involved process of converting the island from a plantation society into a fully functioning naval and air base got underway.

When India Company 3/9 arrived on the island in early 1983, conditions were still relatively simple and the base was not yet even close to developing into the sophisticated, elaborate military complex that it would ultimately become. We nevertheless arrived full of piss and vinegar, as they say, ready to do our duty and defend Diego Garcia.

Just prior to our deployment, we had received formal training in a class aboard an American naval vessel off the coast of South Korea. The subject of our class: Waterboarding. That's right. Waterboarding 101. I need to say here that I have always loved the U.S. Marine Corps with all my heart, and to disparage the institution in any way would be the last thing I would want to do. There are those who might challenge my assertion that the Corps ever delivered such training; but I have buddies who were there who would corroborate my account. In those days, waterboarding was not the hot and controversial topic that it has several decades hence understandably become. I had never even heard of such a thing until that day. Times change, and sensibilities deepen, and I am confident that the Marines deliver no such training today. Nevertheless, with that as context, in 1982 we did indeed receive detailed instructions in how to carry out the process of waterboarding. It's really quite simple: one takes a standard towel, soaks it with water, and then places it over the face and mouth of the recipient of the treatment, while others restrain that person with force. Then one begins to pour additional water onto the towel. The waterboardee very much believes that he is drowning, although he will not. He can't really even be hurt in any way, we were told. Apparently, it is a terrifically uncomfortable feeling. One of my knuckleheaded marines happily volunteered to be the "victim," and as he writhed in agony, it became dramatically apparent that in many if not most cases, this technique might well work for the purpose of extracting information. The sole purpose of the waterboarding procedure was to gain information from the enemy, quickly and efficiently. Needless to say, there was no mention of the word "torture."

At one point during our time on the island we were engaged in a multi-day war game with our British marine infantry counterparts. I commanded our guys. Platoon-sized exercise, with about 30-40 fighting men on each side. Played a lot of cat and mouse in the jungle, trying to evade and ambush each other. My boys succeeded in capturing a British marine, and they brought him to me. I was certain that he knew the location and intended movements of his unit. *But how to get that critical information? Let's see... wait just a tick, I know, I'll put my good Marine Corps training to use. I'll waterboard his ass.* And so I gave the order, and that is what we did. Now, I'm perfectly willing to concede that the young man's thought process almost certainly went something like this: *Bloody hell. How long do I need to let a determined group of U.S. Marines, not a single one of whom could correctly place the United Kingdom on a world map and who, furthermore, collectively, have absolutely nothing else to do this afternoon, torture me? We're not even enemies! (Thank God.) They're not going to kill me, nor will they kill my mates if I rat on them. I'll tell you this in no uncertain terms: not bloody long, that's how long this'll go on. Not bloody long at all.* He was obviously quite shaken by the experience, squirming and struggling as he did, and only lasted about 30 seconds before he sang like a canary. Would have stood on his head and belted out his best rendition of "God Save the Queen" if I had asked him to. But I just needed the coordinates of his platoon's location.

We set up a night ambush and surprised the hell out of the Brits, which allowed us to justly claim victory in the exercise. I wasn't a complete dolt and, at the very least, had the good sense to report immediately to my boss, the commanding officer of India Company. He was one of the best leaders and finest human beings I have ever known – I learned a great deal from him; he described me as a "colorful officer" in the final fitness report of my Marine Corps career, one of the highest professional compliments I have ever received (I think). I recapped the exercise, told him about the ambush and then said, "Sir, you need to hear it from me first before it comes to you some other way.

We captured a Brit yesterday and waterboarded critical locational intel out of him."

"Hmmm... Really? So the waterboarding worked?"

"Yes sir, it sure did."

"Did that intel help you set up the ambush?"

"Yes sir."

"And by virtue of that ambush did we win the exercise?"

"Yes sir."

"Hmmm... Don't worry about it, Lieutenant. Thanks for the update. I'll take care of any repercussions with our friends. Good job."

"Yes sir. Thank you, sir."

An international incident was further averted when, as it turns out, the British lad enthusiastically returned to his unit and merrily bragged about being waterboarded by American Marines. *Whew*.

With all of that said, as I look back these many years later, what I did was really wrong and a serious mistake in judgment, even for a young man. The order that I delivered may have been legal in the technical sense, but it was still wrong. I would profusely apologize to the individual, if I ever knew who or where he was. As noted foreign correspondent and author Andrew Solomon says in his travel memoir, *Far and Away*, "If it is disappointing to grow old, it is likewise embarrassing to have been young. One is startled by what one did then but wouldn't do now." To this day, my good friend John Youngblood repeatedly, emphatically and indignantly reminds my two daughters, "Girls, not only did your father order that another human being be tortured; the victim wasn't even the enemy – he was an ally!" There's no other way to say it: I was a dumbass.

After the creation of BIOT, in the late 1960s and early 1970s, Great Britain and the United States hatched and executed a plan - in the interests of clearing the island to make way for construction of the American military facility - to close the plantations and exile all of the islanders of Diego Garcia. These people were primarily Seychellois who were under contract as laborers, but a significant chunk were also "children of the islands," known as Ilois (and also Chagossians), mostly descended from slaves and indentured servants, who had been born and raised and spent their entire lives on Diego Garcia. In many cases, these families had lived there for generations. The total number of civilian inhabitants to be resettled has been estimated at as many as 2,500.

The BIOT administration based its plantation closure and deportation decision on the grounds that the islanders owned no immovable property on the island and therefore had no permanent right of residence. Many Chagossians left the island of their own volition, especially when essential supplies from the British government became deliberately scarce. For the islanders who remained when construction finally began in 1971, the process of being forced from their homes was particularly painful. It is said that working donkeys and dogs, including family pets, were herded into sealed sheds and gassed and burned before the very eyes of their horrified owners as they awaited their own fate (some donkeys had previously stolen away into the wild, and their descendants apparently remain on the island to this day – I sure saw a lot of donkeys when I was there.) The people were then required to board overcrowded cargo ships. With little choice in the matter, they were transported primarily to Seychelles or Mauritius.

As British diplomat and former BIOT Commissioner Richard Edis states in his book *Peak of Lamuria*, "The resultant trauma, especially for those families who had worked and made their homes on Diego Garcia for generations, is hard to imagine; harder still the sadness of their final Creole mass in the East Point chapel.... The bitterness caused by these removals has rankled for a generation and the yearning, especially of the older islanders, for their former way of life in 'les iles la haut' – the islands up there – is all too understandable." The British government made attempts over the years at compensation, but insufficient to reconcile many of the displaced islanders to the cruel deportation they had experienced. Chagossians have since brought numerous claims against the U.S. and British governments seeking further compensation and the right to return to their homes. The appellate arm of the British House of Lords rendered judgment in 2008 ruling that the government position – that the natives have no right to residency in the islands and cannot even visit without authorization - be upheld. The European Court of Human Rights rejected a Chagossian lawsuit in 2012, asserting that the islanders' claims were inadmissible in that jurisdiction.

———◆———

The BIOT took measures in the 1980s to protect the Chagos environmentally through efforts to restrict commercial fishing, limit the incursions of sloppy yachtsmen, and adhere to current environmental treaties and standards. Unfortunately, the BIOT lacked the resources to enforce its will.

Climate change also began to have its insidious effect. A study in 1996 found significant coral decline from the rich abundance of the 1970s. In 1998, El Nino contributed to a catastrophic bleaching event which caused 90% of ocean coral in the Chagos to perish, including 95% of the seaward reefs of Diego Garcia. With warming oceans - the Indian Ocean rapidly continues to heat up, and is the warmest ocean in the world - come acidic and rising waters, constituting a further threat of inundation for many of the lowest lying islands of the Chagos.

Fortunately, in the new century, the reef system of the Chagos has had something of a rebound. In 2010, The British government designated the archipelago as a fully no-take marine reserve. According to the website of the nonprofit Chagos Conservation Trust: "This declaration makes it the largest such reserve in the world... The combination of tropical islands, unspoiled coral reefs and adjacent oceanic abyss makes this area comparable in global importance to the Great Barrier Reef or Galapagos Islands. As a fully protected marine reserve, all extractive activities, such as industrial fishing and deep sea mining, will be prohibited in the Chagos. This decision will safeguard the rich diversity of marine life found in the area."

Yet danger remains, and complacency will be punished. Richard Edis says, "Forecasts are not of course the stuff of history, though history is replete with accounts of the failure to heed forecasts. What *this* history tells is the unfinished story of one of Nature's treasure stores, which man has exploited but not emptied and which can serve him well for some decades yet, given good stewardship. Whether that stewardship is forthcoming rests with two governments."

I waterboarded an ally on a whim. The colonial powers enslaved people in the Chagos to further the economic interests of wealthy plantation owners. Great Britain and the United States forcefully repatriated, against their will, the entire native population of Diego Garcia. Manmade greenhouse gases and the resulting global warming have caused oceans to heat up and to rise, with potentially devastating effects on marine life in the Chagos and elsewhere. Individuals do stupid, thoughtless things, and so do nations, and so too have we as a world community, done stupid thoughtless things. I fear it may ever be thus.

But perhaps there is reason to hope.

CHAPTER TWO

THE ROOF OF AFRICA

MOUNT KILIMANJARO, TANZANIA

"...there, ahead, all he could see, as wide as all the world, great, high,
and unbelievably white in the sun, was the square top of Kilimanjaro.
And then he knew that was where he was going."

— ERNEST HEMINGWAY, FROM *THE SNOWS OF KILIMANJARO* —

The sound began faintly, gently, like the tinkling of wind chimes in the distance. The climbing party, plus guides and porters, had awakened at the ungodly and pitch-black hour of 3 a.m. After a breakfast of porridge, toast with peanut butter and hot tea, they donned their full array of cold-weather gear, secured their helmets, strapped on backpacks, and then turned on their headlamps to light the way up the notorious Western Breach of Mount Kilimanjaro. Three American climbers had been killed by falling rocks there in 2006 and the route had been temporarily shut down, pending an investigation. It was eventually reopened, but the Tanzanian authorities decreed that rocks released by melting ice were still a hazard and from that moment forward all climbers must wear helmets on the Western Breach. The party had been marching back and forth - but ever upward - in a switchback pattern for perhaps two hours. Though they were at around 17,000 feet in elevation, they were not even halfway through their arduous journey up the potentially deadly path to the interior of the Kibo Crater.

The guide's ears perked up. *What is that?* The sound grew in volume, like a wave slowly gaining momentum in the ocean. Suddenly, with great urgency and near panic he shouted, "Rockslide! Everybody get down!!" In an instant, all hands hit the deck and protected themselves as best they could. One climber covered his helmeted head with his right arm, reckoning that a fractured arm was better than a fractured skull. A desperate father shielded his beloved daughter with his own body. A man who had not prayed in decades beseeched the Lord for divine intervention. Now the sound was a locomotive that had just achieved full speed. It was violent and deafening and relentless and coming straight for them.

At the base camp far below dozens of porters, who were about to begin carrying the climbing party's food, water, cooking equipment and camping gear up the very same precipice, had been watching the 13 twinkling headlamps as they slowly made their way higher, like stars in the night sky. The porters clearly heard the rockslide. Then, in the blink of an eye, the cascading rocks, some the size of small boulders, passed directly through the position where the lights had last flickered. The slide missed the porters as its fury subsided; they breathed a sigh of relief for themselves. But then they looked back up the mountain, deeply concerned, straining to see and hear. There was only darkness and silence above.

◀━━━━━━▶

I had been intrigued by the possibility of climbing Kilimanjaro for many years. I am far from a mountaineer and in fact, though there are not many things that I am afraid of, I willingly acknowledge that heights is one of those things. Since I was a small child, I have always gotten a queasy stomach and a dull ache in my balls any time I am in a situation where I could be hurt or die from a fall. I don't like to be on the open balcony of a tall building, even if protected by a sturdy railing. I was terrified when I was made to rappel off of cliffs and out of helicopters as a Marine infantryman. I feel safe enough in an airplane, but whenever there is basically nothing - or at least not much - between me and the possibility of a long fall, I am insecure and unhappy.

But the word on Kilimanjaro, as I understood it, was that while challenging, the climb was a "walkup." No technical training or skills required, no ropes, no ice axes, no crampons. One simply needed to be fit enough for an arduous uphill hike and to be able to adapt to the altitude. It was the failure to adjust at altitude that caused most of the problems and, frankly, the occasional fatality for those attempting "Kili." I believe that each of us should periodically challenge ourselves to do something extremely difficult, both personally and professionally. I have always appreciated the quote from T.S. Elliott, "Only those who will risk going too far can possibly find out how far they can go." Kilimanjaro would be just such a challenge for me, especially so as I approached the end of my sixth decade on the planet.

I did some research and checked out a number of outfitters. I finally chose one that offered a late-January excursion. This was a highly reputable organization and, adding greatly to the appeal of the journey was the fact that if I made it to the top, according to their itinerary, I would summit Kili at sunrise on my 59th birthday, January 29, 2017. I liked that idea very much and so booked the trip.

⟷

Mount Kilimanjaro, located near the northern border of the East African country of Tanzania is, at 19,341 feet, the tallest mountain on the African continent as well as the world's tallest freestanding mountain. It sits just three degrees south of the Equator and towers over the enormous, desolate plain known as the Great Rift Valley. Kili is a geological masterpiece that was forged 750,000 years ago from volcanic fire and glacial ice. Originally it was a configuration of three massive volcanoes that formed when molten lava broke through the earth's surface and erupted skyward. Shira, the oldest volcano, collapsed ages ago. There remain two peaks: Kibo, at 19,341 feet, and Mawenzi, seven miles to the east, at 16,893 feet. The gorgeous and forbidding desert that separates them is known as the Saddle. Kibo is the youngest of the rugged formations and is considered to be a dormant, rather than extinct volcano (it last erupted 350,000 years ago.) The position on Kibo's snow-covered rim known as the Uhuru Peak represents the highest point in all of Africa. All Kili climbers strive to reach the Uhuru Peak so they can have their picture taken in front of the well-worn and iconic sign that congratulates them for their feat of endurance in making the summit. That coveted photo will give them bragging rights for life.

I left the Twin Cities on Inauguration Day, January 20, 2017. Several of my friends who are not Donald Trump supporters suggested that I was smart to get out of the country and should stay away. I connected in Amsterdam, then flew directly into Kilimanjaro International Airport, arriving late at night. I secured a Tanzanian visa, cleared customs, and was met outside the gate by Ben, who would be our guide for the entire trip, and Michael, one of our drivers. The weather was warm as we piled into a sturdy, well-worn Toyota Land Cruiser and made our way to our first base camp, at the Arusha National Park. It took us probably 90 minutes to arrive at the gates of the park, and then Ben let me know we had another half hour along a narrow, winding and rutted dirt road to the camp. We saw a small herd of Cape buffalo right alongside the road. The famous writer and big game hunter Robert Ruark once said of a Cape buffalo he encountered, "He looked at me as if he hated my guts. He looked at me as if I had despoiled his fiancé, murdered his mother, and burned down his house. He looked at me as if I owed him money." Even in the darkness, I could see that Ruark was right; these animals indeed have an intimidating way of staring at you. Then a family of giraffes ambled across the road in front of us, illuminated by and unafraid of our headlights. Even the baby of the brood looked to be at least 15-feet tall. When we were about half a mile from the camp, we encountered a massive tree which had fallen directly across the road. Our path was completely blocked. What was interesting was that, as Ben explained, this tree had to have fallen in the last three hours or so, because when Ben and Michael left camp to pick me up the road was clear. The tree had obviously come down to earth with suddenness and great force. Clearly a vehicle crusher. How surreal it would have been to travel all the way to Africa to climb a large mountain, only to be killed by a falling tree before the trek even began.

Ben called the crew at camp via walky-talky and they drove out in another vehicle from the opposite direction. There were four of them and they had brought with them a small bow saw which, after much animated conversation in Kiswahili, one of the guys proceeded to wield with great energy in an attempt to cut the tree in half and clear a path. The saw broke. The men cursed. Then they sort of sat on and wrestled with the tree near the partial cut and it finally snapped and dropped to the ground, violently, to everyone's surprise. No one was hurt. The men laughed, pushed the bulky impediment off to the side of the road, and we were on our way again. I was now profoundly fatigued; it was well past midnight, local time, and my body clock was all screwed up. All but two of our party of seven climbers had already arrived at camp hours before and were snug in their beds. For me, Ben insisted that I join him for a multi-course meal: pea soup followed by quiche and a baked potato, topped off by a dessert of cake with fresh fruit. After the approximately six meals, plus countless snacks, that Delta Airlines had fed me (and several glasses of red wine; it's a pretty crummy Merlot in economy class but it's free on international flights) on the way from Minneapolis, the last thing I needed was more food, but I acquiesced and did my best to clean the plate(s). I shouldn't complain, as the meal was delicious. Ben seemed well pleased, and I was finally released to the comfort of my spacious tent and a fitful night's sleep.

Our base for the next day-and-a-half, known as the Itkoni Seasonal Camp, sits at 6,000 feet in elevation. The idea was to give our group of climbers (I will call us "Team Kili") the advantage of altitude right away. The more time we could spend acclimatizing, the better our chances of reaching the summit. Itkoni is located at the edge of Mount Meru, which at 14,764 feet is Tanzania's second highest peak. I loved the concept of this "special campsite," so designated by the Tanzanian National Parks. The camp sits removed from the main tourist trails, in a tropical forest. A genuine concern for the environment is apparent in everything that happens at Itkoni. Water is hauled from Park Headquarters, about an hour away, and usage is minimized through the practice of "bucket showers" (you get a bucket of hot water, once a day, and that's it; as with the classic "Navy Shower," you get wet, stop the water, lather up, and then use the rest of your precious allotment to rinse off – you had best be efficient.) Chemical toilets at Itkoni use virtually no water at all. The camp runs on solar power – no wood or coal is burned, nor is there a generator. Gas and sustainable "briquettes" made from sawdust and coconut fiber are used for cooking. The tents, textiles and leathers used in the camp are sourced in Arusha, while the Western-oriented menu – which was consistently excellent - features locally grown foods. The camp stays in place for the entire season to reduce the need to drive in with heavy equipment and trucks, which can damage vegetation and cause soil compaction. The wildlife around the camp is varied, abundant and noisy, especially the countless baboons and monkeys, who love to chatter loudly back and forth all day and, it seemed, all night as well.

Team Kili met for the first time on our second day. Our two late arrivals, whose flights had been delayed, finally joined us. They were Dave, a San Jose-based litigator, and his buddy Matt, a venture capitalist, also from San Jose. John and his daughter Alysa, also Californians, were both engineers. Barry was a retired litigator from Boston and Raymond was a semi-retired business owner from New York City. Both Raymond and Matt had backgrounds in engineering, and since I am a recovering lawyer, we soon realized that we were four engineers versus three attorneys. Potentially pretty boring stuff. But we also discovered right away that there was nary a Trump supporter among us, so we had a lot of fun discussing our new president. Our comedic commentary, however, was also mixed with significant consternation especially since, among other grave concerns, the new administration, constituted mostly of climate-change-deniers (starting in the Oval Office and cascading downward), espoused the theory that climate science is a hoax which - if we weren't already convinced there was a problem - directly contradicted the abundant evidence we all saw over the next week of the very real effects of global warming on the mountain.

Nevertheless, it readily became apparent that Team Kili consisted of a great bunch of people. We ate every meal together for eight days, and literally climbed a mountain together. You get to know people really well under those circumstances. By the end of our time, there were hugs and even tears as we parted ways. We became like a family.

In the afternoon on Day Two, our chief guide, Ben, and his second-in-command, a young fellow named Tom, checked out everyone's gear one item at a time to make sure that we were all properly outfitted to begin our climb. The guides then provided us with a detailed briefing on our upcoming journey, which included a map orientation session from Tom. We threw on our backpacks and took a short hike along the forested slopes of Meru, which was cut short by a driving rainstorm. We began to get a flavor for how rapidly weather patterns would change on the way up the mountain. Meru, like Kilimanjaro, is a long-dormant volcano which last erupted 250,000 years ago with such force that half of the mountain was blown away. Since then, gigantic and lush forests of African cedar and podocarpus trees have filled in Meru's crater and slopes. Animal life in the area includes all variety of baboons and monkeys, bushbuck, duiker, Cape buffalo, giraffe, and even elephants and leopards. We observed abundant bird life such as colorful touracos, hornbills and parrots. After our wet hike, all of the members of our party enjoyed hot, albeit brief showers back in our tents, and then dinner. Sleep on Night Two was again sporadic. The circadian rhythm was still off, and I was becoming excited to get our adventure underway.

←■■■→

On Day Three, we arose at 7 a.m. and enjoyed a breakfast of three-egg omelets, fresh fruit and coffee. We gathered up all our equipment and climbed into two vehicles for the two-and-one-half hour drive from Arusha to the starting point for the Machame Route up Kilimanjaro. We saw many Tanzanian towns and villages along the way and were struck by the hustle and bustle of activity, the colorful garb (especially for the women), but also by the spare conditions and dire poverty. I did notice a certain number of people, especially it seemed, unfortunately, young men, who appeared to be doing nothing more than idling the day away.

Tanzania won its independence from Great Britain in 1961. The country holds democratic elections but the party known as Chama Cha Mapinduzi (CCM) has by far been the dominant player in the political life of Tanzania since independence. Ben and Tom told us that with the recent election of a new president, John Magufuli - who won thanks to the backing of the CCM machinery - there was hope that corruption might be reduced, government spending brought under control and the economy energized. Time would tell. For now, Tanzania remains one of the world's poorest countries, in the bottom 10 percent of nations in per-capita income. More than one third of the population lives below the poverty line. Nevertheless, real GDP appears to be growing, with agriculture accounting for more than one quarter of GDP and employing 80 percent of the workforce. Mining is also a significant industry and, in recent years, enormous gas reserves have been discovered off the Tanzanian coast in the Indian Ocean. (I wish that mining and offshore drilling were not necessarily the engines for growth, but economics are complicated in developing nations.) And of course, especially in the northern part of the country, tourism is incredibly important and a vital source of foreign currency.

Tanzania is a vast country, more than twice the size of California, with a diverse population in excess of 50 million, split into 130 different tribes. Blessedly, more than one quarter of the land mass has been set aside for national parks or game reserves. The Selous and Serengeti parks are world famous. Still, despite its gargantuan size, land set-asides and awesome beauty, the country is beset by serious environmental problems including deforestation, desertification, soil degradation and erosion, as well as dying reefs. Tanzania is at once a complex and contradictory place of profound troubles, but also of great promise.

When we finally arrived at the starting point for the Machame Route, four miles past the village of Machame and on the southwest side of Kilimanjaro, there were many dozens of climbers and hundreds of porters, all from various outfitters and looking fresh, hopeful and full of vigor as we assembled to begin the ascent from about 6,400 feet in elevation. We were dressed in shorts and otherwise prepared for warm weather; the temperature was probably somewhere in the mid-70s. The Machame Route is the most popular and, therefore, the busiest of the six ascent trails up the mountain, as we clearly witnessed. The hassle of crowds is well worth it, however, as the natural beauty that one passes on this route is simply breathtaking. But it is also challenging and regarded as a much tougher proposition than the alternate, well-traveled Marangu Route. Machame is therefore called the Whiskey Route and Marangu is the Coca Cola Trail. Ironically, statistics indicate that climbers who tackle Machame actually have a higher success rate in summiting than those who attempt other routes. Perhaps this is because the journey takes longer, thus allowing more time to acclimatize. Or it could be that the climbers who choose Machame are generally more fit to begin with. Whatever the reasons, as we embarked upon what began as a gently rising ascent through cloud forests, I am quite sure we all liked our odds.

The climb quickly became difficult, with steeper grades and occasionally unstable footing. Our guides encouraged us to maintain an easy pace. "Pole', pole'," they repeated over and over, which means "slowly, slowly" in Kiswahili. It soon became apparent to me that this whole thing was probably going to be a more intense proposition than I had reckoned upon. I also became concerned that the primary risk that would prevent me from reaching the top was not a lack of fitness or failure to acclimatize, although those might turn out to be problems too, but rather the chance of injury as a result of a slip and fall. *Watch where you are putting your feet, Chowder Head.*

Ben told us that there were eight porters, cooks and other support personnel for every individual climber. That meant that for the seven of us climbers we had nearly 60 people helping to get our lame asses up the mountain. Ben called it our "moving village." The porters were simply amazing, and one of the true highlights of the trip was watching these guys glide up the mountain, sometimes carrying what seemed like the equivalent of their own body weight in gear, with baskets and rucksacks balanced precariously on their heads, some of them wearing tennis shoes - I laughed out loud when I saw a porter in a pair of well-worn white Chuck Taylor Converse high tops, just like the ones I wore in ninth-grade basketball. During the course of our eight days together, just when we thought it couldn't get any worse for us and we were struggling to breathe and put one foot in front of the other, a porter would blow by us, practically running, shout out "Jambo" ("Hello"), all while carrying six times the load any of us had on our backs. It was, to say the least, a perspective check on who is tough and who is not. I told Ben that I served as a Marine infantry officer, and I would take his team of porters as foot soldiers in my rifle company, any day. They were incredible.

In his excellent guidebook, *Kilimanjaro: The Trekking Guide to Africa's Highest Mountain*, author Henry Stedman, in discussing the effects of high altitude on the human body, says, "The need to urinate and break wind frequently are also typical of high-altitude living and, far from being something to be concerned about, are actually positive indications that your body is adapting well to conditions. As is written on the ancient tombstone in Dorset:

'Let your wind go free, where e'er you be,

For holding it in, was the death of me.'"

If all of this is true, and I have no reason to believe that it is not, then I can say, unequivocally, that our Team Kili was adapting very well indeed. The higher we got, the more frequently the gas began to fly. At first, understandably, people were a tad embarrassed. But as everyone eventually joined in the fun - whether voluntarily or not - and we became more like a family, our inhibitions let down. One team member who shall remain nameless (it wasn't me – I know, I know: 'he who smelt it dealt it and he who denied it supplied it' - but it really wasn't me) was particularly active and also fragrant on the trail. I think, perhaps, he harnessed the energy somehow to help propel himself up the mountain. Anyway, I learned to either hustle to get ahead of him in the walking lineup or to put several people between me and his anus if I was behind him. Nice guy, but *Sheesh Dude, what are you eating in your snack mix?*

    The team was also incredibly windy not just while climbing but at night, too, after dinner and lights out, in our tents. In the spirit of true diversity, we delivered on every variety of gasser: your standard, quick-ripping "toots"; loud "poppers" that surprised everyone, including even he who dealt it; the occasional "squeaker," also sometimes known as the "one-cheek-sneak"; the rat-a-tat-tat of the "machine gun"; the multi-tonal and sustained "singsong"; the massive, very loud, hard to ignore, I-just-ate-a-huge-meal "foghorn"; and once, even the dreaded "shart," which woke everyone up as someone stumbled to the toilet in the middle of the night (again, it wasn't me.) We even got to the point where we would comment on each other's efforts:

    "Hey, wow, that was a real dandy [whoever it was]. You held on for a good long time and I liked the flourish at the end. It was almost musical. Well done."

    "Thanks."

    "I hope you're feeling better."

    "I am. Thanks again."

    Can there possibly be any doubt that ozone-depleting gasses are man-made?

Ben is an excellent guide and a terrific human being. I would have guessed him to be perhaps in his early to mid-40s. He was a porter in his youth and had been guiding on Kili since 2001. He estimated that he has been to the summit 150 times. Even with that, I was heartened to watch him sweat and huff and puff with the rest of us as we ascended. He told us that he sees and experiences something new each time he climbs and therefore has never tired of the work. He was both highly fluent in English and a bit of a Zen philosopher. He would say, "I'm not interested in learning how many years 'old' you are. I want to know how many years 'wise' you are. I guided a boy up the mountain who was only 12-years-wise. I also guided a woman to the top who was an astounding 82-years-wise." Ben said, "The summit is not our destination. We are merely passing by. Our goal is the journey." He would ask us, "What's not happening today?" On the simplest, most obvious level, we would come up with responses like, "Well, it's not raining." He would just smile. When one thinks about it, though, the question can be more deeply interpreted. "What's not happening today, you ask? Let's see. Kilimanjaro's glaciers are not restoring themselves." Indeed, Ben lamented the state of his country's environment, with particular and understandably personal concern about the multiple glaciers on Kili; "They are not melting," he would say, "because that implies that they can be restored. They are disappearing, and have been, gradually at first but then more rapidly, every single year I have been on the mountain. Soon they will be gone forever." He spoke these words with genuine sorrow in his voice.

Kilimanjaro's glaciers began to form in 9,700 BC. Almost 12,000 years later, at the beginning of the twentieth century, Kibo's ice cap was estimated at 12 square kilometers. As of 2015, the ice cap sat at a meager two square kilometers. It is vanishing before our very eyes. Some scientists reckon that at the current rate it will disappear completely as soon as 2020, which makes one glad to have had the opportunity to gaze upon its phenomenal beauty before that sad day comes to pass. *I once saw the glacier atop Kilimanjaro. It's not there anymore. The snows of Kilimanjaro are gone.*

The ice cap is melting because of reduced snowfall at the summit but also as a result of increased temperatures, which are the obvious outcome of global warming. Interestingly, the sun's radiation is not the direct cause; in fact, the brilliant blue and white ice does not absorb but instead reflects most of the solar heat. The melting, disintegration and breaking apart of the ice is caused by the sun-baked black lava rock - which does absorb the heat - that undergirds the ice. The rocks get hotter, and then the ice melts. It is true to say that there have been other episodes in the last millennium when the glaciers of Kilimanjaro have receded and then been restored. As always, the issues around climate change are complex. What concerns scientists about the present situation is the rapidity and extent of the melting. The repercussions of a Kilimanjaro without snow and ice are consequential, particularly for the people who live in the mountain's shadow, for whom the glaciers are a source of water. And the larger concern, of course, is whether Kili's vanishing glaciers represent a microcosm for what will happen across the globe, in the future. Or, perhaps, the future is now.

$$\longleftrightarrow$$

At the end of our Day Three hike, we settled down in a very busy campsite near a place called the Machame Hut, at about 10,000 feet in altitude. The porters, with their dutiful efficiency, had everything set up for us upon our arrival. Each of us had his own small tent, and they had assembled two small, tented "outhouses" with chemical toilets inside. We all crammed into the dining tent - which accommodated nine people (seven climbers and our two guides) if we sat absolutely shoulder to shoulder - and had "high tea" at 4 pm. The team was tired, but still really exhilarated.

That night, after dinner, as we lay our heads down exhausted, one of our colleagues who shall remain nameless (not the same guy with the excess flatulence), snored the night away so loudly that several of us got no sleep whatsoever. I was particularly unlucky as his tent was right next to mine and he slept probably six feet away. One of the things that I had thought about packing in my Dopp Kit but decided to forego at the last minute was earplugs. Big mistake. After about an hour of listening to the racket, hoping it would subside but realizing that it would not, I sat up, turned on my headlamp, and searched desperately for something I could use as hearing protection. I tried tissue paper but it was no good. I looked in my kit and, aha, I had some pills. What were they? Aha, stool softening pills! I checked out their size. I wagered that one of them would fit perfectly in each of my ears and block out all sound. *Yay!* So I stuck one of those bad boys in my left ear, just to see if it would work, but it was just a tad too small. It quickly moved deeply enough into the ear canal that I could not remove it with my fingers. *Oh no.* The more I tried using my fingers to remove it, the more deeply it became embedded. Now, here's the thing that worried me. I was not a science guy in school but I know that the ear canal and the oral cavity are somehow connected by various passageways inside the skull. If that stool softening pill dissolved and its ingredients made their way down into my throat and then my stomach, well, I'd be shitting uncontrollably all over the mountain. I had been as regular as rain so far, and did not need any help in that regard. How long would it take? *Oh no.* The climb, for me, could be in grave jeopardy.

So now a frantic search began for a tool that I could use to extract the fucking pill from my ear. If I couldn't get it out, I would be deaf in that ear until it dissolved. Then I could hear, but I'd be shitting all over the mountain. But there was hope, because one thing I also debated about bringing and finally decided in favor of, was my trusty Swiss Army Knife: the kind with about 72 tools in it. And one of those tools is the good old plastic toothpick. I slid that thing out of its placeholder at the base of the knife and commenced to picking at my ear. Now, here's the thing that worried me. If I went too deep with this sharp object into my ear (I could hear my mother admonishing me), I might damage the ear drum, and then I might be permanently deaf in that ear. At this point, I kept remembering the vivid and tragic story of John Hanning Speke, a 19th century British explorer; on one of his African adventures, a beetle lodged itself in Speke's ear and he became so crazed that he finally stabbed the thing with a knife, killing the insect but rendering himself without hearing in that ear. What if I never got the pill out and perforated my ear drum? Then I'd be shitting all over the mountain and deaf to boot! I became profoundly concerned. I breathed deeply to calm myself. Finally, after about ten minutes of effort, I extracted my little nemesis by tilting my head to the side and yanking hard on the ear lobe, thereby expanding the hearing canal and creating easier access. I was sweating, and wiped my brow in relief. Then

I lay back down and listened to my buddy snore the rest of the night away. It was okay. I had received the gift of perspective.

Our climb on Day Four was a tough one. Though we would only be hiking for four or five hours, the trail out of the giant heather and up to the Shira Plateau was exceedingly steep. Increasingly, the small, loose stones known as scree that covered the mountain caused our footing to become precarious. One step forward, half a step back. I had told friends back home, based on my imperfect understanding of how the climb would go, that there was no point on Kilimanjaro where, if one made a misstep or became dizzy or somehow lost balance, that a fatal fall could result. How wrong I was. On this day we scrambled (a mountaineering term that describes hand-over-foot climbing) and there were several instances where a wrong step would indeed have resulted in certain death. And please recall that I hate heights. It was at this point that I made an important decision which would help me immensely in the effort to get to the summit. I decided that I would not look down, as that would cause me to shit my pants in fear of how far I might fall. I also determined that I would not gaze in an upward direction, as that would result in absolute demoralization in seeing how far we had left to ascend. So I just focused my vision and all of my physical and mental energy on the 3x3x3x3x-foot square – the nine square feet - right in front of me. Where should my foot go? *Look*. Where do my hands need to be? *Concentrate*. Do I have stable footing before attempting my next step? *Don't let the mind wander*. I'm sure I missed a whole bunch of great scenery as a result of my new laser-focused, tunnel-vision technique, but it saved me. So, frankly, I didn't care.

Our stopping point, called the Shira Camp, sat at 12,650 feet and commanded panoramic vistas of both the Shira Plateau and the plains to our west. After a terrific dinner of fried tilapia and chips, tomato and cheese salad, and fried bananas for dessert, we lay our heads down to sleep. (The lead chef, Dan, and his team consistently produced outstanding meals.) Our snoring friend agreed to locate his tent some distance from the rest of us, which was certainly considerate on his part. I read very briefly and then had my first really good night's sleep since I had left the States.

The next morning, as I slid out of my tent, I dropped my eyeglasses in the mud and stepped on them, thus rendering them unwearable. Fortunately, I had another pair, but it was still 75 bucks down the toilet because of my clumsiness. As I stood there fiddling with them, one of the porters brought me fresh water for the day. I thanked him but did not look up, and he said, "Do you even know my name?" I gazed into his face and had to admit, though I knew I had met him along with probably a dozen of the other porters on our first day, that I did not remember his name.

"I am Peter," he said, *and I am a human being that you should look in the eye and recognize by name.* Virtually all of the porters had some kind of an anglicized name, undoubtedly to make it easier for their dumbass Western clientele, who are either too lazy or ignorant, or both, to pronounce an African name. In our defense, I watched with comic enjoyment as one of the porters tried to pronounce the name of our young, female member of Team Kili, Alyson. He could not say that name for the life of him. They all called me either "Boss" or "Mr. Jeffu" (where the 'u' at the end came from I do not know.) I never failed to call Peter by name from that point forward, he was always very helpful to me, and we became good friends before the trip was over. Lesson learned: don't be an arrogant prick. *Thanks Peter.*

As we got higher on the mountain, not surprisingly, the weather cooled. We had started in the wet rainforest jungle; then we moved up into the heath and moorland zones, which would eventually give way to dry alpine desert; at the summit, conditions are arctic – no plant or animal life survives there. Since I am a descendant of the Vikings and hail from the north country of Minnesota, I was designated, rightly or wrongly, as the resident expert – particularly for our four Californians – on weather and temperature.

"How cold do you think it is right now, Jeff?"

"Folks, in Minnesota during the winter we have three stages of coldness. They are: 1) cold, 2) really cold, and 3) fucking cold."

"Okay, where are we on that scale right now?"

"Between cold and really cold."

"You're kidding. This isn't fucking cold?"

"Not even close."

"Oh no."

Our Day Five ascent took us from the Shira Camp in an easterly direction toward the Kibo Massif. Again, the work was arduous. We had just a few flat sections of terrain as we followed a rocky ridge, with the rest of it steep and treacherous, as always. Our mid-march objective, where we would stop for lunch, was a large rock outcrop called the Lava Tower, at 15,100 feet. It was at this point, as we got close to 15 grand in elevation, that I began for the first time to feel the effects of the thin air. It seemed as if, all of a sudden and unbeknownst to me, I had consumed a double Jack Daniels on the rocks, and swiftly. Just downed that sucker. That is really the best way I can think of to describe the sensation. *Whoa, daddy, what's goin' on? I just got shitfaced.* I think perhaps others were experiencing the same effect, because with perfect timing Ben stopped us for a break. We sat down, drank some water, had a snack, and simply rested for a few moments. We all soon felt better. The Lava Tower is an awesome geological feature, massive in size, and we enjoyed the scenery as we ate our lunch of corn fritters, tuna salad sandwiches, cheese and sausage slices with fresh fruit.

Then it was in a downward direction toward the Great Barranco, which is a huge canyon that leads to the Western Breach Wall. The descent was tougher than I thought it would be, and we all used walking sticks to stabilize ourselves. There was some frustration that we had climbed to a certain point and then had to go back down again to reach our encampment for the evening, which was the Barranco Camp, at 13,000 feet. The idea, of course, was to assist us in the all-important process of acclimatization. The Barranco Valley is really impressive, and sports some of the most unusual trees, called Giant Groundsels, that I have ever seen. Narrow at the base and becoming multi-pronged like a cactus, with flowery green protrusions at the top of each arm, these are enormous plants that look outlandish and otherworldly, like something straight out of Dr. Seuss. But magical, mystical scenery aside, we needed to pay attention and be careful. The footing on the way down was terrible, and for the first time people started to fall down. I watched Raymond hit the deck right in front of me, and his right knee twisted awkwardly. I suspect he had sprained it, and it bothered him for the rest of the climb. John took a tumble too. Within a minute of that unfortunate event, I was also on the ground in a blink, both my feet having simultaneously slipped out from underneath me. I landed on my butt and sprawled flat on my back. I slid slowly but steadily down the Barranco Valley, out of control, until my left thigh made pretty good contact with a small rock outcropping, which stopped me. Hurt like a sonofabitch. I was okay, got up and dusted myself off, but I was chastened. I felt as if the mountain, the Mother Goddess of Africa, had just sent me a not-so-subtle message: *I just kissed you, not a soft, flirtatious kiss but a real hard smack. You had best respect me. And you even need to love me, too. You really do. You need to be my lover boy, whether you like it or not. Don't take your eyes off of me or let your attention wander to another lover. Look at how beautiful I am. Me and only me, for as long as you insist on being astride me. You need to do all this, to do as I say, because I could really, really hurt you if I wanted to...*

"Yes ma'am, I understand."

The great mountaineer Reinhold Messner once wrote, "Mountains are not fair or unfair – they are dangerous." Yes they are; they do not play favorites.

When I stripped down in my tent later that evening I looked in vain for a bruise on my thigh, but could not find one. It was quite strange, because I knew that I had banged myself real good. It was only when I got back home to Minnesota, after a shower, and while looking in a full-length mirror, that I saw the softball-sized contusion on my left ass cheek – the rock had hit me higher up and further back than I had initially thought. It was a great souvenir from the trip: "The Kiss of Kilimanjaro."

From the Barranco Camp, on Day Six, we left the official Machame Route and struck out toward the famous Western Breach ascent route. I had left the United States not realizing that the Western Breach represents by far the most difficult and dangerous route that amateur climbers on Kili are allowed to attempt. My friends from California explained this reality to me. There are only a couple of outfitters who will bring clients up the Western Breach, including ours. People had been killed in rockslides on the Western Breach. The ice thaws and occasionally releases rocks as the day gets longer. This is why one must be helmeted and attempt the Western Breach only before sunrise. I may have reconsidered had I known this fact, but I did not do enough research, and it was too late now. Sometimes, ignorance is indeed bliss. The outfitter is of the opinion that the Western Breach is challenging, yes, but also quick and direct, and with impossibly stunning scenery as an added benefit. If people can just get through the Western Breach, then the ascent to the summit is relatively fast and painless (they say). As Ben continually reminded us, "It's doable. It's doable."

Rather than continue around the southern slopes of the mountain, we headed upward and westward over rocky ridges and scree. By now, Team Kili was starting to feel pretty fit. Everyone seemed to be acclimatizing well and no one lagged behind. The spectacular Western Breach wall ultimately came into view, and after about five hours of hard climbing we arrived at the Arrow Glacier Camp, at 15,300 feet. We had open views to the west and the entire Shira Plateau lay below us. It was now starting to inch closer to "fucking cold," and the full panoply of cold-weather gear came out in abundance. Weather patterns were fascinating and changed rapidly on the mountain, sometimes literally from moment to moment. Foggy, then sunny, then much colder and with tiny snowflakes, then foggy again. We never knew what to expect, and so we dressed in layers and either bulked up or stripped down depending on circumstances.

We spent the next day more or less resting and continuing to allow our bodies to acclimatize. There was a significant degree of psychological preparation as well. We were keenly aware that Day Seven would be the most arduous of them all as we made our ascent over the Western Breach wall to the Crater Camp at the edge of Kibo's crater. We would end up at 18,300 feet. From there, the summit was a mere 1000 feet above us. But first, the Western Breach. Ah, the Breach.

We arose early, at 3 a.m. There were seven climbers, four porters, and two guides, 13 of us in all. We were bundled up and relied on head lamps attached to our helmets to light our path. About two hours into this immensely fatiguing climb, I became a bit short of breath and one of my walking sticks broke. I asked Ben if we could pause for a few minutes while I regrouped. Several of us sat down. At that precise moment, we experienced a rock slide that came our way with great suddenness and which we could not see, but only hear. We hit the ground and covered up as fast as we could. I put my arm above my head. Father John protected daughter Alyson with his own body. Some people prayed. I found myself not fearful but rather intensely curious as the infernal noise came our way. *I wonder how this will turn out?* It might have been the last thought I ever had, and it was so mundane. As we braced ourselves for some kind of impact, we were peppered by small rocks and scree. The slide came directly at us, passing both right and left, as well as straight over our heads. Miraculously, no one was hurt. A couple of the guys reported that multiple good-sized boulders had bounded right over us. Ben, who has been up and down Kili 150 times since 2001, later related that this was the most violent rock slide that he had ever witnessed. We were stunned and glad to be alive, much less uninjured, like victims of a horrific car wreck who step out of the ruined, twisted vehicle unscathed. Our eyes were big as we checked in with each other. *Is everyone okay?* We laughed nervously. *What the fuck was that!?*

Later that evening, at dinner, I asked everyone what they had been thinking as chunks of Kilimanjaro came hurtling our way. One guy said, "I was thinking that I if I die right now, my wife is going to kill me." In a similar vein, another fellow had thought, "My wife is really going to be pissed at me if I die here today." John thought of only one thing, God bless him: "My daughter and her safety." Apparently, according to Ben, several porters were so frightened by what they had seen – when we all hit the ground our lights appeared to be extinguished to the people below, so they thought that we had been wiped out - that they refused to continue the climb. Basically, they had quit the expedition.

We had made it to this point. It was an electric feeling. Tomorrow would be summit day. Our aim would be for an early wake up, a short but rigorous climb, and sunrise on the mountaintop.

◄———►

Each of the members of Team Kili wished me a very happy birthday, on the day I turned 59-years-wise, as we basked in the morning sun's brilliance, above the clouds, at the highest point in Africa. We had all made it to the summit, together. I was very touched, and it will forever be one of the unforgettable moments of my life.

What goes up must come down. We spent perhaps 20 minutes at the summit (I would guess the temperature was somewhere around 10 degrees Fahrenheit, right between 'really cold' and 'fucking cold'), exhilarated, hugging each other, taking photographs, staring breathless at the surreal, panoramic expanse of the scene, realizing how small and insignificant we all are in the grand scheme of the earth and the universe, feeling sadness at the vastly diminished glacier, now wanting nothing more than a hot shower and a safe return to our homes and loved ones. So we headed down, and it would not take nearly as long as it did to go up. But for me, the trip back to sea level would prove more excruciating than anything that had happened up to that point.

We descended on the Mweka Route, past Barafu, which is a direct rather than a meandering descent of Kilimanjaro. We would be down in a day-and-a-half, over generally rugged and steep terrain. I was initially in fine form, but had neglected to do something important, which was to wear an additional layer of socks and to tighten up my boots. I just did not think of it. The pace became rapid as gravity took effect, and despite doing my best to brace myself with walking sticks, I succeeded in tearing both of my big toenails, and the nails on three other toes, off of the foot. Just lifted them right up. Oh goodness, the pain; 'twas exquisite. We came down more than 9,000 feet that day to the Mweka Camp. That night I removed my boots, examined the damage (considerable) and did my best to clean the wounds, apply disinfectant ointment, and wrap the injured digits in heavy-duty adhesive band aids. I was a victim of the curse known as, "The Toes of Kilimanjaro." The next day's hike, more than five miles, would be an absolute bitch.

It just so happened that I had been reading Hampton Side's heart-rending book, *Ghost Soldiers*, over the past several days. It is the story of American survivors of the Bataan Death March in WWII, who became prisoners of the Japanese in the Philippines. They were ultimately rescued in a daring commando raid, but their suffering knew no bounds. The book provided me with a terrific perspective check as I faced the rigors of Kili: *At least I'm not going through what those guys had to endure.* But I thought of our final day on the mountain as my own mini-Bataan Death March – nothing even close to what those brave men experienced, of course, but a test of grit nevertheless. John and Alyson were ever so kind and thoughtful, in that they stayed back and marched with me the whole way, at the pace of a 90-year-old man, as I struggled to walk. They kept up a cheerful chatter, stopped for photos, and just generally behaved as good sports. People asked me subsequently if I cried at any time that morning. I can say emphatically that I did not, but there was most assuredly a great deal of quiet whimpering going on. At one point, with about an hour to walk, we finally came upon an improved road, the first one we had seen in a week. Our guide, Tom, who had also slowed his pace and kept a watch on me, asked if I wanted a ride back to our final base camp in an ambulance that was sitting there available. I replied, "By golly Tom, I got up the mountain under my own power, and I will come down under my own power. So thank you anyway."

We arrived at the lovely Moivaro Coffee Plantation Lodge in Arusha, exhausted and ready for a hot shower, some champagne, and a final celebratory meal together. I examined my feet again, and the bandages I had so diligently applied the day before now refused to come off. The adhesive glue was strong, and I cut away what I could, but my toes were now a real mess, with dirty bandages contributing to the general unpleasantness of the whole situation. I put the best face on things and we enjoyed our last evening as Team Kili. Then it was off to the airport. I flew home, again through Amsterdam, and after 16 hours of flying, upon touching down in Minneapolis, I was barely able to pull my shoes on as a result of badly swollen feet. The next day my doctor cut away the bandages, cleaned things up, took one look at those two nasty, seriously infected feet, and prescribed painkillers and penicillin. I took photos with my iPhone and sent them off to a couple of friends. "Not even the Pope would kiss those feet," said one.

<hr />

After dinner on summit day, my birthday, a very long and eventful day which had entailed both triumph and travails, our chef Dan and his wonderful team brought a cake into our dining tent, to my great surprise and delight. It was a lemon pound cake, with icing that spelled out 'Happy Birthday', and it sported five candles which burned brightly in the darkness of the tent. Dan and the guys sang:

"Happy birthday to you
Happy birthday to you
Happy birthday, Mr. Jeffu
Happy birthday to you!"

I said, "Gee, thanks so much…" but they were not done. They sang again. One of the cooks possessed an absolutely magnificent tenor; he was really good, with a fine, rich, full, even operatic voice. He led the chorus as they filled the tent with the power of their collective volume. I said, "Oh, you really shouldn't have…" and they interrupted me and sang again. Then again. I finally just shut up, smiled, and let them finish. Six stanzas later they finally ran out of gas, reluctantly. All of the Americans laughed hysterically, as we had most certainly in all our lives never heard this ever-so-familiar ditty sung with so much enthusiasm, so much energy, so loudly, and so many times. Even as I winced in pain because of my feet, I could not help but join in the raucous laughter and thunderous applause that followed this inspired performance. I blew out the candles, they gave me the gift of a brightly colored t-shirt that said 'Tanzania,' and we all enjoyed a delicious piece of cake. I was profoundly moved by their generous, heartfelt gesture. It was a really nice thing that they did. Tears came to my eyes.

I thought later, after I got home, that my surprise birthday party was a very representative moment of our time on Kili; it contained spontaneity, exhilaration, friendship, laughter, joy, generosity, and a bit of pain, all at once. And it really had nothing at all to do with getting to the top of the mountain. As Ben told us, "We are just passing by the summit. Reaching the summit is not the point. It is the journey that is the goal." The journey was our goal. It is the memory of the journey, and the journey alone, that I will always cherish and never forget.

CHAPTER THREE

A NIGHT AT THE OPERA

SANTA FE, NEW MEXICO

"In the beginning there was nothing where the world now stands: no ground; no earth; only darkness, water and cyclone; no people, fishes or living things."

— JICARILLA APACHE CREATION NARRATIVE —

The oral history is a bit cloudy but apparently the story goes something like this: Years ago, two men on horseback rode slowly along a lonely stretch of remote and desolate terrain at the very edge of the vast reaches of the American Southwest, just outside the town of Santa Fe, New Mexico. The scene they beheld was magnificent. As they peered into the distance from their position on a low hill, they saw gorgeous mountains jutting to the heavens, table-topped mesas, and steep-sided arroyos, gouged from the earth eons ago. They might have been traversing the surface of a far distant planet. The endless expanse of sky was a dazzling shade of blue. But these men had no time to enjoy the view. They were on a serious mission, which required them to be armed with rifles and ever vigilant. Occasionally they were compelled to take a shot. They listened carefully as the gunfire echoed.

The year was 1956. The two men were Jack Purcell – an acoustician from Boston – and John Crosby, the visionary founder of what would become the world famous Santa Fe Opera. Their purpose in firing a number of rifle shots from a variety of different spots was to determine where best to locate the outdoor opera venue that Crosby desired desperately to build. They finally found the perfect, rough-and-ready corner of high desert terrain – where the explosive boom reverberated most musically to their ears - and the rest is artistic history.

◄────►

Opera is weird and wonderful. I'm not sure exactly why, but I have always loved it so (perhaps it is because I am, if not wonderful, at least a bit weird.) I have always maintained that the most amazing musical instrument of them all is the human voice. There is no force of nature that I have ever experienced that compares to a stage full of trained opera singers, working together, pounding out a finale all at once. You can feel the G-forces as your hair blows back, your eyes begin to water, your nose runs, and the skin on your face becomes contorted and stretched. My wife Faith and I have been past patrons of the quite accomplished and well-regarded Minnesota Opera. We have sat rapt through *Carmen, The Magic Flute, La Boheme, The Marriage of Figaro, Turandot, Madame Butterfly* and *Das Rheingold*, among many others. We have enjoyed virtually every opera we've seen, with the exception of *Nixon in China*. Sorry, had to leave at the intermission of that one. It was discordant, dissatisfying, and in the end we had to cut things short (just like with Nixon's presidency). We walked from the Ordway Theater across the street to the St. Paul Grill for a stiff drink and an early steak dinner.

But opera at its best represents a brilliant spectacle and a particularly compelling way to tell stories, uniquely and entirely through words set to music. If one is willing to be open of mind and heart (and eyes and ears, of course), to suspend disbelief just for a few hours, then opera can be astonishing in its capacity to enlighten, entrance and entertain. I have more than once been so moved by opera that I have gotten a lump in my throat and shed quiet tears. This is a powerful medium.

Which is why I was so very excited when my beloved cousin Richard Paulson's oldest son, Andrew, actually became a professional opera singer.

◄────►

Claudio Monteverdi, who was born in Cremona, Italy in 1567, did not invent opera, but he became its first great composer. With the debut of his *Orfeo*, in 1607, came opera's first undisputed masterwork. It is one of only six of Monteverdi's 19 stage works that have survived to the present, and it is still performed to this day in operatic repertories the world over. *Orfeo* combined musical and dramatic art - such as they existed in early 17th-century Italy - in unforgettable fashion. With Monteverdi's achievement, the new genre called opera would continue to grow and flourish for the next four centuries and beyond.

Interestingly, at just about the same time that Italian opera began to develop into a recognized and popular form of entertainment, Spanish explorer Juan de Onate first laid European eyes on what would turn out to be a future American mecca for the arts and for opera: Santa Fe, New Mexico. Santa Fe became the capital of the New Mexico territory in 1609, as decreed by Spanish officials, who then began to construct the Palace of the Governors, today the central feature of downtown Santa Fe and the oldest surviving non-Native, continuously occupied public structure in the United States.

Several years ago my older brother, Tom, and his husband, Charlie Newman, left their architectural jobs in Philadelphia to retire to Santa Fe. They live in a comfortable, sprawling adobe home, within walking distance of the plaza downtown. They love their many friends, their dogs, their gardens, the artistic scene, the galleries, the history, the restaurants, the farmer's market, the spectacular desert landscapes and the clean, fresh air. Although he would be too modest to ever acknowledge the fact, Tom is an excellent painter who spends his days in a small studio, adjacent to their *casa*, creating his distinctive abstract renderings, primarily in oil on canvas. He has participated in some gallery showings and, if we drag the information out of him, will even admit that he has sold a few paintings. I have purchased a couple myself – and he has given out others as gifts - and they proudly adorn the walls of our home in suburban Minneapolis. My brother is a superb artist. Faith and I, along with our daughters Anna and Lucia, have enjoyed visiting Uncles Tom and Charlie in Santa Fe on a number of occasions over the years. Nevertheless, the timing had never been right for us to see the legendary Santa Fe Opera, which we had always very much wanted to do. That was the case until Faith and I made a visit in the late summer of 2016, the 60th anniversary of this fantastic enterprise.

←——————→

I set out to learn more about the Opera prior to our trip. The founder, John Crosby, was a trained musician who came from a privileged Eastern background but had fallen in love with New Mexico during a visit as a schoolboy. He kept coming back. His parents eventually purchased a summer home just north of the city. Crosby understood the very welcoming tradition of Santa Fe toward artists of all types and the enormous potential appeal of the place to tourists. In the mid-'50s he began to formulate the idea of establishing an opera house, but with a twist: his would be an open-air theater so that, simply put, he could present opera *al fresco*. When a 76-acre ranch property – whose succession of previous owners had grown pinto beans, raised foxes and, later, run a pig farm – became available near his parent's home north on the road to Taos, Crosby borrowed $200,000 from his father, secured the parcel, and set about the work of building an opera company.

At the time, there were only three major American opera companies. With just a few exceptions, when the summer months rolled around operas and orchestras throughout the United States shut down, and musical artists made their way to Europe to continue to hone their craft. Crosby sought to reverse this trend. He envisioned a grand summer festival, international in its scope. He further envisioned nothing short of the development of a truly and uniquely American style of opera. His creation would be futuristic in its outlook, with a focus on providing opportunities for talented young American singers and new, rather than strictly tried and true operatic productions. The Santa Fe Opera, in John Crosby's way of thinking, with its daring, modern approach and spectacular location, would become a sacred place of musical pilgrimage, a must-have experience for artists and a must-see entertainment for their audiences.

Construction of the original house, seating 480, was completed in early July 1957, just in time for the opening-night performance of Puccini's *Madame Butterfly*, directed by (who else?) John Crosby. There were 10 curtain calls that evening, all six of the initial performances sold out, and the game was on.

Ticket prices were an eminently reasonable $2.40, $3.60 and $4.80. The simple yet awe-inspiring venue featured folding chairs and wooden benches for its patrons, who sat outside, unprotected from the elements, facing a covered stage with redwood walls. The audience peered west through the open stage to the spectacular Jemez Mountains in the distance. For maximum acoustical effect a small, crescent-shaped reflecting pool sat between the orchestra pit and the seating area. Patrons took their chances as the weather in northern New Mexico was then and continues to be iffy, changing on a moment's notice. There had been discussion from the very beginning of covering the entire house, especially as wild summer storms with cold, soaking rains caused the postponement of a number of performances in that initial season. But The Santa Fe Opera remained an open-air enterprise and the people continued to come in droves.

On July 27, 1967, the venerable opera house burned to the ground, leaving nothing but charred and twisted metal beams and the remnants of a concrete staircase. No one knows how or exactly when the fire started. Crosby, his board of directors and community-minded, opera-loving Santa Feans immediately came together to rebuild. A new and even more magnificent theater, with a seating capacity of 1,887, rose from the ashes and opened in time for a comeback performance of *Madame Butterfly* in July 1968. This bold architectural statement featured two gigantic, curved roofs reaching desperately toward each other but not quite meeting in the middle, thus preserving the outdoor tradition. But now at least some patrons, if not all (534 seats were still open to the elements) would remain dry during a rainstorm.

Finally, in 1991, Crosby was compelled to act. During that season, 22 of 37 performances were dampened or inundated with rain. Gift-shop ponchos became a valuable and then scarce and ultimately non-existent commodity as they entirely sold out. There had not been another summer like it in Crosby's memory, and so he made a decision to put the wheels in motion over the next several years to fully protect his audiences from the vagaries of Mother Nature.

The current house, by far the most astonishing structure of them all, cost $20.5 million to build. It is fully roofed and accommodates 2,100, with additional standing room capacity of 100. The opening performance on July

3, 1998 featured, once again, *Madame Butterfly*, exactly 41 years to the day after John Crosby's vision first became reality. The new house sits on the old footprint with large concrete columns framing the corners of the original stage. The two graceful curved roofs – weighing a massive 435 tons - are now linked and held steady by a network of masts and tension rods. The auditorium remains open on either side. Eight tall and slender wind baffles are positioned south of the theater to provide protection from gusty high desert winds. As before, the stage has no back wall so that audiences can still enjoy a distant glimpse of dramatic western mountains and picturesque sunsets. Of the modern-day Santa Fe Opera House author Phillip Huscher says, "... the juxtaposition of its dazzling, sculptural theater and the hardscrabble land – the totally modern and the very ancient, a state-of-the-art facility in a timeless setting – is as unexpected as the pairing of opera and the American West itself."

My Cousin Richard Paulson's mom, Peggy, was my Dad's older sister and his father, Stanley, was one of my Dad's closest and dearest friends for many decades, until Stan's passing. Rich has two sons, Andrew and Mark. Rich's lovely wife Denise has been a kind and loving step-mom to the boys for many years. They are a great family, and Rich has always been one of my favorite guys – cousin or not – in all the world. We've known each other all our lives, for goodness sake.

Andrew is a tall, good-looking, red-bearded young man of 26. I thought that, for some incomprehensible reason, I had never met him prior to the summer of 2016. Rich later reminded me that I had met Andrew, when he was a toddler, at a family get-together in 1991. Rich forgave my oversight; at the time, he explained, "Andrew was almost two, but he was very short and not much of a conversationalist so he would have been easy to miss." The grown-up Andrew has penetrating brown eyes, with which he studies you closely. My first impression was that he was a soft-spoken, serious guy, but upon getting to know him his vivid personality, curiosity about the world, charm and humor came to the fore. While Andrew was in junior high school it became apparent that he was deeply interested and had a significant talent in music.

His parents signed him up for piano. But like so many other kids who take music lessons for years, at one point he told his father he wanted to quit. Rich would not let him. *Ain't gonna, happen young man.* By the time high school rolled around, with training and practice, it became obvious that the kid could really sing. I mean really belt out a song. Like someone who might be an opera performer someday. His father tells a hilarious tale about how, after a particularly dramatic and powerful solo in a high school musical, rendered masterfully in his fine baritone, all of the girls in the audience surrounded him and swooned, "Oh Andrew, Oh Andrew..." He wasn't quite the Beatles but it was pretty damn close. This is the story Rich tells in response to the question, "When did you have the first inkling that Andrew might be a star someday?"

Andrew matriculated to Westminster Choir College where he received a Bachelor of Music degree in Voice Performance, *magna cum laude.* He furthered his studies at Florida State University, earning a Master's in Voice Performance. And then, by golly, the intrepid fellow was on his way. Andrew has performed in concert as a baritone soloist with the Tallahassee Community Chorus and the Florida State Baroque ensemble. He has had stints with the Sarasota Opera, Opera Colorado, Central City Opera, Opera on the Avalon and the Sugar Creek Opera. He has received recognition in numerous competitions such as, among others, the Mobile Opera Competition (second place), the Denver Opera Lyric Guild Competition (third place), and the Florida Suncoast Opera Guild Competition (fourth place). Did you ever know that opera singers were so competitive? Along the way, Andrew met and married his vivacious and irrepressible wife Abigail Rethwisch, who is also an accomplished young opera singer. In 2016, Andrew was in his second season as an Apprentice Artist with the Santa Fe Opera (Abby, who is a soprano, will be in the apprentice program in Santa Fe in 2017.) That summer, Andrew would perform as Happy in Puccini's *La Fanciulla del West*, a Diener (morgue worker) in *Capriccio* and was Mercutio cover (backup) in *Romeo et Juliette*.

As apprentices in Santa Fe, Andrew and Abby are part of a long and honored tradition. When John Crosby founded the opera in 1957, youthful and talented American singers who wanted to develop their skills had no other recourse but to travel to Europe for additional learning and stage experience. Crosby determined to put an end to this. He said, "My own personal experience in the field of opera when I was a youngster rather soured me with regard to what might be called 'alleged apprentice programs' in which a great amount of work was extracted from young people with a minimum of training and help offered, and an extremely poor caliber of instruction provided. Perhaps it has been with these personal experiences in mind that I have always wanted to feel The Santa Fe Opera Apprentice Program was in every way meaningful, helpful, and honest about the service it expects from the apprentices and the instruction with which it provides them."

There were 11 apprentices in the first season who sang as the chorus and, in some cases, had the opportunity to perform in bit roles. A new way of developing American operatic talent had been established. From 300 auditioning hopefuls by 1967 to more than 800 during the 1980s, the program grew in scope and significance. Andrew told us that he was one of around 1,000 applicants; of that number something between 300 and 400 received a tryout; from that total, a mere 40 were selected. Unless my math is off, an initial applicant therefore had about a four percent likelihood of ultimately becoming an apprentice (as Jim Carrey famously observed in the movie *Dumb and Dumber*, "So you're telling me there's a chance!") The program opened up to theater technicians in 1965 and, all told, more than 4,000 aspiring performers and backstage techies have gone on from Santa Fe to careers in the opera business.

Andrew gushed as he described not only the fun of working as a member of the chorus but also the master classes he has taken from a variety of experts, the diction and acting coaching he has received, and the excitement of participating in the annual apprentice evening of scenes from the company's repertory. Ironically, Andrew took his turn on apprentice night as Henry Kissinger in a scene from *Nixon in China*. My brother saw the production, but I did not; Tom said Andrew was very good in the role, and I'm sure he was; I never told Andrew that I think that particular opera is a complete piece of shit - I'm quite positive he wouldn't give a rat's ass what I think, especially about opera, which is as it should be. We all got a huge kick out of watching Andrew walk us through the choreography of a sword fight: every move is numbered, like a dance step, and must be precisely executed or else, well, someone might get hurt. In that spirit, Andrew relayed a story about a fight scene he was in during a rehearsal in which his opponent – one step behind in the count, apparently - inadvertently socked him in the face. Hazards of the profession.

$$\longleftarrow\longrightarrow$$

The Santa Fe Opera is regarded as a festival of international importance in significant part because of its focus not just on the old, reliable operatic standards, but on the new and the different. From the very beginning, the Opera opened itself up to untested productions and the possibility of changing perceptions through an approach that was and remains distinctly American. Let's just say it: the Santa Fe Opera is entirely unpretentious and, frankly, a little bit funky. And funky is one the words that popped into my mind when we had the great pleasure of watching Andrew, as a member of the chorus (but with a name, "Happy") sing and dance and have a hootin,' hollerin,' rootin'-tootin' time in Giacomo Puccini's *La Fanciulla del West (The Girl of the Golden West)*.

On the day that we were going to see Andrew perform, Faith and I met Rich, Denise, Andrew, Abby, Tom and Charlie for lunch at the Museum Hill Restaurant, adjacent to the splendid Santa Fe Botanical Garden. I loved my chicken soup with a Greek salad, and Rich and I enjoyed an ice cold Santa Fe Pale Ale, a local craft brew highly recommended by Andrew. We then headed back to Tom and Charlie's place for a chance to get to know Andrew and Abby better. We had a discussion not only about opera but also concerning what the weather might bring - a necessary consideration when, after all, we would essentially be sitting outside all evening. Our intention was to tailgate prior to the production, another great Santa Fe tradition. Tom and Charlie mentioned that the weather had gotten strange in New Mexico over the last period of years. Charlie called it not global warming but "global weirding."

Indeed, according to the Nature Conservancy, more than 95% of New Mexico has experienced mean temperature increases over the last 30 years. While some say that if one wants to avoid natural disasters the safest state in the union is New Mexico (not a lot of earthquakes, hurricanes, or tornados and the like). Still, temperatures throughout the American Southwest are rising, streams are drying up, drought conditions prevail, forests are dying, and wildfires are becoming more frequent and deadly. Just prior to our visit a massive wildfire had devastated neighborhoods in the East Mountains area of

New Mexico. What became known as the Dog Head Fire burned nearly 18,000 acres and destroyed a dozen homes.

As it turned out, a strong downpour spoiled our tailgate, so we ate indoors at Tom and Charlie's: sandwich wraps, grapes, chips, cookies, and some really good Pinot Noir. Perfect summer picnic fare. Andrew had been entirely calm all day – no pre-game jitters - and had to be on his way some hours before the show. We would see him backstage afterwards. Just as we finished our meal the skies cleared and gave way to what would become a cool but comfortable, light-jacket kind of evening. We arrived at the opera house with the sun still mostly warm and bright, and admired the view of the Jemez Mountains to the west, beyond the Rio Grande. Looking east, we could see the Sangre de Cristo range. There is a prominent mountain in that direction affectionately known as "Santa Fe Baldy," that sits 12,622 feet high. And to the north, amazingly, one can see 90 miles, all the way to San Antonio Mountain and the Colorado state line. We took some pictures, had a glass of Cabernet just beyond the entrance plaza in the outdoor foyer, and then settled into our seats for a night at the opera.

La Fanciulla del West, with music by Giacomo Puccini (1858-1924) and libretto by Guelfo Civinini and Carlo Zangarini, premiered at the Metropolitan Opera in New York in 1910, with the legendary tenor Enrico Caruso and soprano Emmy Destinn in the leading roles. The production is sung in Italian with English and Spanish opera titles. It was first introduced in Santa Fe in 1991. It is said that Puccini never actually visited any of the places he attempted to portray in his operas; nonetheless, it is obvious that he had done his level best to depict frontier life during the California Gold Rush. But trust me, one truly has to be willing to take a trip to make-believe land here, which is almost a prerequisite for opera in general, as I can't imagine any actual scenario in the Old West where a bunch of rugged cowboys and grizzled gold miners, all heavily armed, stood around bellying up to the bar in a rough-and-tumble saloon, singing loudly to each other in Italian. As I say, this is why opera is really fun.

The basic storyline goes like this: Minnie, the central character, is a strong and self-sufficient Western woman who owns a bar called the "Polka," but also teaches Bible lessons on the side. She is highly independent and takes guff from no man. Anyhow, unfortunately for her, Minnie falls for a charming no-goodnik named Dick Johnson. He is an outlaw whose real name is Ramirrez, and he leads a band of cut-throats. Really bad dudes. When Minnie finds out Dick's true identity, she is upset but eventually comes around. Sheriff Jack Rance, who has been spurned by Minnie, not surprisingly goes hunting for Dick. Dick gets shot. Minnie tends his wounds, then makes a deal with Rance and wins Dick's freedom in a card game (*do not mess with that woman*.) Tough luck for Dick though, when his sorry ass gets captured by a posse and there is an interminable final scene during which an angry mob has a noose around Dick's neck, but they just keep singing and singing. The mob sings, then Dick sings, the mob, then Dick. Back and forth and back and forth. *Will you please just hang the son of a bitch already?!* Anyhow, Minnie steps in at the last minute, totin' and wavin' a pistol (*do not mess with that woman*) and pretty much saves Dick's life. The angry mob is chastised. Gosh, they're sorry. They skulk away. Minnie and Dick disappear over the horizon together. The End.

Andrew spent a good deal of time onstage, and he was great, although of course we could not hear his individual baritone but for the noise of all the other singers, who of course all sing very loudly. Abby told us that the way to identify Andrew was that he had on a really pointy cowboy hat (he did) and that he wore high-water dungarees (ditto that). I poked my brother in the ribs, "There he is, do you see him?"

As for Puccini's music, the noted fine arts critic Barrymore Laurence Scherer has written, "His melodic richness is irresistible. Crowned with thrilling high notes, the melting beauty of his arias captivates the ear. Enhancing this appeal is the opulent chromatic beauty of his harmony – even to listeners untrained in music theory, the basic sound of his suave harmonic language is like an audible signature. Moreover, Puccini's music glows with the polychrome magnificence of his instrumentation, which blends the flexible, full-bodied orchestral style of Verdi's 'Otello' and 'Falstaff' with the plush instrumental timbres of Massenet." *Say what? What you talkin' 'bout, Barrymore?* All I know is that everyone present concurred that the music in *La Fanciulla del West* was fantastic. Good job, Mr. Puccini.

Andrew was very gracious backstage; he looked each of us in the eye and thanked us all up and down for taking the time to share in his special moment. I would not have missed it for the world. What a kid.

⬅━━━➡

They say that the popularity of opera is on the wane. How will we ever get Millennials, with their allegedly limited attention spans, interested in this art form? I don't know the answer to that question but I do know that it makes me happy that talented young singers like Andrew Paulson and Abigail Rethwisch are pursuing their operatic dreams with great diligence and high energy. And as long as The Santa Fe Opera – and other like-minded companies all over the world - continues to determinedly envision new ways of doing things and to invest in the future, I cannot help but believe that the proverbial fat lady has not yet begun to sing and that opera will be around for a good long while to come.

CHAPTER FOUR

DÉJÀ VU ALL OVER AGAIN

VENICE, ITALY

"Each night, when I go to sleep, I die. And the next morning, when I wake up, I am reborn."

— MAHATMA GANDHI —

I do not believe in reincarnation. I am a practical man and a strong skeptic with respect to all things paranormal. I had never traveled to Italy. More specifically, I had never traveled to Venice, Italy. I had never read a book about Venice. I had never looked at a map of Venice. I didn't know jack shit about Venice. But when I finally got there, several years ago, I was pretty damn sure I'd been there before. Because I remembered it. I remembered Venice.

⬅—➡

I have since come to learn a great deal about Venice. Usually, and especially with such an important venue, I do significant research in advance of my travels so that I will have better context for what I am seeing and experiencing. But the crush of work and domestic business travel had prevented me from even thinking about Venice at all, until Faith and I actually arrived in the city called the "Queen of the Adriatic." We would only be there for a day, just typical tourists, but what an interesting day it turned out to be.

The original Venetians thought of themselves as Romans. The glory that became Venice started as a series of independent settlements, spread out over a cluster of marshy islands in the northern Adriatic Sea, whose occupants had fled the terror of barbarian hordes. The Roman Empire could no longer defend its many far-flung citizens, and so the first Venetians sought the protection of remote and stout island redoubts which they knew that even the Goths, the Huns, and other marauding, uncivilized ruffians of their ilk would never dare attack. Those fierce and nomadic warrior tribes, over the centuries, slowly but inexorably, like crazed and frothing hyenas after a wounded zebra, would ultimately bring down the Roman Empire.

Over time, the Venetians allied themselves with the Byzantine Empire whose capital, Constantinople (modern-day Istanbul), had become a sophisticated, diverse center of civilization, representing the last vestiges of the Roman Empire. The Venetians were now a part of what was in essence an Asian empire and they adjusted their sights accordingly, to the East. They built countless, sturdy ships and immersed themselves in the pursuit of riches through extensive trading. In a controversial turn of the tables, French crusaders sacked Constantinople in 1204. In effect, Christian attackers had overtaken the Christian seat of the Eastern Roman Empire. This was the culmination of the Fourth Crusade and a violent looting in which Venetian mercenaries enthusiastically participated. When all was said and done, many of Constantinople's most precious treasures and valuable monuments had been unceremoniously uprooted and transported to Venice. By the 15th century, an independent Venice had become the supreme maritime and commercial power of Western Europe. But the Byzantine influence in religion, art and architecture can still be seen in Venice today. In his book *Venice: A New History*, author Thomas Madden sums up this fascinating legacy: "Although later Venetian authors tried to clean up the details, Venice was nonetheless the child of chaos, uncertainty, and fear. Yet it was also the product of courage, defiance, and resolve. The first Venetians were Romans, proudly refusing to cooperate with a world in collapse, and clinging to a glorious past that had no hope of return. That proud, conservative outlook tempered with a pious devotion to God and his Church was woven deeply into the Venetian character from its earliest years."

The island city of Venice is just three square miles in size, is of course built on water and, as a result, its major thoroughfares are canals. There are no motorized vehicles. The "Canal Grande" (Grand Canal) meanders through the middle of the city; from the west, a traveler passes under such bridges as the Calatrava, the famed Rialto, and the Accadamia. Eventually, one arrives at the "Piazza San Marco" (St. Mark's Square) to see the magnificent Basilica and the sublime Doge's Palace. The "Ponte dei Sospiri" (Bridge of Sighs) is the notorious enclosed bridge, made of white limestone and containing windows with formidable stone bars, leading from the Doge's Palace to what was once a prison. Legend says that convicts who crossed the short span on their way to lonely, dank and rat-infested confinement turned one last time, wistfully, to witness the splendor that was Venice, and sighed.

The city is organized into six districts, called "sestieri," and each of them has some kind of distinct identity. Venice's most amazing churches can be found to the west, in Santa Croce. In the north, the Jewish population once resided in Cannaregio. And San Marco and San Polo, along the banks of the Grand Canal, were once thriving hubs of commercial, governmental and administrative activity.

Interestingly, though Venice is actually relatively small – one could walk across it in an hour – it is dense and a bit of a maze. In the guidebook *Walking Venice – The Best of the City*, produced by National Geographic, the authors say, "With its complex network of at least 175 canals crossed by as many as 400 bridges, the city is riddled with narrow alleys, secret courtyards, twists, turns, and dead ends.... You can reach all major sights on foot and, outside of the San Marco/Rialto areas, the city is relatively crowd free. But be warned – Venice is notoriously difficult to navigate. The many canals and bridges can be disorienting and you will get lost without a reliable map..."

The flamboyant libertine Giacomo Girolamo Casanova was born in Venice, and lived there off and on throughout his eventful lifetime (1725 – 1798). In his 2016 biography, *Casanova: The World of a Seductive Genius*, author Laurence Bergreen states, "Superstition ruled Casanova's Venice. It was believed that magic and the devil caused people to lose their way in the city's labyrinthine streets or even to go mad. Venetians routinely acknowledged the existence of ghosts. To this day some Venetians swear that when they place their fingerprints on the wall of a house, they can feel the presence of the departed and hear their voices."

Faith and I traveled into the city on a cool and sparkling late-autumn morning by waterbus - a motorized, covered boat called a "vaporetto" - with a small group and our tour guide, a young 20-something Venetian woman named Lucia (we were naturally inclined to be fond of her because she has the same name as our youngest daughter.) We entered the Grand Canal from the east, and made our way past a series of spectacular buildings. We snapped photo after photo of a seemingly endless array of gorgeous, ornate, highly-differentiated structures, showing Byzantine, Gothic, Renaissance and Baroque influences, and each with a fascinating story that Lucia simply did not have time enough to tell. Lord Byron used to take his daily exercise when he lived here by swimming in the canal. The wealthy American heiress, Peggy Guggenheim, established a world-renowned art museum. Elton John, among other present-day luminaries, has a place in Venice, for goodness sake. As with so many whirlwind, "touristy" experiences, there was a bit of sensory and information overload.

We finally came to a stop, I don't know exactly where (I was unfortunately not journaling at the time and therefore was not paying close attention), disembarked the vaporreto, received a brief preview of our upcoming walking tour, and then sat down outside at a lovely café on the waterfront to enjoy a "ciaoccolata calda" (hot chocolate – very tasty) and some cookies. I had been carrying a backpack for Faith. There was nothing particularly valuable inside, just an extra light jacket, water bottle and snacks, maybe a pair of sunglasses and some sunscreen – but no camera or iPhone. This is perhaps why I forgot about the backpack, which I had casually draped over the back of my chair, when we got up to start our tour. We were headed in an indirect fashion to our final objective, St. Mark's Square. Lucia gave an expert description of the landmarks along the way and a succinct recitation of Venetian history. About 20 minutes into the tour, Faith realized that I did not have the backpack with me. *Oh-oh, I fucked up.* We asked Lucia to stop, told her our predicament, and I indicated that I would head back to get the lost article. She graciously put in a call to the café and asked them to hold onto the backpack. Next, she gave me less than precise – dare I say confusing? - instructions as to how to get back to where I needed to go and then, finally, how to complete the return journey to rejoin the group at St. Mark's Square. *Uh, okay, what did she just say?* She did a lot of pointing in the general direction of this, and then turned around and sort of waved toward the approximate location of that. She then smiled, said, "You'll find us," and sent me on my way. Faith looked worried, but we were in cell-phone contact and so, at worst, a search party could hopefully be sent out before I was discovered several days later floating face down and naked in the Grand Canal. I went off to glory with a spring in my step.

◆━━━━━▶

We had asked Lucia whether Venice was sinking. She gave a rather long-winded answer, the gist of which was, "No one is precisely sure what is happening, but it does seem that we are sinking. How fast we will sink is anyone's guess." Indeed, there is no denying that, at the very least, Venice is vulnerable to flooding. The Grand Canal, key to the city's well-being, was once a river that emanated from the Italian mainland and drained into the Adriatic. Over time, sediment formed barrier islands at one end of the river, cutting Venice off from the sea and forming a lagoon. Today, tides run to and from the ocean, cleaning out the Grand Canal and its smaller, connected waterways with massive amounts of water flowing in and out, twice on a daily basis. Enormous, heavy buildings were erected on the city's marshy islands by placing them on top of wood pilings driven into the clay. But Venice is in continuous peril because the ocean tides are strong, highly variable and can create serious damage to the city's many superb but aging waterfront structures. A recent article in the *Encyclopedia Britannica* explains, "...the lagoon requires careful husbandry to prevent it from threatening the very existence of Venice. The deepening of channels in the 20th century, the over extraction of fresh water from mainland aquifers, the rising of the Adriatic Sea, and the geologic sinking of the Po River basin have all combined to lower the land level, creating a serious flooding problem. On a regular basis, when high tides combine with winds from the south and east, the waters of the lagoon rise and flood the city, creating the 'acqua alta' (high water) so familiar to Venetians, and elaborate raised platforms are laid out in main squares to allow tourists and others to walk around the city."

A serious flood inundated Venice in 1966, sparking widespread alarm and an effort to study and solve the problem of high water. Disagreement was fierce, however, as to both the causes of high water and what steps to take. Venice had flooded periodically throughout its history, but never so much as it has since the 1970s. Acqua alta has occurred more than 50 times per year since 1980 and, in some years, much more often than that. In 1994, the Higher Council of Public Works approved a scheme to build a network of submerged gates that could be inflated with air when the water rose, thus completely blocking off the lagoon. The proposal was and remains highly controversial, and has been subject to lawsuits, appeals, endless environmental studies and bureaucratic infighting. Construction of the system, known as MOSE ("Modulo Sperimentale Elettromeccanico" or Experimental Electromechanical Module) got underway in 2003, but is not scheduled to be finally completed until the summer of 2018. It will probably end up costing around six billion dollars. In the meantime, it seems that Venice remains just as vulnerable to flooding as it was in 1966. The Venetians, as ever, are resilient and hold out hope. About their beloved city, they have a favorite saying, "Sempre crolla, ma non cade" ("It is always crumbling, but it never falls.")

↔

I just knew where to go and that's all there is to it. When I left the tour group in search of the missing backpack, I was very certain of the way to get there. Everything seemed eerily familiar. I did not retrace our steps from the café, which I could not have done if I had tried; we had taken far too many twists and turns. I know that naysayers who have been to Venice will say, 'But there are certainly some sporadic street signs, and especially signs pointing to major landmarks,' but I can tell you that I did not reference any signs. They will say, 'He must have had a map,' but I did not. Surely, they will say, 'He asked a native Venetian for directions.' Again, no. They will scoff, 'There are several major thoroughfares, such as the Mercerie and Fabbri. He just took one of those easier routes.' Nope. I took a brisk and direct walk, with nary a moment of hesitation, a left turn here, two right turns, over this bridge, and so on. I was back at the café in less than 10 minutes. I thanked the server for the backpack, and then turned around and took a completely different route to St. Mark's. Lots of side streets and alleys, several more bridges, no dead ends; as close to a bee line as one can achieve in Venice. In 15 minutes I spied Faith in the distance across the square, standing in front of the Basilica. She looked surprised.

"How did you do that so fast?" she queried.

"I don't know. That was actually really weird. I just knew how to find you." Lucia was right.

The best way I can think of to describe what I experienced is this: early in my professional career, when I was in my thirties, I worked for a number of years in downtown Minneapolis. I spent several years practicing law out of the IDS Tower, and then began my Fortune 100 business career, with the Target Corporation, in the International Multifoods building. Those who know downtown Minneapolis know that we have an elaborate skyway system (a heated, glass-enclosed walkway one story above street level), primarily as a means of allowing people to get around easily and comfortably in our ridiculously frigid and snowy winters. I spent endless hours over the years traversing the skyway, and got to know the rather Byzantine system well. If you plopped me in the skyway near my old haunts today, even though it has been some time, I would know where to go. I had the same sensation when I was in Venice; I just knew my way, as if I remembered those streets, alleyways and bridges because I had traversed them many times. But it was all so odd because, of course, I had never been there before.

In the early 1960s, when the great New York Yankees sluggers, Roger Maris and Mickey Mantle, who were in the prime of their athletic prowess and batted next to each other in the Yankees' lineup, repeatedly hit consecutive home runs, their sage teammate – and King of Malapropisms – Yogi Berra observed, "It's déjà vu all over again."

The *Merriam-Webster Dictionary* defines the term "déjà vu" as follows: "1a:

the illusion of remembering scenes and events when experienced for the first time; b: a feeling that one has seen or heard something before." Note the word 'illusion.' In a 2010 *Psychology Today* article, Dr. Judith Orloff states, "Déjà vu is a common intuitive experience that has happened to many of us. The expression is derived from the French, meaning 'already seen.' When it occurs, it seems to spark our memory of a place we have already been, a person we have already seen, or an act we have already done.... [There are] many theories to explain déjà vu: a memory of a dream, a precognition, a coincidental overlapping of events or even a past life experience in which we rekindle ancient alliances. What matters is that it draws us closer to the mystical. It is an offering, an opportunity for additional knowledge about ourselves and others." Those who believe that déjà vu is merely an illusion posit that there is some kind of a physical cause, such as a neurological discharge; déjà vu has also been linked to seizure activity in temporal lobe epilepsy. The scientific community readily acknowledges that it is an extraordinarily difficult subject to study, yet it is said that well over two-thirds of the population has had a déjà vu experience. Déjà vu is almost always reported as a brief, transitory sensation. Here in a blink, then gone.

For me, I understand that many great religions of the world and countless intelligent, thoughtful people believe in reincarnation. I do not. But I also don't think that I had any kind of neurological discharge (not even sure exactly what that term means) that would account for my remarkable, unerring walk in Venice. I am also, very thankfully, not epileptic. My sense of familiarity and directional confidence was sustained in its power, not fleeting in any way, as is supposedly typical. There was no illusion to it. I got to where I intended to go, easily; the fact of my successful and timely arrival at the right location – not once, but twice - proves it. So I am stumped.

━━━▶

When I told her this story, my daughter Lucia smiled and suggested, "I think you were a merchant who lived in Venice, 300 years ago." Pragmatic, no-nonsense person that I am, I find that or any similar scenario to be highly unlikely. But the human condition is deeply mysterious, as is the universe, and there is so much that we simply don't understand, and never will. There is unseen energy all around us. In the end, the longer I live and the more I learn, the less I know. With regard to my most excellent adventure in Venice, I can only say – and this is true of so many things in life – I know what I experienced; I just don't know how to explain it.

CHAPTER FIVE

BOTTLED POETRY

NAPA VALLEY, CALIFORNIA

"Beer is made by men, wine by God."

— MARTIN LUTHER —

In the spring of 1976, a British wine merchant and publicist living in France named Steven Spurrier organized a wine tasting in Paris. This unique, one-time event would become forever known in the lore of the industry as the Paris Tasting or, more grandly, the Judgment of Paris. Spurrier had for years enjoyed tasting California wines, and he became determined to test those wines against the highest-quality French Cabernets and Chardonnays. At the time, no one questioned the world-wide dominance of the French; certainly no American wines could compare. Spurrier decided on a blind tasting, and that the panel of judges would all be Frenchmen, among them some of the best-known wine tasters and critics in the world. The forum was public and the press had assembled. The various bottles of reds and whites sat on tables before the judges, anonymously wrapped and numbered. One taster said, "Finding these Californians is easy... Smell this one. Almost no nose... Definitely Californian." (The wine was French.) Another judge declared, "Ah, back to France... nervous and agreeable... a good nose." (The wine was Californian.) A third taster opined, "The magnificence of France. It soars! Certainly a *premier grand cru* of Bordeaux." (The wine was Californian.) First prize among the Cabernets that day went to a 1973 *Stag's Leap*; winner among the Chardonnays was a 1973 *Chateau Montelena* (Both were California wines.) The French cried

"*Foul!*" California vintners did not gloat but collectively smiled and quietly reaped the benefits of millions of dollars of free publicity. Sales soared. For the California dreamers, who had toiled so long and hard to make world-class wines, their time had come and nothing would ever be the same.

Our trip to the Napa Valley had been a long time in the planning. Finally, in the early spring of 2016, we were able to get everyone together. Faith and I would rendezvous with John and Jennifer Youngblood; Danal and Wendy Abrams; Pete and Nancy Ross; and Dmitri and Robin Pauli at the Hotel Meritage on Bordeaux Way in Napa, California. The 10 of us, all good friends for many decades, would spend five days exploring wine country.

The Napa Valley is not quite 30 miles long and only five miles across at the widest point. Ages ago it lay at the bottom of a gigantic inland sea but over millennia, as tectonic plates collided violently deep beneath the earth's surface, molten rock forced its way above the briny waters to form California's coastal mountain range. Napa's soils, originally composed of volcanic ash and the remains of ancient sea creatures, became rich as they were gradually mixed together by the meandering Napa River. Like the rest of the north coast, Napa enjoys bright sunlight most of the year, coupled with the moist, cooling air that rolls in through the mountain gaps from the Pacific Ocean.

Vineyards in southern California can be traced to as far back as 1818, but it was not until 1858 that wine was first produced commercially in Napa by John Patchett. Charles Krug, a Prussian immigrant, opened his Charles Krug Winery in 1860. He was followed by such winemaking pioneers as Gustave Niebaum (Inglenook Vineyards, 1879), Louis Michael Martini (Louis M. Martini Winery, 1933), and Cesare Mondavi (Sunny St. Helena, 1937). Cesare Mondavi's son, Robert, played a huge role over many years in the exponential growth of the American wine industry.

Napa's early winemakers won accolades in New York and even overseas for the quality of their wines. In the late 19th century, however, many of Napa's vineyards were devastated by the scourge of phylloxera, a voracious insect that had destroyed the vineyards of France and been transported to the United States by ship from Europe via diseased vine cuttings and rootstock.

Napa winemakers suffered another blow with the prohibition against the manufacture and sale of alcohol in the United States. Beginning in 1920 and over 13 long years before repeal of the Volstead Act, more than 230 California wineries closed. In Napa, by the 1930s, prune trees and walnuts grew on much of the land that had formerly produced grapes.

Ironically, Americans spent an estimated $36 billion on liquor during the era of Prohibition. The law was widely flouted. Wine consumption more than doubled—thanks to a provision in the Volstead Act that allowed families to produce wine at home for their own consumption—from approximately 60 million to 150 million gallons. At the same time, the perception of wine as a beverage either for unsophisticated southern European immigrants or for wealthy, snobbish oenophiles who imported their wines from France was fading. In the U.S., wine now teetered on the precipice of becoming an accepted part of mainstream culture. Over time, through the efforts of people like Robert Mondavi, the Gallo brothers (Ernest and Julio) and Jess Jackson, among many others, America became a wine-drinking nation from coast to coast.

In 1981, the Napa Valley became California's first American Viticultural Area (AVA). Today, the Napa Valley AVA is home to almost 475 wineries. The AVA, with 43,500 acres of vines, is about one-sixth as large as the total wine acreage in Bordeaux, France. The Valley eventually became subdivided into 16 smaller AVAs, also known as appellations. An appellation is a geographical area in which winemakers are officially authorized to identify and market wine – 85 percent or more of the grapes used must come from a specific AVA in order for a wine to carry that designation on the label. The Napa AVAs range in size from 3,300 to over 16,000 acres. Many vintners choose to blend grapes from multiple appellations, and even though some might legally be allowed to use the name of an individual appellation on their label, the prestigious words "Napa Valley" more than serves their purpose.

◀━━━▶

Faith and I woke up to snow in the Twin Cities – no surprise – and our flight was delayed due to the necessity for de-icing procedures. No problem: I am all for de-icing when airplane wings are frozen, especially when my loved ones and I are aboard said plane. John and Jennifer met us at the San Francisco airport and the four of us got on the road to Napa. We had missed lunch and so stopped at an In-N-Out Burger joint. Had a great cheeseburger, wrapped properly so that no juices escaped, but the fries were pretty average-tasting. We had a hunch that the quality of the cuisine would pick up soon.

The rest of the crew would not arrive until later in the day, so the four of us took the opportunity that afternoon to visit the Larkmead Winery, at the northern end of the valley in Calistoga, for a tour and a tasting. Larkmead, established in 1895, is one of the oldest family-owned wine estates in the Napa Valley. The location is lovely, quiet and absolutely idyllic. Our guide explained to us about the diversity of soils that permeate the 150-acre vineyard. Centuries of alluvial flow created a concentration of hundreds of feet of ancient, well-drained riverbed gravel. This variety gives the wines their character, and the Larkmead winemakers work to vinify small lots in order to capture nuance and complexity.

We tried four wines: a light and exquisite Sauvignon Blanc; a Cabernet Sauvignon (my tasting notes said, "big, bold, lusty" – I know this is what good Cabs are supposed to be, but could I possibly sound any more trite and unimaginative?); a wonderful, rich Merlot; and, finally, our favorite, a terrific blend called *Firebelle*. We ate crackers and cheese and drank water between tastings to start fresh with each new wine. My wife has combined undergraduate majors in food science and nutrition, and worked for many years in quality control for a large company in the food industry. She is a trained taster – of food, anyway - and our guide had fun trying to trick her palate by having her look away and then mixing in some additional, different wines. For me, after tasting several wines (I know you're supposed to spit the wine out, but I hate doing that: first of all, it's expensive; secondly, it's delicious; thirdly, spitting is gross; fourthly... I forget the fourth reason), I'm lucky to be able to differentiate between red and white. But Faith was among the best amateur tasters the guide had ever seen, or so he said, and she could not be fooled. She aced the exam. We all laughed hard and gave her a round of applause. I was very proud of her.

That evening we connected with the rest of the team and enjoyed dinner at the Farmstead at Longmeadow Ranch in St. Helena. The food is farm-to-table American fare, served in a renovated barn. Our friend John is always budget-conscious – which we all greatly appreciate about him – and he had learned that we could bring our own wine to the Farmstead and drink it for a $5 corkage fee, the proceeds to be donated to charity. The proverbial "win-win," as they say. The food was delivered family style. We devoured a tray of deviled eggs, passed massive plates of chicken, pork and meatballs, and were even good to ourselves by eating a great big serving of kale salad. I noticed that the men and women sat apart from each other, which we agreed we would correct going forward. I asked and, apparently, while the men discussed the battlefield tactics of ancient warfare, the women talked about the nuances of bikini waxing, among many other subjects. Not sure I wouldn't have rather sat in with the ladies for that part of their conversation - I know a bit about ancient warfare, nothing about bikini waxing.

The next morning, the entire 10-person "Team Napa" motored to the Sonoma Valley to experience the Kistler Trenton Roadhouse tasting room, located just north of the Kistler Vineyards in Sebastopol. Our friend Dimitri Pauli is an accomplished New York City-based restaurateur, and through his contacts was able to arrange several of our private tastings, including the visit to Kistler. The Kistlers established their vineyard in 1978, and it has been a family affair ever since. They are notably famous for their Pinot Noirs and Chardonnays, and produce around 35,000 cases per year. We marveled at the spacious, sunlit tasting room; among many other interesting things related to its classy design, there were about a dozen jars of the various types of soil that can be found on their land, all lined up together on a shelf. When our guide took us outside to observe and walk among the grapes – the morning was cool and slightly misty so we covered ourselves with several large umbrellas – I realized then, if I hadn't before, that winemaking is farming. *Sorry, I grew up in the suburbs.*

The guide explained that all Kistler wines are carefully farmed and produced using what she referred to as "classic Burgundian techniques." The Chardonnay is grown from the same heritage clone of grape that the winery has used for almost 30 years. We learned that when a cutting or bud is taken from a "mother" plant, that this is considered a clone, basically a second plant that will then be identical to the first. Understandably, when winemakers discover a grape that they like, they want to replicate it. The Kistler wines are crafted using solely native yeasts, aged in bespoke French oak barrels, then bottled unfined (meaning no additional trace substances are added to reduce impurities and/or enhance flavor) and unfiltered so that they are considered "natural" wines. There seems to be some controversy as to whether natural wine is better than its more highly processed cousins. We heard a range of opinions as our trip progressed. Proponents of non-organic wines assert that they want to reserve the option of tinkering with their wines in order to improve flavor; there is also a school of thought that organic wines don't taste as good. All of the organic wines we tasted over several days were absolutely wonderful.

Our guide reminded us that California had experienced four years of drought previous to this year. She said, "One more year of serious drought would have really hurt," but that rainfall for the Kistler vineyards had been more plentiful in recent months. "Fortunately," she emphasized, "at least for the white grapes, they really don't need much water." The Kistler winemakers obviously know their craft, and have survived and thrived despite periodically difficult conditions. The wines we tasted were unbelievable. Our consensus group favorite was called the *Trenton Roadhouse Chardonnay*, from 2010. Some of the words people used to describe the wine were, "clear with subtle fruit; hint of vanilla, licorice, and even turpentine (but in a nice way); great, long finish." Faith and I ordered several bottles of the 2013 *Sonoma Coast* Pinot Noir. I love Pinots because when they are good they go with almost any variety of meat; I am a shameless carnivore. My tasting notes for that wine – I was finally attempting to be somewhat more creative – say, "great structure but light; bright fruit, especially cherry; hint of coffee." It was a very special wine.

Next on the agenda, for some of us at least (Jennifer, Robin Jeff, John and Danal – if you were wondering, Danal's name is pronounced just like "Dan" with an "l" attached) came a mud bath at the Indian Springs Spa in Calistoga, which is famous for its mineral waters. I had never taken a mud bath, so had no clue what to expect. I was told it's supposed to be relaxing. We stripped naked (boys and girls in separate areas) and put on robes, then took them off, and then slipped into, as you might have guessed, a mud bath. We each lay in our own tub while a guy just stood there and shoveled more hot mud right on top of us. Only our heads cleared the surface. It was really warm. There was pressure all around. I thought this must be akin to what it felt like to be in the womb, but I couldn't remember far back enough to confirm that. Mud is heavy. And it is mud, so it kind of works its way into all your various crevices, especially when you're buck naked. Pretty grainy. But it felt kind of good.

They say, while you're in the mud bath, that it's really fun to pass gas and then feel the bubbles rise. Heat goes to the surface, you know. The bubbles tickle your legs on the way up. Then there are a series of tiny, silent explosions at the surface. The smell of the steamy mud generally overwhelms any hint of ass whiff in the air. So, no one is the wiser. This is only what I have heard; I am of course well beyond such childishness. Anyhow, after ten minutes in the bath, we took a shower, paying particular attention to the crevices. Jennifer confirmed later that the women had crevice-related issues too. We soaked in a hot tub for another 10 minutes. Then we took a sauna for seven minutes. I was ready to get out of that hot bitch after about three minutes, but John and Danal were not complaining so I didn't either. Finally, we rested on a bed with a cold towel on our foreheads and cucumbers on our eyes. Never did that before. At the end of it all, I guess it was relaxing. Kind of. John said, in summary: "I hate spas."

"What is it about spas that you hate?" asked Danal.

"Everything."

"I kind of enjoyed the experience, and feel pretty good right now," I responded. "Why do you hate everything about spas?"

"I hate being around people who are so stressed out that they have to pay money to relax."

"Okay, we see, good point... let's go somewhere else then."

Assessing the impact of a changing climate on the California wine industry is a complicated challenge. In a fall 2015 article analyzing several recent academic papers on the subject, wine writer Becca Yeamans-Irwin concluded:

"In general, it is predicted that California will see increased temperatures as well as decreases in soil and plant moisture, leading to overall greater stress to the grapes and a reduction in overall wine quality. Some regions of California already on the brink of being too hot for winegrape production may find themselves sooner than later unable to produce high quality wine, necessitating rapid change and adaptations not only at the individual vineyard level but at the state level.... It will become necessary... to create policies and programs to provide support for wine growers to make the necessary adaptations required to maintain economic health. With a $61.5 billion state-wide economic impact, addressing climate change effects on wine production and taking immediate action is of critical importance for the economic health not only of California, but also for the nation."

But California is a big state, and a 2011 scientific study commissioned by the Napa Valley Vintners, a non-profit trade association, concluded that climate effects in Napa Valley are best understood by looking at appellation-specific impacts. Napa shares traits of both coastal and interior climates and, as a result, temperature changes in Napa are not as high as those that have been experienced in warmer inland areas, and not as low as in cooler coastal locations. The Napa Valley Vintners assert, "Climate change can and will affect all fine-wine growing regions worldwide, but the results will not necessarily be a blanket effect, as climate change is not a one-size-fits-all phenomena. This is a very long-term issue, which vintners and growers around the world need to pay attention to and be directly involved with. At the end of the day, vintners and grape growers are farmers. As no two harvests are the same, farmers must successfully adapt, harvest to harvest, season to season, year to year, and have done so for nearly two centuries in the Napa Valley, and for many thousands of years worldwide. For the farmer, change is not only inevitable; it is a way of life."

An additional concern in California, as our Kistler guide pointed out to us, is the prospect of drought. The entire state of California faces a significant challenge in the years ahead in adapting its water management systems to this unfortunate reality. For the vintners, improvements in technology and agricultural techniques around genetics, breeding, and other vineyard adaptations will no doubt help. Some growers, for example, are utilizing sophisticated, energy-saving variable-frequency irrigation systems that allow for more precise, efficient watering. Solar-powered weather stations can sense when temperatures drop too low at night (global warming is not always strictly about too much warmth – there are frequently temperature swings in the Napa Valley), thus activating wind machines that circulate warm air to protect vines. For some winemakers, crops are monitored by drones with moisture-detecting sensors that can indicate nutritional deficiencies or leaky irrigation systems. Basic farming techniques like rainfall capture, planting cover crops such as rye or barley between rows of vines to help keep soil healthy and limit erosion, and even using barn owls to control pests without using pesticides and to frighten away other pesky birds that eat grapes are also in the repertoire of many a smart and resilient Napa vintner. But as Katie Jackson – eldest daughter of the late, great Jess Jackson, and currently vice president for sustainability and external affairs at California-based Jackson Family Wines, one of the largest family-owned winemakers in the country – said in early 2017, "The climate has been getting warmer and warmer, and we're seeing more extremes, from really wet to really dry. Little by little, we're learning." Advanced technologies and improved techniques will be costly, require innovative thinking, and take time. The future is uncertain at best.

◄─────────►

After our afternoon spent lolling in the mud, the full group reconvened and went to dinner at Press Restaurant, in St. Helena. Press is a nationally-recognized steakhouse, featuring a hell of a fine piece of meat called the Cowboy Ribeye. Press has two private gardens, and what cannot be grown there is sourced from local farmers and markets. Once again, John saved us a few bucks by ordering a gargantuan magnum of Merlot - much cheaper than other alternatives from the wine list, and more abundant in quantity as well. *Thanks John, good call on the vino.* Nine of the 10 of us had steak; I won't call out the wimp, who had some form of seafood, pan-seared Alaskan halibut or something ridiculous like that (it was my wife, Faith... sorry, honey.) Steaks were sizzling and cooked to perfection. We savored shrimp cocktail and shared dishes of macaroni and cheese and au gratin potatoes. I don't believe there was a vegetable in sight. Dessert for most of us was a chocolate soufflé with vanilla ice cream. Cup of decaf with cream. No one went into cardiac arrest.

Next morning we ventured to the Darioush Winery on the Silverado Trail in southern Napa Valley. Founded by Darioush Kaladi and his wife Shahpar in 1997, the property is grand and ornate in the style of an ancient Persian palace. Kaladi was born in Iran, worked as a civil engineer for the government of the Shah, and then got out while the getting was good in 1976. He came to America and started a company with his brother that eventually became the largest family-owned grocery chain in California. But he dreamed of becoming a winemaker, and that he has done. His wines are exquisite, and we enjoyed our visit immensely. Hearing about Kaladi's background, I was struck by how many of these stories about the founding of Napa vineyards are great American stories, many of them about immigrants to this country, and some from troubled, controversial places. Sorry, Donald Trump, but it's true. Their sagas are also timeless tales of entrepreneurial grit, vision, taking nothing for granted, incredible hard work and ceaseless effort, finding a better way, risk-taking and, finally, in some cases at least, ultimate triumph. Only in America.

For a change of pace we spent some time exploring the Culinary Institute of America (CIA) at Greystone in St. Helena. A splendid and imposing structure commissioned as a cooperative winery and cellar in 1889, the CIA purchased the building for a song exactly 100 years later when the Loma Prieta earthquake rendered it highly unstable. The CIA exhaustively renovated and refitted the structure, and it now serves as a top-drawer educational center for students seeking associate degrees in culinary, baking and pastry arts. In addition, CIA offers certificate programs in culinary, wine and beverage studies. It is a vast enterprise and we enjoyed our tour of the facilities and, later, browsing the bookstore/giftshop. We ate a snack (as if we needed it) in the student-run Bakery Café by Illy, which serves soups, salads, sandwiches, and out-of-this-world bakery goods. I had a pretty darn fine chocolate chip cookie.

Then it was off to what was, for some of us at least, our favorite venue of the entire trip, the Spottswoode Estate Vineyard and Winery at the foot of the Mayacamas Mountains in St. Helena. Our guide related the Spottswoode story and it, too, is a compelling one. Mary Weber was a Stanford-educated kindergarten teacher in Los Angeles when she married Jack Novak, a medical doctor.The Novaks fell in love with Napa Valley on a visit and, in 1972, purchased the Spottswoode Estate (founded in 1882), moved their family, and set out to learn the wine business by doing. Mary faced a crisis in 1977 when her husband died suddenly of a heart attack at the age of 44 during a game of tennis. She was now the widowed mother of five, but she determined to carry on. Initially, the Novaks had simply sold their grapes to large local producers. When Mary took the helm, she committed in 1982 to begin producing her own wines. From the beginning, the Spottswoode wines were a hit, in particular its Cabernets and Sauvignon Blancs. In 1985, Mary made the decision to become one of the first Napa growers to embrace organic methods. The vineyard is now certified as fully organic. Over time, Mary's daughter Beth joined the business and she is now its president. Daughter Lindy is a marketing director. And in keeping with the theme of an entirely women-owned and -operated business - in what is very much a man's world - Mary hired a succession of women as winemakers. We tasted a 2013 Cabernet Sauvignon, a 2015 Sauvignon Blanc, and the much celebrated 2013 Cab called *Lyndenhurst*. They are all wonderful wines. Mary passed away in September of 2016 at the age of 84, but her legacy lives on. The famous wine critic Robert Parker has said, "When the history of Napa's great vineyards is written, the 40-acre Spottswoode vineyard, tucked behind the quaint town of St. Helena, will be counted among the finest *grand cru* vineyards of the region."

Dinner that evening was in my opinion a bust. I think the team concurred. The only stinker we experienced in Napa. We ate at Ninebark on Main Street in downtown Napa. Service was indifferent. The meal came out family style, starting with some kind of a soggy toast and clam combo. Then there was a weird strawberry and tomato mishmash, and my entrée, duck, was only passable. Dessert was sort of inedible. Some kind of a chocolate hockey puck. So we enjoyed that magical restaurant double-whammy of both bad food and bad service. And as you might expect, it cost just as much as every other dinner we had. We subsequently learned, not surprisingly, that Ninebark closed its doors permanently just a few months after our visit. Something was clearly amiss at that venue. As Dimitri Pauli will tell you, the restaurant business is hell.

Next day was our last full day together. We traveled to our final tasting at the Shafer Vineyards, in the Stag's Leap District of Napa Valley. John Shafer purchased the 209-acre property in 1972, with the intention (as with so many other Napa vintners, he was not formally trained in the complex art of winemaking) of learning the business of growing grapes that would be one day, probably years down the road, transformed into fine wines. The vintage of Shafer's first wine was 1978. Today, annual production is 30,000 cases of Chardonnay, Merlot, Syrah and Cabernet Sauvignon. John remains on board as Chairman, and his son Doug is President. Doug had been head winemaker until the mid-1980s, when he realized that his assistant, Elias Fernandez, would probably do a better job. Elias is the son of a migrant worker, and he is a UC-Davis grad in viticulture. The Shafers credit Elias with taking their business to new heights. During the tasting, we had the privilege of meeting both Doug and Elias, who were gracious enough to stop by and chat for a few minutes. Shafer is justly famous for all of its excellent wines, but in 2008 the Cabernet Sauvignon known as *Relentless* won *Wine Spectator* magazine's prestigious Wine of the Year award. John and Doug named the wine after Elias, who they say is himself "relentless." Faith and I procured a bottle, and we are saving it for some extremely special occasion – perhaps the publication of this book. Elias is a very soft-spoken and modest man. When we asked him which one of the many wines that he so skillfully produces is his personal favorite, he smiled and said quietly, "They are all my children."

Faith and I opted out of dinner with the crew that evening for some quiet time together. We took a walk in downtown Napa, went to see a mildly amusing Melissa McCarthy movie, then came back to the hotel and ate olives, crackers and cheese that we had purchased in the hotel snack shop. We shared the bottle of wine that had come with the room. It was a red, I don't even remember what kind, but it tasted especially good. We sat outside on our deck, breathed in the cool night air, and greatly enjoyed our simple repast.

There is a large wooden sign on the approach to Highway 29 which says:

"Welcome to this world famous wine growing region

NAPA VALLEY

... and the wine is bottled poetry..."

Several months after our adventure in wine country, I had the chance to follow up with some of the participants to get their retrospective on the "bottled
poetry" that we had experienced together in the Napa Valley. Wendy Abrams
was amazed that the 10 of us got along as well as we did. We were indeed
fortunate, as there wasn't a moment of interpersonal stress – everyone simply lived and let live. I think we were having too much fun to get irritated
with each other. Wendy found the Spottswoode story incredibly inspiring.
She said, "They clearly have paid their dues. Women competing effectively
at the highest level in a man's world. I loved the whole gestalt. Everything
was very much back to nature, yet also elevated and pristine." Wendy's husband Danal said, "I came in knowing basically nothing about wine [Danal is
primarily a craft-beer kind of guy] and I learned so much. The complexity
of process that goes into something that is so seemingly basic is mind-bog-
gling." John Youngblood reflected, "The producers are so deeply attached to
their land and their approach... I am amazed at what a competitive business
it is." Pete Ross observed, "The trial and error aspect of the business is fascinating. Small adjustments made today might not see results for years. This
is a science that someone could study for a lifetime and never gain complete
knowledge." When I asked Pete what he liked best about the trip, he summed
it up beautifully: "The scenery was gorgeous. We had fun and learned a lot.
We were with our best friends, eating great food and drinking fine wine. What
could possibly be better?" I'll drink to that.

CHAPTER SIX

OCEAN QUEST

LOS CABOS, MEXICO

"Mexico's doors have been flung open, the welcome mat's brand-new, its cerveza es muy fria, its water has been purified, and the putting greens have a nap as diligently tended as a baron's beard. You get the picture – head south, spend money, relax, party, shake your bottom until the pesos rain out of your pockets."

- BOB SHACOCHIS, FROM *KINGDOMS IN THE AIR* –

In the midst of the crisis that is global climate change, not all is despair. There are oases of hope to be found in many places. Interestingly, it is frequently not the actions of politicians, corporate leaders or university scientists that matter nearly as much as deliberate, thoughtful steps taken by common people - living in regular communities, acting independently of greater forces, trusting each other - endeavoring together to preserve our fragile environment. Today, a number of small seaside towns in Mexico's Baja California Peninsula are working hard to preserve and manage their fisheries, for the benefit of all and with the long term in mind. The lesson is this: each of us has the power to make a difference, both individually and as citizens within our larger community.

———

I have only been to Mexico once, when Faith and I joined John and Jennifer Youngblood for a few days of fun in the sun, in January of 2011. The Youngbloods had swapped into a timeshare at the Grand Mayan Los Cabos Hotel, located at the southern tip of the Baja California Peninsula, in the city of San Jose del Cabo. What once was a cluster of humble fishing villages has been transformed over the last several decades into a sprawling, bustling, mostly upscale tourist mecca. San Jose del Cabo sits on the east side of this peninsula where the Gulf of California (also known as the Sea of Cortez) meets the Pacific Ocean. It is a pretty town, with a historic plaza, a handful of colonial-era buildings and a flourishing art district. Most people tend to think of San Jose as more tranquil and quiet, and significantly less touristy than Cabo San Lucas, situated 18 miles away on the western edge of the peninsula. Cabo San Lucas is where the bulk of the partying takes place. San Jose del Cabo and Cabo San Lucas, together with the stretch of land that connects them, called the Corridor, are known as Los Cabos. The Corridor abounds with beaches, condos, hotels, restaurants and golf courses. The Mexican government has divided this entire expanse of land into various towns and development zones called "fraccionamientos," which comprise the county, or "municipio," of Los Cabos.

I was not journaling back in 2011, had no idea I would be writing a Cabo chapter in a book six years later and so, regretfully, I only have a few specific memories of this trip. Here they are, in no particular order: We visited a friend of John's who was a golf pro at the Diamonte Cabo San Lucas development - at that time it was still under construction – which today consists of a gorgeous resort and three golf courses, two of them designed by Tiger Woods, with dramatic ocean views. We quickly identified a favorite restaurant, called El Herradero Mexican Grill & Bar, and ate there at least four or five times during our stay, breakfast and dinner. They had a rich, creamy seafood omelette that was to die for. After dinner one evening, I walked on the beach and smoked a Cuban cigar (you can't get those suckers in the U.S. unless you know a guy who knows a guy) that I had purchased in a grocery store, but that was kept in a humidor, so I was confident it would be fresh. Damn, if it wasn't the oldest, driest excuse for a cigar I had ever tasted. *Yech.* Faith, John and I went fishing one afternoon. Our guides kept telling us the fish we were catching were king mackerels, sometimes known as kingfish. Later research revealed that king mackerels are much larger than the species we were hauling in and live primarily in a western Atlantic and Gulf of Mexico habitat, nowhere near our location. We concluded that most of our fish were probably a species called Sierra Spanish mackerel. Maybe the guides just liked the sound of "king mackerel" – I don't blame them; it is a cool-sounding moniker. The guides cleaned the fish for us, and we ate some of it raw as sushi later that evening. I remember thinking, *I hope we don't get sick as dogs*. But we did not. I actually think of that fishing trip every day, if subconsciously, because as Faith and I sat in the two fighting chairs at the back of the boat, John snapped a picture of us from behind. The sky is bright and sunny, the ocean deep blue, we have our lines in the water and, even though you can't see our faces, it looks like we are having fun. Which we were. It is my favorite photo of my wife and me, and it is the screensaver image on my desktop computer. In any event, over the course of several extremely pleasant days, our little gang of four did our best to head south, spend money, relax and party. We firmly drew the line at shaking our bottoms until the pesos rained out of our pockets.

←——————→

Unfortunately, Los Cabos has probably grown too explosively for its own good. The region's population in 1990 was approximately 44,000. By 2015, it had increased almost seven fold, to 288,000. In 2016, Los Cabos received more than two million tourists, 75 percent of them international visitors, with the majority of that number Americans. The dramatic increase in population represents an influx of native Mexicans who came to work in the tourist trade, in construction, landscaping, hotels and restaurants. The planning around where all of these new migrants would live has been haphazard, at best. Some of them live within the city limits of San Jose del Cabo and Cabo San Lucas, but most now reside in run-down, underserviced neighborhoods built shoddily in the dusty, hardscrabble desert that extends north from the Corridor. These are neighborhoods where tourists rarely, if ever, dare venture. The random collections of tiny, cinderblock houses with corrugated metal roofs are generally without sewage systems, and frequently lack a municipal water connection. The trash piles up, cars are abandoned, and roving packs of dogs wander about, just a few short miles away from plush locations like the Grand

Mayan Los Cabos Hotel.

To add to what is already a miserable scenario, the cities of San Jose del Cabo and Cabo San Lucas have seen a tragic surge in gang-related violence. Homicides were up almost three fold just from 2016 to 2017. The killings occur virtually exclusively on the streets of the sad little villages I have just described. Criminal gangs are in a savage and merciless battle for control of the drug trade, all throughout the California Baja Peninsula. The situation has become so dire that, in August of 2017, the U.S. State Department issued a heightened travel warning not just for Los Cabos but for the entire Baja Peninsula. However, ironically, tourists have not been murder targets, at least in part because the drug trade that criminal enterprises are at war to dominate is designed to service the narcotic-using habits of some of those very tourists. The Mexican government has clearly focused more on driving tourism than taking care of the workers who sustain the industry. Indeed, many people believe the fundamental problem is simply the absence of any fair redistribution of tourism dollars throughout Mexican society. We certainly have our own problems in the United States, to be sure, regarding the decided lack of parity between the proverbial haves and have nots. Crime, poverty and inequity are rampant in America, too. But it is still a pity, nevertheless, from the standpoint of indigence and violence as well as changes to the environment, to realize what is happening in Los Cabos, such a wonderful natural resource and an amazing, scenic part of the world.

←——————→

As is true in so many other locations, warming waters are transforming the California Baja Peninsula's Pacific Ocean and Sea of Cortez ecosystems. It is an astounding and disturbing fact that more than one quarter of human-generated carbon dioxide ends up in the world's oceans. The resulting warmer waters hold less dissolved oxygen and have a diminished capability to carry oxygen down from the surface to lower depths. As a consequence, low-oxygen zones are increasing in size, driving marine animals to the surface, where their populations become diminished because they are easier targets for predators. Certain types of an algae called "Pseudo-nitzschia" also expand rapidly in warmer water. Enormous blooms of this algae create a notorious neuro-toxin called domoic acid which, when consumed by zooplankton, shellfish and fish, can in turn harm the myriad birds and mammals that subsist on these marine animals. Warming seas are generally more acidic, which reduces calcium carbonate, a substance critical to shell growth for oysters, clams and other species. Not surprisingly, acidic oceans disrupt the brains of fish which, among other problems, worsens their ability to evade predators and to sense the location of their home territory.

One additional man-made problem has also historically bedeviled the Baja Peninsula ecosystem, and that is overfishing. I distinctly remember thinking as we fished back in 2011, with many dozens of small boats just like ours turning smelly, diesel-fueled circles not just in our immediate vicinity but, indeed, for almost as far as the eye could see: *How many fish are there in these waters, and when will they all be gone?*

From the 1940s to the '60s, Baja had gone from a peninsula with spec-tacular biodiversity to seriously overfished, with many species decimated over that time period, and to the present day. The Mexican government exacer-bated the situation with a program called "March to the Sea," begun in the mid-1950s and designed to encourage unemployed laborers to become fisher-men. Starting in the 1970s, out of frustration with the collapse of fisheries, as lone-wolf fishermen and their families moved from place to place in search of whatever fish remained, a handful of communities decided to work togeth-er, along with local leadership, various units of government, scientists and non-profit organizations, to preserve what they had. In a fascinating article from the September, 2017 issue of *National Geographic*, environmental writer Erik Vance explains, "Around the world, fish populations are crashing, and species such as tuna, turtle, and grouper are ever more scarce. Yet, in north-western Mexico, a few communities have managed to protect their under-water resources. These micro-conservation areas were created by or with the support of the communities, which many environmentalists see as the key to conservation that works. How they did it holds lessons for the world's fishing communities."

In a mid-peninsula hamlet called Punta Abreojos, for example, fisher-men delay their quest for abalone for a full three months beyond the government-designated opening of the fishing season. This simple step allows the abalone to become larger in size and more abundant in numbers. Today, Abreojos and other similarly patient villages harvest in excess of 90 percent of Mexico's abalones. They process the seafood in a modern plant, and increase profitability by selling directly to hungry Asian markets. In Cabo Pulmo, a formerly modest fishing village east of San Jose del Cabo, local residents created a marine reserve in the mid-1990s. The community designated a small but well-enforced no-take reserve, 27 square miles in size, called the Cabo Pulmo National Park. By forbidding fishing in this preserve, biomass has increased as much as three times since the year 2000. The resulting income from diving tourism has built a thriving local economy.

Success stories like these don't just happen. Erik Vance says that there are five rules that are "... key to sustainable, community-supported ocean management. First, like Abreojos, it helps if the site is fairly isolated, with just a community or two using it. Second, the community needs a resource of high value, such as lobster or abalone. Strong, visionary community leaders are the third necessity. Fourth, fishermen need a way to support themselves while the resources recover [in a town named El Manglito, fishermen are paid by a non-profit to not fish; instead, they earn a paycheck as they watch for poachers and conduct biological surveys.] And, lastly, the community must be bound together by trust." These are certainly criteria that will not apply everywhere, but to me the ideas that stand out are around the importance of leadership and trust. With those two critical components, anything might be possible in any community, anywhere in the world.

$$\longleftrightarrow$$

And, oh yes, individuals need to feel empowered to change things for the better and to believe that their efforts will have an impact. The actions of concerned and engaged citizens who reside in a number of special communities in Mexico's Baja, such as Punta Abreojos, Cabo Pulmo and El Manglito, are proof of this truth. These oases of hope serve as shining examples for us all. As John F. Kennedy once said, "One person can make a difference, and everyone should try."

CHAPTER SEVEN

HUNT 'EM UP!

ESTELLINE, SOUTH DAKOTA

"Any woman who does not enjoy tramping across the country on a clear, frosty morning with a good gun and a pair of dogs does not know how to enjoy life."

— ANNIE OAKLEY —

I was frustrated. Over the years I had been pheasant hunting in various parts of South Dakota on a number of occasions. In 2015, I and a group of buddies had found a lodge that we really liked, called Dakota Ringneck, in the tiny town of Estelline, just across the Minnesota border about four hours by car from the Twin Cities. I wanted to arrange another trip in the fall of '16, but was having a heck of a time getting people to commit. With just a few short days left before we would need to pull the plug, my friends John Youngblood and Danal Abrams were the only two solid "yeses." Everyone else had dropped out. I was lamenting my fate to Faith. I felt we needed at least one more participant to make the trip worthwhile.

"I'll go," Faith said.

"What?"

"I'll go hunting with you and the guys." This is a woman who loves to fish, and revels in nature, but had never picked up a shotgun in her life.

"Uh. Really?"

"Sure."

"Uh, okay. Sounds good. Thanks for saving the trip. Let's do it!"

Pheasants are not native to the North American continent. Virtually all pheasant species originated in China, Japan, or Mongolia. In 1882, the U.S. general counsel to Shanghai, Judge Owen Denny, imported 50 pheasants to Oregon's Willamette Valley, in the first serious attempt to introduce the species to the wild in this country. Ten years later, in a testament to their prolific reproductive capabilities, 50,000 ring-necked pheasants were harvested on opening day of the first official hunting season.

The birds were gradually introduced across the country and ultimately came to populate 39 states and seven Canadian provinces. Ringneck numbers peaked in the 1940s, with continued healthy populations into the '50s and '60s. In the 1970s and '80s, however, intensive farming practices all but eliminated the best pheasant habitat, with a concurrent plunge in population. In 1985, in recognition of the seriousness of the problem, the Conservation Reserve Program began the process of reversing these population declines by paying farmers and ranchers to convert land to pheasant habitat. Ringnecks rebounded and ultimately came to thrive again, mostly in Midwestern states with farm country consisting of 55-to-70-percent cropland. Corn and soybean fields proved ideal. Pheasants thrive on the small grains, weed seeds, and insects that can be found in grasslands, wetlands, woodlots, thickets, fence lines and ditches. South Dakota, in particular, has historically offered nearly perfect habitat and has come to be seen as the world mecca for pheasant hunting.

The male, or "rooster," pheasant, is flamboyantly beautiful, with a red copper breast, a light blue patch on his rump, and a dazzling white ring around his neck. His head is iridescent in green and black, and he possesses what looks like a bright red, costume-party mask around his eyes. He has a light brown tail that can reach more than two feet in length, with evenly spaced black bars for additional decorative effect. He is a proud and colorful creature, and he exists in stark contrast to female pheasants, known as hens, which have dull beige coloring, the better to camouflage themselves. The rooster can reach three feet from the tip of his beak to the end of his tail and weighs up to three pounds when fully grown. He is polygamous and will breed with many mates. This is the reason why he is highly expendable, come hunting season. In most locales, only roosters may be taken during the season. Even with reduced male numbers, because these birds tend to impregnate as many females as possible, if other conditions are right, there will nearly always be a sufficient overall pheasant population into the next season and beyond.

Pheasants are maddeningly elusive creatures. They depend on sharp eyesight and hearing to avoid their enemies, whether animal or man. They can see the glint of a shotgun a quarter mile away. They hear at 10 times the sound range that humans do. They sit quietly in tall vegetation and look and listen carefully for any sign of danger. They sense ground vibration through "Herbst's corpuscles," which are highly sensitive pressure pads on their feet. The spurs on their feet can kill a rival rooster and have been known to maim a hunting dog as well. Once a ringneck detects danger, it may sit tight and allow a predator to walk right by. Or it may begin to run, and it is swift. It may take off in sudden flight, as far out of range as it can get, with the capability of achieving 28 to 37 miles per hour in cruising mode, and up to almost 50 miles per hour when in full-chase mode. Because the ringneck is as tricky a prey as a hunter could hope to pursue, and because its senses are far keener than a man's (or woman's), well-trained pointing or flushing dogs are essential to a successful hunt.

Our friend John flew in to the Twin Cities from New York City, and Faith and I picked him up on Friday afternoon, September 30th, at his parent's home in Edina. Danal would fly into Rapid City, South Dakota, and drive to the hunting lodge from there. John, Faith and I headed west. The weather was glorious. I love this drive, because it is through God's country, with endless blue skies, wide-open expanses of farmland, and classic western Minnesota small towns. We stopped for lunch at The Broaster, on the main thoroughfare in the tiny town of Bird Island. John enjoyed the smallest side salad any of us had ever seen, approximately six miniscule pieces of lettuce with a couple of carrot shavings. This was really funny because John is 6'6" and goes about 215. He is a big man who needs a lot of food - we laughed and took a picture prior to him wolfing the salad down in less than two bites. John also had the patty melt with tater tots. Faith ate a burger; I decided on the burger with Swiss and potato soup special. All in all, it was a fine lunch.

John and I have a tradition over 40-plus years of seeking out and sampling dive bars and greasy spoons, wherever we may find them, all over the United States. We have been extremely successful in this endeavor; in recent years, GPS technology has aided significantly in our search capabilities. Our clear favorite in rural western Minnesota, discovered by random chance (and GPS) the previous year, is The Rusty Duck Bar & Grill, in Dawson. We love that frickin' place! We stopped for a cold beer later that afternoon, introduced Faith to the honored venue, and then we all bought Rusty Duck t-shirts. Other small towns dotting our path along the way included Danube, Granite City, Renville and Glencoe. Finally, we crossed the Minnesota-South Dakota border, and made it to the Dakota Ringneck Lodge, in Estelline.

Ken and Ellen Hansen own 4,000 acres of contiguous farmland, some of which is always kept as refuge, which they make available to their pheasant hunting clients every fall. Their property abuts the very scenic Lake Poinsett, one of South Dakota's largest lakes, at 8,000 acres. Ken and Ellen are assisted in running the business by their son, Andy, and his wife Kelsey. The Hansens are terrific, salt-of-the-earth people. Their property includes CPR grass, food plots, waterways and sloughs. The Hansens manage the farm to improve pheasant populations year-over-year by placing food plots and grass buffer zones around heavy cattail sloughs; while Mother Nature sometimes has a different idea, the hope is that by doing so, pheasants will have good habitat all year long.

When we arrived, Andy and Kelsey greeted us. Danal drove up shortly thereafter. Faith and Danal (also a shotgun and hunting novice) headed out back of the lodge to shoot at some clay pigeons and get the hang of how to properly lead and hit a rapidly moving target. It is a difficult thing to do. While I was an excellent shot with rifle and pistol in the Marine Corps, despite years of practice, I have never been particularly good with a shotgun. I actually stink at sporting clays. I do what riflemen do: I point at the target, hold the weapon still and pull the trigger. When you do that with a shotgun, seeking to hit a speeding clay pigeon or a flushing pheasant, sorry, but you miss. Under

Andy's expert and patient coaching, both Faith and Danal began to knock down a few pigeons. We could feel the excitement of the hunt, to commence the next morning, begin to build.

◀━━━━━━▶

I am keenly aware that many people object to hunting. They may see it as a form of cruelty to animals, or feel that it is an unnecessarily violent pastime, or believe that no creature should harm another. And, particularly in the case of human beings, who have a number of inherent advantages over the animal kingdom (but not always), the whole enterprise somehow may seem unfair—not sporting, if you will. However, if one doubts whether animals are also cruel to one another, view an hour of a National Geographic special featuring a typical day on the African savanna. What I truly believe constitutes cruelty to animals is zoos – watch a big tiger pace back and forth in his pen - I am a zoo-boycotter for that reason. I understand and respect these anti-hunting arguments, particularly when they come from a thoughtful, principled person, who is perhaps a vegetarian or vegan. What really chaps my hide, however, is when I hear these statements from the mouth of someone who is at that very moment bellying up to a plate of hot roast beef. Then I feel dismay. Those people really do not get it and, to me, their position seems the height of hypocrisy. If you eat and enjoy meat, then you must understand and can't complain that animals must die in order to feed you. There is a nascent scientific movement to develop "clean meat," derived from animal cells; no animal needs to die in the process; while many people are repelled by this idea, I am all for continued research in this area – but I will still hunt.

I came to hunting only in my 40s. My Dad and I occasionally fished together when I was a kid, but he was never a hunter or a gun owner. A group of college friends asked me if I'd like to try hunting pheasants in South Dakota, sometime in the early 2000s. I was, of course, comfortable in handling firearms from my years in the military. I own several pistols, rifles and shotguns and believe in the Second Amendment right of a private citizen to bear arms; I do not, however, appreciate the politics or tactics of the National Rifle Association – I have never been and will never be a member/supporter of that organization – I am not alone in this, as approximately 90 percent of gun owners do *not* belong to the N.R.A. I also believe in sensible gun control laws: no American sportsman needs to own a military-grade assault rifle with massive rapid-firing capabilities, for example.

I found that I enjoyed the sport of hunting and soon expanded into other areas. Over the years, I have hunted small game like rabbits and squirrels; pheasants in South Dakota and ruffed grouse in Wisconsin; black bear in northern Minnesota; whitetail deer in Minnesota and north Texas; pronghorn antelope in Montana; and on and on. I love being out in nature (even a bad day hunting in the great outdoors is better than a good day at the office), I love observing animal behavior, I love the camaraderie of the field and happy hour and a hot meal at the end of a long day. If I am able to take an animal, then so be it, but that is not the point. It would just be icing on the cake.

I have fired many shots while hunting and definitely missed more often than not. I once missed a Montana pronghorn buck with my trusty Model 70 Winchester 30.06 bolt-action rifle, from 390 yards away (my buddy had a range-finder - that's almost four football fields), just over his rear end. We saw the bullet kick up dust. Mr. Pronghorn T. Antelope was lucky that day, and he probably heard the supersonic crack and felt the breeze over his backside. When I hunt pheasant, with most of my shots, the birds are quite safe. It doesn't matter to me. In any instance where I happen to have killed an animal, I always eat that animal. That is what an ethical hunter should do, in my opinion. Squirrel meat tends to be tough and is not my favorite. Rabbit is good. Pheasants can also be dry but are potentially delicious, depending on how they are prepared – I like them stewed in a crockpot with mushroom soup for a few hours, with vegetables and rice thrown in at the end. I shot an eight-point Texas buck and had the meat turned into spicy, peppery venison sausage, which was just superb. On two occasions, I have shot a black bear. In both instances, I watched the animal in its death throes; I watched the guide skin and quarter the bear; I watched as the butcher cut the meat into steaks; I went home and threw the steaks on the grill. Bear is tender and flavorful, probably a bit strong and gamey for some people, but I like it. When I was directly involved in every step of the process, from the harvest of a wild animal to meat on the dinner table for the nourishment of my body, I had never before felt like such a good, deserving and honorable carnivore. The food doesn't just land on our plates, folks.

←————————→

Speaking of food, one of the great things about the Dakota Ringneck Lodge is, as you might have guessed, the food. Wendy, the lead cook, and her very capable crew turn out one fantastic meal after another. On Friday evening, we feasted on ham steak, au gratin potatoes, green beans, and cake for dessert. No one was counting calories. Wendy and her helpers are all down-to-earth South Dakotans, mostly from farming backgrounds, and though they would never say it, they must sometimes think that some of the Lodge's clientele is, you know, just a little bit weird; or at the very least, not native South Dakotans. For example, in 2015, one of our hunting buddies was Eric George, who practices law with our friend Pete Ross. The two of them are the lead partners in a boutique Los Angeles litigation firm. In addition, they have offices in San Francisco and New York City. Eric is a high-powered guy, but also a really nice man and lots of fun. He is, obviously, extremely bright and well-educated. He is a master raconteur, a skill no doubt honed by years of convincing juries of regular men and women of the righteousness of his client's cause. And he is funny as hell. When he tells a story, he stands up, just as he does in court, so as to better command the room, and sometimes he uses big words. He is truly sesquipedalian ("given to or characterized by long words"). On opening day in '15, he told Wendy a long, detailed story, in the fashion I have just described. She looked at him, dumbfounded. When it was all over, even though Eric is a native Californian with no discernable accent to speak of, Wendy cocked her head sideways, looked him in the eye, and asked, "Are you from the United States?" Did we all roar with laughter? Yes (Eric included).

After dinner on Friday evening, Andy walked us through the ever important safety lecture: how to handle our weapons; how we would move in the field; how we would work together to make sure no one gets hurt. He showed us a short video. The demonstration this year, from Andy's point of view, took on additional urgency. Last year, after our visit, while guiding a corporate group, Andy was accidentally shot by one of the hunters. He could have been killed. He was hit by recklessly discharged shotgun pellets in the nose, mouth and, most painfully according to Andy, through the finger. Nobody fessed up, but Andy suspects it was the boss of this corporate team who was the incredibly careless perpetrator - which explains why no one pointed fingers. Andy recovered fully, but it was a hard lesson learned. We assured him we would be extra careful, especially with two neophyte hunters in our group.

The next morning, we ate a hearty breakfast of gigantic sausage patties, crispy bacon, French toast, maybe a couple of pieces of fresh fruit, juice and copious amounts of coffee. You can't get too much protein – we were about to walk nine miles. Then we were on our way. The morning was cool, around 53 degrees when we started, but the day soon turned bright, clear and warm - it eventually got into the 70s. We took a beat-up former school bus, now stripped down and outfitted for pheasant hunters and their dogs, and arrived at Andy's preferred spot. We would pretty much walk spent cornfields all day. I was armed with my Browning Gold Hunter, a 12-gauge autoloader; John had borrowed his Dad's well-worn 16-gauge side-by-side. Danal and Faith had rentals, in Faith's case a smaller, lighter 20-gauge shotgun. We spread out in a linear formation, Andy to our rear so he could keep an eye on all of us, as well as the dogs. He then gave the command that we would hear again and again as the day wore on: "Hunt 'em up!" I looked over at Faith as we stepped off for her first pheasant hunt. She had a huge smile on her face. What a trooper.

One of the most entertaining aspects of pheasant hunting is the dogs. They are amazing as they range tirelessly, back and forth and up and down the fields, until they see, smell or hear a bird. A dog's visual field is 250 degrees compared to 180 degrees for a human; their sense of smell is 50 times greater than ours; and they hear four times the sounds humans do and at twice the frequency. They are weaponized hunting machines, built to find roosters. When they detect a bird they freeze, and let you know that there is about to be some action. *Hunter be ready!* When a rooster flushes, there is great excitement and, usually, a volley of shots. When a bird goes down, the dogs handily execute the retrieve. It is a joy to watch them work.

This year, we hunted with two male German Shorthairs, one named Shaq and the other called Rio. They were large, mature dogs and both excellent pointers. We also were accompanied by a four-month-old male puppy called Bane who turned out to be our favorite. He was a Deutsch Drahthaar (I had never heard of such a breed), also known as a German Wirehaired Pointer. This may have been the cutest dog we had ever laid eyes on. His head was dark grey and his body a splotchy mix of light and darker grey. He had wonderful, soulful, grey-green eyes, and boy was he friendly. He was just a puppy, albeit a big one with huge paws, so he was of course in training. Andy's methodology made complete sense: he just let Bane watch Shaq and Rio work, and Bane figured it out in no time. He delivered on his first retrieve, of a rooster that John had shot, and Andy took a picture of dog and hunter together. Bane was a natural hunter, but he was just as interested in the tiny yellow butterflies – I think they may have been Common Sulphur butterflies - that fluttered around us all day, as he was in pheasants. Sometimes, when he was supposed to be on the run after roosters, Bane would instead just stand still, mesmerized by a butterfly on a wildflower.

We took a break for a lunch of cheeseburgers and macaroni salad back at the lodge, then returned to the field for the afternoon. I made a really dumb mistake when I inadvertently shot a hen (females are strictly off limits). I had a rooster in my sights as he flew directly away from me, and she got into his jet stream, right behind him, like one NASCAR driver drafting in the wake of another, just as I pulled the trigger. For once, I hit the target, and I felt terrible. I apologized up and down to Andy, but he knew it was an honest error and was very gracious. "Just be careful, Jeff." "Yes sir, I will."

We took nine ringnecks that day; the legal limit in South Dakota is three birds per hunter, per day. Danal had three, and for a guy who was a somewhat reluctant hunter (he is a gentle soul and a profound animal lover, especially of dogs) he got into the spirit of things fairly quickly. Faith got skunked, but she pulled off a few shots and had a hell of a time. She could not believe the frantic action that ensues after a flush of birds. It surely makes one's heart pound. Some hunters say it causes "a roaring in the blood." We all compared bruises on our right shoulders when we got back to the lodge – a shotgun will kick. After a shower and a few drinks, it was steak and shrimp, home fried potatoes and salad for dinner. Then a nightcap and more animated talk of the day's adventure. We slept well that night.

There are a number of factors that threaten the future of pheasant hunting, in South Dakota and elsewhere. First, there are deep worries about habitat. In the fall of 2016, South Dakota Game, Fish and Parks (GF&P) official Tom Kirschenmann said, "The number one concern for us is changes to our landscape in habitat. Weather and other factors can change the pheasant population from year to year, but ongoing habitat loss is our long-term concern." Huge swaths of grasslands have been lost to agriculture. In South Dakota, between 2006 and 2012, farmers looking to cash in on soaring grain prices plowed pastures, as well as Conservation Reserve Program (CRP) lands – all potentially superb grassy habitat – to the tune of 1.8 million acres. This is extremely disquieting, as pheasant hunting is big business in South Dakota, supporting more than 4,000 jobs. In 2015, 85,000 nonresident hunters (22,000 of them Minnesotans) spent an estimated $140 million in the state. Sixty five thousand resident hunters added another $30 million in revenues. In August 2016, GF&P reported a 20 percent decrease in the pheasant population which, in turn, resulted in a five percent decrease in license sales for both resident and nonresident hunters. In classic domino fashion, decreased license sales reduced GF&P revenues by $500,000, money that would have been spent in significant part on, what else: habitat programs. Kirschenmann explained, "Our agency doesn't receive any state general fund dollars, so any downturn in license sales plays into decision making going forward." He added, hopefully, "This doesn't mean we're going to do less with pheasant management."

Historically, CRP contributed to increased pheasant habitat by paying rent to farmers to take marginal land out of production and converting it to pheasant-friendly grasses and plants. From 1995 to 2005, the CRP program helped boost pheasant numbers from 4.9 million to a healthy 9.2 million. Good years followed, with an immense population of almost 12 million pheasants in 2007. Recent numbers have hovered between six and eight million. But the decline of CRP acreage continues. When the U.S. Congress last debated the Farm Bill, agribusiness interests prevailed. Fertilizer companies, chemical manufacturers, and the implement industry all argued that farmers (and, of course, themselves) would benefit more from production-oriented subsidies, rather than CRP set-asides. South Dakota now has around 950,000 CRP acres, which will decline to 800,000 by the time debate renews in the U.S. Congress, in 2018, on a new Farm Bill.

But there might be reason to be cautiously optimistic. The state of South Dakota may use other financial resources in the attempt to reclaim lost grassland. There are also cohorts of wildlife conservation leaders and non-governmental conservation partners, such as Pheasants Forever, a wonderful organization of which I am a proud member, that work diligently to help. There is hope that, despite the proclivities of the anti-conservation Trump regime, a renewed emphasis around increasing CRP acreage will come out of the next Farm Bill. And with grain prices, in some cases, significantly reduced (as of the fall of 2016, corn was down from seven dollars a bushel to three dollars) landowners may be more inclined to listen to a pitch which rewards them for working their best land, while setting the rest aside for pheasant habitat.

The second threat to pheasants is climate change and, more specifically, drought. In June 2017, Governor Dennis Dauggaard declared a drought emergency across South Dakota. As a result, farmers and ranchers were permitted to cut and bale state highway ditches adjacent to their properties, which destroys cover for pheasant chicks and their nesting mother hens. The federal government also declared a drought, leading to the opening of CRP lands on an emergency basis to haying and grazing. Adequate pheasant cover protects chicks from predators and promotes the production of the tiny insects that constitute 95 percent of a chick's diet during the first two months of life. The lack of morning dew, a further outcome of drought, not only damages insect populations, but also deprives young birds of a key regulator of their body temperature. The situation is particularly disappointing, said Pheasants Forever South Dakota state coordinator, Matt Morlock, who lamented, "Going into spring, we were really optimistic because our bird numbers looked good and conditions were good for an excellent hatch... When you don't get rain, and you don't have dew, you don't have insects. In drought, the only insects we have are grasshoppers, which are too big for pheasant chicks." Sadly, in late August, the South Dakota Pheasant Brood Survey Report revealed that statewide ringneck numbers for 2017 were down 45 percent and average brood sizes were the lowest they have been since at least 1949.

Finally, declining hunter participation and the lack of interest on the part of young people constitutes a serious threat to conservation, hunting, fishing and other outdoor sports. American hunters are some of the most dedicated conservationists on the planet. In 1937, President Franklin D. Roosevelt signed into law the Federal Aid in Wildlife Restoration Act, better known as the Pittman-Robertson Act. Hunters lobbied extensively in favor of the law, even though it created an 11 percent tax on firearms and ammunition, a tax hunters would pay with every gun and bullet they bought. All of that new tax revenue would be distributed to state wildlife agencies, based on the size of the state and number of licensed hunters. Most of the funding goes to research, surveys, wildlife and habitat management, and land acquisition. The program is sometimes referred to as the North American Model of wildlife conservation. In effect, for the last 80 years, hunters have willingly taxed themselves to pay for preserving, protecting and growing the sport that they love. As a result of the $11 billion that has been spent since the late '30s, many species that were threatened then are thriving today: white-tailed deer, black bears, elk, turkeys, pronghorn, and even non-game species such as songbirds.

But roadblocks to continued progress abound. Howard Vincent, President and CEO of Pheasants Forever, says, "We all know the great challenges facing Pheasants Forever and the country to keep the North American Model of wildlife conservation going strong in this new millennium. A long-term decline of hunter numbers, an aging demographic of hunters, inadequate numbers of young people taking up the cause of conservation and hunting, rampant habitat loss and increasing urbanization." Pheasants Forever works hard to develop and deliver conservation-focused youth education programs, recently raising nearly $2 million for that purpose. But the going is tough. So, if you have a chance to do it, introduce a kid to the beauty and majesty of the great outdoors. And let that child know that unless we all speak up and get involved, nothing is forever.

◄──────►

On Sunday morning we would hunt for only half the day, till noon, as people needed to get home to resume their lives. But it was a good half day. The weather continued to be gorgeous, warm and sunny. And we bagged 10 roosters, one more than we had in hunting all day on Saturday. So our aim improved slightly. Faith got off a few shots, again, but had no luck. The process of watching a rooster flush, taking the shotgun off safety, raising the gun to her shoulder, tracking the bird, hitting the bird, and then quickly reloading again proved to be a challenge for her, as it would for any beginning hunter. But she did not care – she had a blast, both literally and figuratively, I guess you could say. She also, unfortunately, stepped in a gopher hole and did a face plant, dropping her weapon. It did not discharge, thank goodness. This type of accident obviously could have happened to any one of us; our footing was somewhat treacherous throughout the hunt. She initially felt okay and continued to walk, but when she got home, first her ankle and then her Achilles tendon began to hurt. Probably just a bad sprain of the foot. She had the trace of a limp for weeks, but she is a hardy one.

I asked Faith many months later how she thought about the whole experience, upon further reflection. Was she bothered that she did not get a ringneck? An emphatic "No." What did she like best? She said, "The thing I enjoyed most was the camaraderie with you, and John and Danal. You guys were all really nice to me, and I felt like an equal partner. Andy was especially kind and patient as a coach, guide and teacher. I learned a lot. But with that said, as good as it was to hang with the guys, I think it would be even more fun to hunt with a bunch of my outdoorsy girlfriends. Now that would be great." Maybe someday. Faith also enjoyed the dogs, commenting on how neat it was to watch little Bane turn from a butterfly-loving puppy into an avid hunter, before our eyes. Her overall sense? "It was a totally unique experience, something I had never done before. The novelty of it was thrilling."

It seems to me that taking on new challenges with gusto and learning from them, just as Faith had done, is at least in part what a life well-lived should be all about.

CHAPTER EIGHT

DOWN UNDER

AUSTRALIA

"Don't worry about the world coming to an end today. It is already tomorrow in Australia."

— CHARLES M. SCHULTZ —

On January 26, 1778, 11 vessels – remembered forever afterward as the "First Fleet" – sailed into what is today known as Sydney Harbor, on the southeastern coast of Australia. The squadron had set out from Portsmouth, England in May of 1787, and covered 15,000 grueling and treacherous miles of open ocean over eight months with the mission of delivering (give or take a few) 548 male and 188 female convicts to penal exile on the remote, expansive, unknown continent. The powers that be in Great Britain had made a decision to send their criminal element (mostly petty thieves) as far away from the homeland as possible. The policy represented more a culling of the under-class than a banishment of dangerous criminals. Since rebellious colonists had achieved independence and now prevailed in North America, Australia seemed a satisfactory alternative location for a penal colony. The legendary Captain James Cook had explored Australia's eastern littorals in 1770, and pronounced the region more fertile and habitable then it actually turned out to be. The first white settlers struggled mightily to sustain themselves, but with time and diligence ultimately began to make progress. Over the entire 90-year period of the convict transportation program more than 160,000 men, women and children were shipped far away from the land of their birth to endure what essentially amounted to a life sentence in a harsh environment. Never before had a European government forcefully moved so many people, at such enormous expense, over such a vast distance. No other country in the world has had such a unique beginning. But this amazing creation story is just one of many reasons why Australia, among all of the places I have ever visited, is most compellingly unique.

◄──────►

I learned a new word just prior to our departure for Australia: *antipode*. I had never heard it spoken or seen it before in all of my reading. It is a noun defined as "the direct opposite of something else." For example, the antipode of any location on the earth is the point on the earth's surface which is diametrically opposite. As Faith and I, with our daughters Anna and Lucia (we call her Luci), explored Australia over 10 days in November of 2018, the term antipode kept popping into my mind. Australia is, if not exactly diametrically opposite on the globe from Minneapolis, Minnesota, pretty damn close to antipodal. It is a long-ass ways away. We flew out from the Twin Cities, starting at around 6:30 pm on Tuesday November 13, on our way to a connecting flight in Los Angeles. Then it was around 16 hours to Sydney. Because it is such an extended flight and because Sydney is 15 hours ahead of Minneapolis, we did not touch down until Thursday morning. Wednesday was just, well, gone - an entire day erased. Ironically, Wednesday the 14th happened to be Luci's 25th birthday; I told her that because we were essentially in a time machine during her milestone event, and that the 14th of November therefore never happened, she could choose to remain 24 for another year, or just skip ahead to 26. She said 25 years old was just fine.

Australia is the antipode in other ways. When it is summer there it is winter where we live, and vice versa. Northern Australia is generally hotter than Southern Australia. The constellations in the night sky are seemingly, to my eye, upside down. Even the moon just doesn't look right. After a few drinks it really doesn't look right. Crazy shit. They drive on the left-hand side. Pedestrians on a busy Sydney or Melbourne street also walk on the left-hand side. I kept running into people until I figured that out; it took me several days. The steering wheel in their cars is on the right. Australians will write 14 November rather than November 14. They are on the metric system. They watch different sports (have you ever tried to figure out the game called cricket? I have, and it can't be done.) Aussies are required by law to vote (they pay a small penalty if they don't); how would that go down in the U.S.? Australians are more laid back than we are in the States; their most common catchphrase is "no worries." Faith and I joked that in America, more often than not, our catchphrase is "fuck you." People in the service industry don't expect a tip – because they are relatively well-paid, they don't survive on gratuities. They appreciate a tip, but don't expect one. Australian animals are bizarre – they are nothing like anything we would ever see in the States (I give you the kangaroo, for example.) Flora and fauna in Aussie Land evolved in a world apart. The people supposedly speak the English language Down Under, but I didn't understand much of what they said to me. Apparently, "he's got 'roos loose in the top paddock" translates as: "that guy is nuts." It's all antipodal. And I could go on.

But one of the truly wonderful things about travel is that it allows a person, from time to time, to experience an alternate universe, just as I and my family did in Australia. We learn this lesson: our way of seeing the world and doing things is not the only way; in fact, there's a good chance our way might not even be the best way. I'm so glad that our daughters were a part of it. Luci is an honors graduate in English from the University of Minnesota. As an undergraduate, she spent a period of time living and studying in India. When she finished her degree, she spent nearly a year in China, teaching English as a second language to Chinese schoolchildren. In the summer of 2018 she earned a master's degree in global thought from Columbia University in New York City. She is truly a citizen of the world. Luci is now back in the Twin Cities - we are very happy about that - working in marketing and communication at her alma mater, the U of M. She aspires to be a university professor and contribute to global educational policy someday.

Her sister Anna, who is 27, was an honor-roll student at the University of Saint Thomas in St. Paul, majoring in psychology, with minors in family studies and business. She spent time traveling in Europe as an undergrad. She is extremely interested and currently working in the food and wine industry in Austin, Texas. She has studied hard and completed initial certifications with the Court of Master Sommeliers and the Wine Society Education Trust, and is considering working toward the formal sommelier designation. It's great to have a true food and wine expert in the family; I know only enough to be dangerous. Anna also aspires to additional higher education someday, subject area to be determined. Our daughters are both intelligent, vivacious, funny and a joy to spend time with. They are beautiful on the inside and the outside.

As is their mother. Faith worked early in her career in the food industry. When Luci was born, she opted to stay home as a full-time mom. As the girls got older, Faith became a master gardener and developed an interest in landscape horticulture. She went to technical college and earned an associate's degree in that discipline, and then worked to attain many additional qualifications. Among other things, she is a Board Certified Master Arborist, a Tree Risk Assessor (I call her the "tree whisperer"), and sits on the board of directors (otherwise all male) of the Minnesota Nursery and Landscape Association. She has built her own nicely profitable little company, Tree Quality, LLC, and made her way successfully over the last decade in what is truly a man's world. She has been dismissed, denigrated and openly discriminated against in the industry based on her gender, but she has persevered. Oh, how she has persevered. She is a great example to working women everywhere, but most especially she has been an inspiration to her two daughters. Please excuse me for bragging about my family, but I am mighty proud of all three of my girls (sorry, women). It goes without saying that I love each of them with all my heart.

←——————→

We received news just prior to our departure that our flight into Los Angeles might be disrupted due to the historically catastrophic fires that were raging in California. We had just recently gotten word that a cousin of mine and her husband had lost their home and virtually all of their material possessions when Paradise, the lovely Northern California retirement community that they had happily moved to several years ago, was completely incinerated. Her spouse was at work, but my cousin had barely escaped with her life in the exodus, as the inferno closed in. Nothing remained of their home but the chimney.

On the day we departed, the *New York Times* reported on "the deadliest and most destructive wildfire in California history," which had to that point caused 42 fatalities and razed 6,453 homes. More than 200 people were unaccounted for. The Camp Fire, as it was known, had burned 113,000 acres and was only 25 percent contained. President Trump cited "gross mismanagement of the forests," as the cause of the fires. Scientists vehemently disagreed with that assessment, asserting that both nature and humans are to blame. High natural winds whip fires that burn more rapidly as a result of human-caused climate change, which kills and dries the shrubs and trees that fuel the fires. A University of Utah fire scientist, Philip Dennison, stated that while there are many factors at work in a fire of this magnitude, "forest management wasn't one of them." The president subsequently went on to astutely observe that if Californians only spent more time "raking and cleaning and other things," then they wouldn't have such a big problem.

Needless to say, the entire affair provided a gigantic perspective check for all of us. As it turned out, our flight was delayed by only a few minutes, and we would easily make our connection to Sydney. If a brief flight delay is the worst thing that happens to you in a day, then you are suffering from what are known as "first-world problems." We sent my cousin and her husband a note of condolence on their horrific loss - but acknowledged how thankful we were that they were alive and safe -and a check, and wished them the best as they work to rebuild their lives. We were reminded of how fortunate we are, and that all life is so fragile – everything can be taken away on a moment's notice. Everything.

◄———————►

We arrived in Sydney having missed sleep completely on the long ride over. Faith says she did not slumber – I think she is sandbagging; she looked pretty conked out to me, most of the way, with her eye shades, neck brace, ear plugs and blankie. We cleared customs and checked into the hotel - The Vibe on Coulburn Street - and took a walking tour. Sydney is a big, vibrant, diverse, cosmopolitan city, with a population as of 2018 of more than five million. We saw Hyde Park, the Botanical Garden, the ANZAC Memorial and Archibald Fountain. We had a lovely lunch, each of us with a salad: lamb, salmon, pasta and Caesar. Our daughters were immediately and overwhelmingly impressed with the handsomeness of the men. I kept my thoughts to myself, but the women were not bad either. The Aussies are good-looking people.

In the late afternoon we rendezvoused with our tour guide, Kerry, and the rest of the group we would hang out with for the next 10 days. All really nice people. Though the evening was foggy and rainy in Sydney Harbor, we boarded a boat for a dinner tour. The harbor is immense, one of the biggest in the world. We got a bit of Australian history, had some good wine, and ate a nice supper of beef, salmon and prawns (contrary to popular belief, Australians don't call shrimp "shrimp" – they call them prawns; the idea of them talking about "shrimp on the barbie" is a fallacy.) We marveled at the unforgettable landmarks, primarily the Sydney Harbor Bridge and the world-renowned Opera House, which were both especially beautiful at dusk. Our captain Mike and his first mate, Joe, were engaging and hilarious. They were typical of what we came to see as the Aussie personality: outsized, outgoing, outspoken, smart and good-humored. We had a great time with all of the native Australians that we met.

The next morning we were up at the crack of dawn to catch an early flight to Cairns (pronounced "Cans"), in Queensland to the northeast, the coastal region that is adjacent to the Great Barrier Reef. We were excited to see this wondrous place that we had heard and read so much about. We landed to hot and sticky weather, then took a bus ride north to the Mossman Gorge Centre, which is owned and operated by the Aboriginal people called the Kuku (pronounced "goo goo") Yalanji. Apparently, Mossman Gorge is the site of a sacred battleground from long ago. We took a tour of the Daintree rainforest, led by a young Aborigine man named Mason. The Kuku Yalanji who live in this area retain their native language and culture; they forge a living through tourism by sharing their stories, art and heritage with visitors from all over the world. Mason was a kick: knowledgeable, irreverent, quick-witted. We could tell that he clearly loved to scare the shit out of tourists by bragging about all of the poisonous species, both plant and animal, that can kill you in the rainforest. Faith, ever fascinated by such things, followed Mason around shoulder-to-shoulder through the entire tour, asking questions and then gasping at this answers. "This plant will kill you if you touch it, m'am."

I had an embarrassing moment; have you ever blurted something out in front of a group and then known immediately that it was among the stupidest things you've ever said? On the short bus ride with Mason out to the location where we would begin our walking tour, I sat with my family in the back on the right-hand side. Mason sat up front on the left, in an elevated seat so he could turn and speak to us. From where I sat, this young man was responsible for driving the vehicle on a winding, hilly dirt road, yet he was not facing forward and was using both hands to gesticulate. I was dumbfounded, and suddenly exclaimed: "Guys, we are in a driverless vehicle! I've never ridden in one before..." It just seemed to me like that was what was happening. Anna quietly whispered, "Dad, the driver is on the right-hand side. You just can't see him" (in my defense, he was a short guy.) By that time, half the bus was chuckling about the knucklehead who thinks we're in a driverless vehicle. No one said anything, they were nice enough about that, but they all gave me that knowing, sidelong *you sure are one dumb motherfucker* look. But hey, when we are used to seeing things in a certain way, an alternate reality is sometimes hard to perceive. Right? Nevertheless, I vowed to be more thoughtful and circumspect in my commentary going forward. As the ancient philosopher said: "It is better to appear stupid, than to open your mouth and remove all doubt."

Australia's Great Barrier Reef is, quite simply, a fabulous, unforgettable place to visit. It is the largest coral structure on earth. While its exact dimensions are not precisely known, it is at least the equivalent in length of America's west coast. It covers more than 130,000 square miles and can actually be seen from outer space. It is a huge component of Australia's economy, providing 70,000 jobs and billions of dollars in tourism revenue. The reef was initially formed 18 million years ago; it consists of around 3,000 separate reefs and more than 600 islands; it contains gloriously diverse coral and aquatic life in all shapes, sizes and colors; and it has been awarded UNESCO World Heritage

Status. Perhaps 1,500 species of fish roam its domains; there are many types of sharks, turtles and whales; and more than 400 varieties of coral, 4,000 different mollusks and trillions of tiny coral polyps decorate this lustrous habitat. But the reef also represents one of the world's most delicate ecosystems and, tragically, it is dying before our eyes. Lest there be any doubt, we are the ones who are killing it. In significant part, the Appelquists just wanted to see the mystical Great Barrier Reef before it is completely gone.

On Saturday morning we woke up to a cacophony of bird calls – I haven't heard nature in such a commotion since Africa. We donned swimsuits, gathered up our hats, shades and sunscreen, proceeded to the Reef Marina at Port Douglas harbor, and then boarded a boat called *Calypso*. She is a large, well-outfitted catamaran that is able to accommodate up to 80 aquatic adventurers at a time. *Calypso* has a substantial back deck with a submerged platform for easy water access. Her crew did an excellent job; they outfitted us with all the necessary scuba and snorkeling accoutrements, and on the 90-minute ride out to our dive location at Opal Reef, they served hot tea, cookies and pastries. One of the guides delivered an excellent interpretive lecture on all of the wondrous life forms we would experience that day. As part of the tour package, we all paid a small fee to help maintain the reef, which we were happy to do. There was a blazing sun with temperatures in the high 80s. The wind was at a very manageable 10-15 knots, perfectly fine for diving and snorkeling.

Luci and I had gotten certified as open-water divers by the Professional Association of Diving Instructors (PADI) in 2012, but had only had a chance to dive together on one or two occasions since then. For this reason, as a safety precaution, we took a little refresher course and practiced in a local pool just prior to our Australia departure. Scuba diving is potentially hazardous; I know this from personal experience. I had actually first become certified way back in the mid-1990s, and had during that time done quite a bit of diving and taken several courses beyond the basic level. One time, in the midst of a dive as part of a PADI wreck-diving course, I had a close call in Lake Superior. Conditions were icy as I descended with my buddy, both of us in dry suits to prevent hypothermia. As we reached more than 100 feet in depth and began to explore the wreck that lay in that spot my regulator - the essential piece of equipment that you hold in your mouth which allows you to breathe underwater – froze open. *Oh-oh. This is bad. Even potentially fatal.* The precious and finite air from my tank was just gushing, uncontrolled, out of the front of the regulator. I did what any high-tech guy such as myself would do: I wacked it a couple of times, essentially punching myself in the face at the same time, but to no avail. I could still breathe through it but was rapidly losing air and would soon run out. Fortunately, we were only minutes into the dive, and had only just arrived at that depth when the problem arose. I did not panic or shit my dry suit, but I knew I needed to surface posthaste. I signaled my buddy and then began to ascend steadily but quickly. If I had been down for much longer, as part of standard diving procedure, I would have needed to take at least one safety stop prior to reaching the surface to allow excess nitrogen to escape from the body. If a diver does not do this, tiny bubbles in the bloodstream can rupture and cause what is known as the "bends." Serious injury and even death can result. The bends will ruin your day. Fortunately, I surfaced successfully and uninjured. So, once again, this cowboy got lucky. Why? I don't know. Perhaps so that one day in the future I would have a chance to dive the Great Barrier Reef with my family. Winston Churchill once said, "Life is a whole, and luck is a whole, and no part of them can be separated from the rest."

The diving in the Barrier Reef was comparatively easy and enjoyable. We had a skilled, knowledgeable guide with us the whole way, were in warm, clear and relatively shallow water, and swam along at an easy pace. I had a scuba session with Luci, and then went snorkeling with Faith and Anna. Visibility was incredible and the sights we saw were stunning. When the girls were little one of their favorite Disney movies was *Finding Nemo*, and we were all reminded of that vividly colorful animated classic as we closely observed the vast variety of fish that swam into view: orange and white Clown fish – apparently the most photographed fish in the ocean; blue and green Wrasse; delicate striped Angelfish; bright yellow Butterfly fish; iridescent blue Damselfish; Gobies, Groupers, Parrotfish, schools of fish, individual fish, big fish, little fish, shy fish, curious fish, good-looking fish, ugly fish, and on and on. We were dazzled. But we also observed, to our great sadness, many pockets of gray and even white bleached coral. Several of the areas we surveyed appeared to our untrained eyes to be thoroughly dead.

⬅━━━━━➤

Corals depend for their life on an organism called zooxanthella, which lives inside the coral. Zooxanthella is a photosynthetic algae that not only produces bright colors, but also supplies critical energy, oxygen and waste filtration for the coral. When ocean temperatures become too warm, corals release their zooxanthella, which causes the coral to lose color, appear "bleached," and become more susceptible to death. The Great Barrier Reef was struck in both 2016 and 2017 by horrible back-to-back bleaching events. No such thing – the reef being severely impacted two years consecutively - had ever happened before. The tragic result was a mass die-off of half of the reef's coral - thirty percent of the coral died in 2016, and another 20 percent in 2017.

Before the 1980s, large-scale coral bleaching incidents of this sort around the world occurred roughly every 27 years. The pace since 1983 has increased to an average of one event every six years. Nature is resilient and, amazingly, coral has the ability to reabsorb zooxanthella and therefore recover after a bleaching event. But even under good conditions, the fastest-growing coral species typically take at least a decade to come fully back to life. With higher ocean temperatures will come an increased frequency and severity of bleaching events, thus not allowing enough time for even hardy coral to bounce back.

A study published in the early spring of 2018 in the journal *Nature* lamented that the Barrier Reef may be forever changed. Terry Hughes was the lead author of the report and is a senior researcher and director of an Australian government-funded center for coral reef studies at Queensland's James Cook University (more on that institution in a bit). As quoted in the *New York Times* in April, 2018, regarding the study, Hughes said "The reef is changing faster than anyone thought it would... One thing we can be sure about is the reef isn't going to look the same again... What the paper shows is that [a mass die-off] is well underway... That transition is happening here and now." Another publicly-funded Australian research institute, the Climate Council, published a study in the summer of 2018. In it, scientists lamented that unless greenhouse gas emissions are drastically reduced, by the 2030s, bleaching events will occur as frequently as every two years. Martin Rice, chair of the Climate Council, said "This would effectively sign the death certificate of one of the world's largest living marine structures... It should serve as a serious warning for governments around the world to act now."

Australia has additional environmental challenges. As reported in the *Wall Street Journal* in August of 2018, "A severe drought has gripped an area of Australia more than twice the size of Texas, turning normally fertile crop areas into dust bowls, draining water reserves and leaving wine-producing regions parched. Hungry kangaroos are turning up in cities." (Indeed, the only wild kangaroo I saw during our entire visit was sitting in the front yard of someone's home in a residential area outside of Cairns – he looked lean and hungry.) Australia has a historically progressive record on a range of issues such as gun control, health care, wages, and same-sex marriage. The country can boast of what has arguably been the world's most successful economy over the last several decades, enjoying steady and uninterrupted growth. Yet Australia has struggled to address the crisis of global warming. In August 2018 Prime Minister Malcom Turnbull, succumbing to pressure from conservatives in his own party and powerful coal-mining interests, abandoned a modest proposal to reduce energy emissions. (Coal was discovered in New South Wales less than a decade after the arrival of the First Fleet in 1778 – millions of tons have been mined since then.) Despite the fact that recent polling shows that 59 percent of Australians believe that "global warming is a serious and pressing problem" concerning which "we should begin taking steps now even if this involves significant costs," the government fails to act. In a *New York Times* article from August 22, 2018, an Aussie cancer biologist, Dr. Darren Sanders said, "It's incredibly hard to describe how utterly sad it feels to be a scientist and dad in a country being dictated by a small group of science-denying clowns putting their own short term political gain over the long term public interest." Can we feel his pain?

◄———————►

In the evening after our day spent on the Barrier Reef, exhausted members of our group were almost without adequate words to describe what they had seen. Wondrous, unforgettable, indescribable. My journal for that day reads, "We were awed and humbled." Kerry, ever the generous hostess and a fabulous cook, prepared an authentic Aussie barbecue for our enjoyment outside on the hotel's patio. She called it our "family dinner." The delicious spread included salmon starters and salad, followed by lamb loin chops, chicken, veggie stacks, and our first sampling of kangaroo, all cooked up on the 'barbie.' Dessert was a berry and pomegranate pavlova – it was all a hit. We discussed our impressions of the kangaroo meat; I thought it was beef-like in texture with a gamey flavor; it also reminded me of liver (I have always loved liver and so does my father; however, my mother hated liver and so does my wife, so Dad and I never got it – we had to go to a restaurant on our own if we ever wanted to eat it.) I liked 'roo – not surprisingly, Faith did not. Some folks said it reminded them of venison.

The following morning we explored the bustling Sunday market in Port Douglas. Anna bought a broad-brimmed hat and I picked up a beautiful boomerang, fashioned and painted by hand by a local Aboriginal artist named Kel Williams. I had a fascinating discussion with him about his art. The boomerang was made from the wood of the Black Wattle tree, and depicts a colorful kangaroo in its center and ornate, symbolic Aboriginal designs at either end. It came with instructions about how to throw it, but I vowed never to do that and instead to display it proudly and safely in our family room back home.

We headed south again to Cairns, stopping for a break along the way. Kerry picked fresh mangoes up off the ground and tossed them to us; we peeled them and reveled in their juicy succulence. We paused at a place called the Rex Lookout, a steep cliff with a panoramic view of the Pacific far below. There we observed a paraglider, after many failed launch attempts in quite windy conditions, finally take off and float effortlessly over the ocean. It seemed incredibly perilous; Luci asked, "Dad, how would you ever be able to practice for that sport? You have to get it perfectly right every time or you die." She makes an excellent point. How some people get their kicks. I believe we can safely say that guy has 'roos loose in the top paddock.

We arrived at the previously-mentioned James Cook University, which is in Cairns and surrounded by rainforest-covered mountains, in the late afternoon. Four thousand students study there, and the University houses a world-renowned research facility/aquarium that contains some of the most venomous and poisonous sea creatures in the world. We learned that a venomous animal secretes and injects venom via a bite or sting; a poisonous animal or plant produces a toxic substance that can cause injury or death when absorbed or ingested, but not by a bite or sting – if you eat or even sometimes just touch a poisonous plant, for example, you are up shits creek; did you know the difference? I did not.

Aussies take great pride in the number of deadly species that inhabit their continent. It is said that of the 10 most venomous snakes in the world, all 10 are from Australia. We met a researcher at the University, Jamie, who showed us around. Gosh they have some nasty critters there. Kerry calls them "dangerous beasties." Stonefish look just like a stone in the sand; I casually leaned up against the glass of one of the aquariums not realizing that a stonefish rested just inches away. This is one of the most venomous fish known to man; his sting is potentially lethal and incredibly painful. I only saw him when Jamie put a stick with food in his face, and he lunged to eat it. Scared the crap out of me. Even nastier is the box jellyfish. There are many varieties of this species, but Chironex Fleckeri is supposed to be the largest, baddest of the bunch and he causes the most fatalities in Australia. Even though there are comparatively few people who have ever died this way, the sting on occasion can bring on cardiac arrest within minutes. We wondered why endless stretches of Queensland's idyllic, sandy beaches sat empty without a single human being in sight. Now we know why. And isn't it interesting that they told us about all these deadly creatures the day *after* our time in the water at the Great Barrier Reef? Our wetsuits were supposed to have protected us from any stings, we were assured, but I'm not certain how confident most of us would have been had we had this very enlightening tour the day *before*. We might have thought twice. *I'll just sit in the Calypso's galley and drink beer while you guys go in the water, if that's okay. Have fun!*

That night we had a fabulous meal at a Cairns restaurant called the Raw Prawn. The fresh seafood was great: Faith had trout, Anna enjoyed mud crab, Luci ate scallops, and I devoured prawns and grubs (small lobsters) slathered in butter. We shared a skewer of grilled 'roo and crocodile meat; the croc was very good, a bit chewy like calamari and chicken-like in flavor (you know, 'tastes like chicken.') We uncorked a nice Aussie Merlot called *Bay of Stones*. The food and wine scene everywhere we went was just outstanding.

The next day, Monday, we ventured to the Tjapukai Aboriginal Cultural Park north of Cairns and took a skyrail ride up above the rainforest canopy. The views were awesome. We made several stops along the way to (according to the brochure) "discover this ancient living museum via boardwalk tours and interpretive signage." We proceeded on to the village of Kuranda. This was not my favorite site of the trip. In my journal that evening I wrote, "We toured the village which was set in a gorgeous natural environment but was in-and-of-itself a grossly overpriced ($50/person for the bird sanctuary – we passed), charmless, tourist-trappy-crappy-tschotske-mart." (I think maybe I sound like a grumpy Tom Wolfe there.) We did have a nice lunch al fresco, and enjoyed walking the nature trail around the perimeter of the village. We hopped on the Kuranda Scenic Railway, which provides a grand, 90-minute return ride to Cairns. The train, high up on the hillside, travels over dozens of bridges, 93 curves, and through 15 tunnels. The whole thing was constructed by hand more than 100 years ago by hardy North Queensland pioneers. These guys dug tunnels through rock with pickaxes; needless to say, it took years to build. Apparently, and not surprisingly, many laborers died in the process. Again, the scenery was spectacular, but none of my girls saw any of it. They sacked out the minute we got underway. Lights out, baby. I showed them photos of what they missed afterward.

I had heard about the fabled Australian Outback since forever ago, and was anxious to finally see it firsthand. We flew to Alice Springs on Tuesday, then connected to Yulara Airport. This is in the central part of the country, but it is considered the Outback. When we stepped outside the terminal to get on the bus to the hotel, the first thing that happened to Luci was that on a stinking hot and extremely windy (35 mph) day, she got a faceful of sand. Welcome to the Outback! We got settled in and then proceeded to Uluru (which has also been known as Ayers Rock.)

Uluru is one of the world's largest monoliths; it rises above the flat plain that surrounds it to an elevation of more than 1,100 feet, and seemingly changes color throughout the day. The Anangu people own the land around it and, to them, it is a holy place. It should be to all of us. The Anangu speak of a creation period which they call Tjukurpa (the "Dreamtime"). They believe they are direct descendants of the creatures who populated the earth during the Dreamtime, animals such as pythons, lizards, snakes and emus. These animals created all of the land and such remarkable individual features as Uluru. A sign at the base of Uluru reads in part: "We, the Anangu traditional owners, have this to say: Uluru is sacred in our culture. It is a place of great knowledge. Under our traditional law climbing is not permitted. This is our home. As custodians we are responsible for your safety and behavior. Too many people do not listen to our message. Too many people have died or been hurt causing great sadness... [almost 40 tourists have perished while climbing Uluru over the years from falls, heart attacks, etc.] Please don't climb. We invite you to walk around the base and discover a deeper understanding of this place." Even despite this incredibly polite and solicitous request, people still feel compelled to scale Uluru. They poop and pee when they get to the top. They hit golf balls from the summit. And occasionally they die. It is all so profoundly sad and disrespectful. Fortunately, commencing in the fall of 2019, the climbing of Uluru will be prohibited altogether by law.

Kerry led us on a wonderful, informative tour around the base of the rock. We saw that up close it is not smooth and red, as it often appears to be from a distance in the sunlight, but gray and pockmarked. We were encouraged to touch the rock at certain locations; but there were also sections where, at the request of the Anangu, no touching or photos were allowed. In fact, the stories associated with a number of those places were reserved exclusively for the Anangu people. Kerry did not know the stories, and never will. So we just took in the grandeur of Uluru. They say the rock has healing powers. I had suffered from a touch of sciatica just prior to our departure, and continued to have pain in my leg during the first part of the trip. The long plane rides did not help. On the morning after our visit to the rock, my pain was gone. And it stayed gone.

After our walking tour, we spent time at the nearby cultural center to learn more about the lives, history and art of the Anangu people. It is a great facility, the staff is friendly, and we absorbed a lot of information. But I could not help but feel a touch of regret for the historical fate of the Aboriginal people of Australia. Trust me, I understand full well that we in the United States are in absolutely no position to judge: we enslaved one race of human beings and committed genocide against another (see Chapters 9 and 16 in this book). But the fate of the Aborigines was similarly sorrowful. Anthropologists believe that when the First Fleet arrived in 1778, there were perhaps 300,000 Aborigines, speaking as many as 300 different languages. They had first arrived in Australia as far back as 60,000 years ago. No one knows for sure. They were, and are, an incredible race of people. In his book *In a Sunburned Country*, Bill Bryson says, "They... mastered the continent. They spread over it with amazing swiftness and developed strategies and patterns of behavior to exploit or accommodate every extreme of the landscape, from the wettest rainforests to the driest deserts. No people on earth have lived in more environments with greater success for longer. It is generally accepted that the Aborigines have the oldest continuously maintained culture in the world... Their art and stories and systems of belief are indubitably among the oldest on earth." But, tragically, over time, European diseases to which they had no immunity decimated populations; white men encroached on Aboriginal land and enslaved the people. There were wars and massacres. Just as in America, the white people took over. Aboriginal numbers plummeted as a percentage of the overall Australian population, which in 2018 is 25 million. As of a couple of years ago, according to the Australian Bureau of Statistics, "The first results of the 2016 Census of Population and Housing... show that Aboriginal and Torres Strait Islander peoples [a people who are distinct from other Australian Aboriginal groups and who are generally referred to separately] represented 2.8 per cent of the population counted in the 2016 Census – up from 2.5 per cent in 2011, and 2.3 per cent in 2006." And so it goes, sadly, in so many places around the world and throughout human history.

We worshiped at the cathedral of Uluru that evening at sunset. I was reminded of the chills that went up my spine the first time, years ago, that I laid eyes upon the ceiling of the Sistine Chapel. We stared at the great, otherworldly monolith, sipped champagne, there was a distinct nip in the air as we huddled together, and we all spoke in reverent whispers as we marveled at the kaleidoscopic beauty of the sacred, magical, healing place.

◄————————►

Kata Tjuta, while considerably less well-known than Uluru, is just as fascinating. Sometimes called the Olgas, Kata Tjuta is a configuration of three
dozen enormous rock outcroppings that features a maze of endless crevasses
and gorges. On Wednesday, we made the drive to Kata Tjuta, 33 miles west of
Uluru, and took a trek called the Walpa Gorge Walk. Our group was virtually
alone in this vast, mysterious venue. Once again, the atmosphere was cathe-
dral-like, and we whispered to each other – except when we chose to shout,
which caused a haunting, resounding echo. We saw numerous bird species, as
well as several monitor lizards (I kept thinking, *This is a mini-me version of what
the dinosaurs looked like*) who froze in place, eyed us carefully, and then meandered on their way. Small pools of water contained hundreds of tiny tadpoles.

In the afternoon, the Appelquist family witnessed the whole astonishing wonderland from the air, during a 30-minute helicopter ride. None of my
girls had ever ridden in a chopper before, so weren't sure quite what to expect.
For me, as a former Marine infantryman, I had on dozens of occasions flown
in whirlybirds, but not since the early 1980s. One of my fondest Marine Corps
memories is sitting tethered in but with the door wide open and the wind
rushing through on a Bell UH-1 Iroquois, called the "Huey," speeding along
at probably 120 mph just above treetop level. I remember the surge of adren-
aline. What a thrill for a young, fearless idiot such as I was. Well, I survived
those years, and the family survived our ride above Uluru and Kata Tjuta. On
a bright sunny day with endless visibility, it was remarkable to see the entire panorama from 3,500 feet. When we finally landed, however, reviews were
mixed: Luci's comment was, "Okay. I've done that. I've flown in a helicopter.
Now I don't ever have to do it again." Been there, done that. That evening we
had dinner at our hotel, the Outback Pioneer. They had giant grills set up in
the dining hall so that we could cook our own steaks. I had a beer called *Iron
Jack Lager*. I was starting to like Aussie beer just as well as Aussie wine. *Iron
Jack*, a wicked-good porter called *Cascade Stout*, and *Great Northern*, another
outstanding lager, became my three favorites.

The next day we finally got a chance to really sleep in. It was Thursday and Thanksgiving, back in the States. The Americans in our group quietly wished each other a happy Thanksgiving - we do have so much to be grateful for. We flew for the final leg of our Aussie adventure from Yulara to Melbourne (the natives pronounce it 'Melbun') and landed in a storm that was sufficiently violent that the airport closed just as we were disembarking from the plane. The weather cleared and we were able to walk from our hotel, the Rendezvous, to dinner that evening at a fine establishment called Saint & Rogue. Faith spilled water all over the gentleman next to her. I spilled red wine in Faith's direction and she, of course, had white pants on. Bummer. I hadn't even had a sip yet. It was all just general clumsiness. We consumed what remained of the wine, which was a really fine Shiraz called *McPherson's Three Vineyards*. For my Thanksgiving meal, it was a scrumptious leg of duck. No turkey on the menu, but the duck was a fine substitute.

We loved Melbourne, the capital city of Victoria. It is a lovely, lively, immensely livable city with bustling markets, exquisite food and wine, sports, nightlife, culture and arts. Melbourne's population as of 2018 is right around five million. The architecture is eclectic, with very modern, even abstract buildings sitting beside splendid Victorian structures that were built during the great gold rush in that part of Australia. The Yarra River cuts through the city center. The southern bank of the river was once basically a run-down slum; now it teems with vibrant, upscale restaurants, entertainment and artistic venues.

On Friday our family headed east to the Yarra Valley, about an hour away, with our wine tour guide, Peter. He is a retired gent who has boisterous good fun with his business, which is showing people the fabulous wineries in one of Australia's versions of the Napa Valley. He was an engaging and knowledgeable guide. The weather was chilly and rainy the whole day, but we had a really nice time anyway as we toured four different vineyards. In just the last several decades Australia has emerged as one of world's premier wine-growing regions. The climate varies significantly from place to place, but there are many areas where the terroir is perfect for producing extremely high-caliber Shiraz (known in other parts of the world as Syrah), Pinot Noirs, and Reislings, among others. Only France and Italy export more wine to the

United States than does Australia. For the Aussies, this industry contributes nearly six billion dollars annually to the overall economy. Wine is a booming business Down Under. As is true in the Napa Valley and elsewhere around the world, Australian vintners are becoming more interested in environmental sustainability, and are increasingly producing organic and biodynamic wines. But winemakers, like other farmers throughout Australia, have also been adversely affected by the aforementioned drought.

The Yarra Valley features a generally cool climate and a diverse combination of volcanic and clay soils, ideal for harvesting any number of different grapes. Local wineries feature Chardonnay, Pinot Noir, Gewurztraminer, Sauvignon Blanc, Malbec, and many other fine varietals. Our first stop, the Domain Chandon, was a really fancy-pants kind of place. A sign just outside read, "Please, no picnics, ballgames or BYO alcohol. Enjoy your visit." Our favorite wine was a Sparkling Pinot Noir Shiraz. It was redolent of cherries and blackberries, deliciously sweet, and the bubbles made their way up our noses. Next stop was a winery more to our liking. The family-owned and operated Yering Farm vineyard features a sort of tin shack as its main tasting room. Everything is very rustic. Their menu is hand-written on a chalkboard. The family owns a scenic 30-acre vineyard and a 70-acre orchard. Yering produces excellent Chardonnay, Pinot Noir and Cab; we were fond of everything we tasted. Next was Rochford Wines, where we were particularly impressed with a Sauvignon Blanc. Finally, it was the Oakridge Winery. In addition to our sampling, we enjoyed a lunch of oyster blade of beef with a spring beetroot salad. The reds were excellent. We bought several bottles at Oakridge to take home with us. Finally, we capped off the afternoon at the Yarra Valley Chocolaterie & Ice Creamery for macaroons and salted caramel ice cream.

Our final full day in Australia was Saturday. The highlight was a walking tour of Melbourne led by a funny and borderline zany woman named Zelda. She walked us all over, gave us a download on the interesting history of Melbourne, and introduced us to the incredible diversity of the food scene. We stopped at an Asian fusion place called Lucy Lui for a crispy pork bun and barramundi and scampi dumplings. Wow. Then it was off to the Mess Hall for Italian. A nice bottle of Tuscan red called *Remole* complemented our noodles, peas and wild boar. The gnocci was delectable too. Our last stop was the Gelateria Primavera for a gelato. The banana and almond were particularly special. I made the determination then and there that I would not be weighing in immediately when I got home. *Not gonna step on the scale for a week or two, until I have worked off the excess blubber.*

←———————→

My, we had a grand time in Australia. We were incredibly tired but still absolutely exhilarated by the experience when we finally arrived home. We left Melbourne at around 12:30 pm on Sunday, and arrived home in Minneapolis at around 4:30 pm on that same Sunday. Really, then, the journey only took about three hours, or so I told the girls. They did not believe me, and groggily shook their heads no. But we were still euphoric.

We had been so impressed with the Land Down Under, with its utter immensity, stark beauty, and with the people. I was fascinated by its diversity, both in natural and human terms. Australia, like many other countries around the world, has historically had its share of controversies with respect to immigration. Not everyone is in favor of open borders. Nevertheless, 28 percent of the population in 2018 was born somewhere else. Half of the people are either immigrants or the children of immigrants. And they are wonderful human beings, who should be proud of their country and culture. We can learn so much from them.

Bill Bryson captures it well: "Let me say right here that I love Australia – adore it immeasurably – and am smitten anew each time I see it…. The people are immensely likeable – cheerful, extrovert, quick-witted, and unfailingly obliging. Their cities are safe and clean and nearly always built on water. They have a society that is prosperous, well ordered, and instinctively egalitarian. The food is excellent. The beer is cold. The sun nearly always shines. There is coffee on every corner. Rupert Murdoch no longer lives there. Life doesn't get much better than this."

CHAPTER NINE

SACRED GROUND

GETTYSBURG, PENNSYLVANIA

"We have appointments to keep in the past, in what has gone before and is for the most part extinguished, and we must go there in search of places and people who have some connection with us from the far side of time."

- W.G. SEBALD –

Paddy O'Rorke was an outstanding young man. He was born Patrick Henry O'Rorke in County Caven, Ireland, in 1837, and immigrated to the United States with his parents as an infant. He grew up in New York, attended public schools, and in 1857 received an appointment to the military academy at West Point. He graduated first in the class of June 1861. His classmate, George Armstrong Custer, was the goat of the class, graduating 34th out of 34; at Gettysburg, O'Rorke was a 26-year-old colonel, while Custer outranked him as a 23-year-old brigadier general, having just been promoted; so much for the merits of high academic achievement. At the time of the American Civil War's monumental contest at Gettysburg, Pennsylvania, in July 1863, O'Rorke - called Paddy by his many friends and admirers - commanded the 140th New York regiment. By every account, he had a brilliant future in front of him.

On the afternoon of the second day of the battle, Thursday July 2, a desperate and bloody struggle took place for control of an elevated piece of terrain known as Little Round Top. The steep, rocky precipice anchored the southern flank of the Union Army of the Potomac, but General Gouverneur K. Warren, the army's chief engineer, discovered it to be only lightly defended at a critical moment in the battle, as crack infantry from the Confederate Army of Northern Virginia rushed up the hill to attempt to take the position. Warren frantically searched for reinforcements to bolster the meager defense. He approached a column of troops marching on the Wheatfield Road, behind Little Round Top, and saw that it was the 140th New York, commanded by Warren's former underling, Colonel O'Rorke. Warren spurred his horse forward.

"Paddy, give me a regiment," shouted Warren. O'Rorke explained that he had been ordered to follow his brigade commander.

"Never mind that, Paddy! Bring them up on the double-quick – don't stop for aligning! I'll take the responsibility!"

O'Rorke immediately responded, promptly speeding his regiment to the top of the hill. He saw Confederate attackers - hardy, veteran troops from Alabama and Texas - about to win control of Little Round Top unless he could push them back. O'Rorke dismounted, brandished his sword, and exhorted his men forward: "Down this way, boys!" One of his soldiers described what happened next: "It was about this time that Col. O'Rorke, cheering on his men and acting as he always does, like a brave and good man, fell, pierced through the neck by a Rebel bullet." He was killed instantly. But his men rallied furiously around their beloved, fallen leader. It is said that the Rebel soldier who killed O'Rorke became riddled with 17 Yankee bullets in angry response. The Confederate assault was repulsed, and Little Round Top would remain in Union control for the duration of the battle. The charge of the 140th New York represented, arguably, a battle-winning turn of events.

Today, a small monument stands on the spot where Paddy O'Rorke died. It was erected by New York veterans in 1889, in commemoration of the courage of the stalwart 140th regiment and their esteemed leader. There is a relief image at the front of the monument, made in bronze, of O'Rorke's handsome face. Visitors to the National Park at Gettysburg will note that Paddy's nose seems to be well worn, shinier than the rest of his visage. There is a tradition that those who rub Paddy's proboscis, whether they be Irish or not, will have good luck.

I have had a passionate interest in Civil War history since I was probably six years old. I don't know why for sure, but it may have something to do with the fact that my father – also a great history buff - purchased a book for me at that time, called the *Golden Book of the Civil War* and, even as a squirt, I became fascinated with the story of this momentous, cataclysmic event in the life of our country. My reading skills were of course rudimentary at that point, but I remember poring over the pictures. There were a number of intricately drawn battle scenes with elaborate, colorful landscapes, populated by hundreds of detailed, tiny soldiers, depicting the movements of troops for each particular battle. I could not get enough and sat for hours riveted by that book. I know what you are thinking, and it's true: I was a weird little fella. But that early fixation on Civil War studies would, over time, develop into an idea for a business and a critical component of my professional livelihood during the past decade.

Here is my long career in one paragraph: I served for three years as a Marine infantry officer after graduation with a B.A. in political science from Carleton College. I attended the University of Wisconsin-Madison and earned a combined J.D. and master's degree in public policy and administration. I practiced law, unhappily, for four-and-one-half years as a litigator with two poorly-run, young-associate-unfriendly Twin-Cities law firms. I quit the law, opened a franchise restaurant, worked my ass off, couldn't turn a profit, lost all our savings, declared bankruptcy, and was unemployed for seven months. While Faith supported us and I looked for work, I was the primary caregiver for our daughter Anna, then a toddler; we played together and read books all day long and have been very close ever since. Alas, it's true, we do learn more from our failures than from our successes. I worked eight-and-one-half years for the Target Corporation in property development, community relations, store management, distribution and, finally, human resources. During those years I volunteered in the community and served briefly on our local city council. I moved across town to the Best Buy Company and spent another seven-and-one-half years as an HR generalist, supporting a multitude of different business functions out of Best Buy headquarters in suburban Minneapolis. While at Best Buy, in 2007, I tapped into my deep love of history and high fluency in "corporate-speak" to develop an experiential leadership program based on visits to the Gettysburg and Little Bighorn (site of Custer's Last Stand) battle-fields. Best Buy was, in effect, my angel investor, and I am forever grateful for their support. Thank you, Best Buy. In 2009, with the economy swirling down the toilet, the company offered a buyout to all of its corporate employees. I and 500 of my close friends took the generous severance and I formed my own company, now called Blue Knight Leadership, LLC. I weathered the Great Recession, wrote some books, and have been doing leadership and business consulting - as well as taking corporate teams to the battlefield - ever since. They say that if you're going to work for an idiot, it might as well be yourself. That may well be true, but I will also tell you that, my many shortcomings aside, I am still by far and away the best boss I've ever had.

When I bring a team to the battlefield, we start with an afternoon session going through a series of preparatory exercises. My goal is to help business leaders come to understand how lessons from history can be extremely relevant in their day-to-day professional lives. Oliver Wendell Holmes, Jr. said it well: "We... must remember that for our purposes our only interest in the past is for the light it throws upon the present." The next day, after breakfast, I give a short lecture on the strategy and tactics of the battle, and I show the team maps depicting the places we will see. We then hop on a bus and take a more-or-less chronological tour of the battlefield, stopping along the way to learn the story of what happened at each spot. We talk about the importance of establishing common purpose, communicating clearly, building strong relationships and trust, and making good decisions, among many other leadership principles.

After a long day, we have dinner at my favorite Gettysburg restaurant, the Dobbin House, which was built as a private home in 1776, the year the Declaration of Independence was signed. Dobbin House may have served as a stop on the Underground Railroad (a system that transported escaped slaves to safety and freedom in the North) prior to the Civil War, and was a field hospital during the three days of the battle. Some people say the Dobbin House is haunted; I am unsure about that. The next morning, we spend a few more hours digesting and synthesizing what we experienced together. We formulate some ideas, tips and tricks for how we can take the new learning back to our places of work. We also discuss the enormity and the meaning of this epic event, the largest battle in the history of the Western Hemisphere. Over the three days, 50,000 young Americans were killed, wounded, captured or went missing. About half the time, someone sheds tears – sometimes it is me – during this final session. Despite the tragic magnitude of the human suffering at Gettysburg, and the undeniable heaviness of the subject matter, I take great satisfaction in being able to share this unforgettable story with my teams. We need to better understand America's past – all the good, the bad and the ugly of it. In the end, people almost uniformly come away genuinely moved and changed by what they have seen and heard – many of them tell me so. My heart sings when that happens. I am most richly blessed, for I love what I do.

◄━━━━━━►

In her outstanding book, *The Hour of Land: A Personal Topography of America's National Parks,* author Terry Tempest Williams includes a chapter on the Gettysburg National Military Park, to which she is deeply drawn. In it she says, "Gettysburg is at risk of becoming a place of war worship. In our desperation to perceive valor and courage that may not be present in our own lives, we glorify a terrible slaughter of men and boys. The myth that war propagates and that our national memory perpetuates is that all soldiers are valiant and brave, and that American history is a history victorious instead of shadowed and scarred."

I have had a number of people over the years who have not been through my program firsthand wonder, without saying so directly, whether there might just be some element of war worship in it. They will tell me, "Oh, that's a guy thing," or "That's a war thing." My emphatic response is that "It's not a guy thing, and it's not a war thing; it's a leadership thing. And leaders come in every shape, size, race, creed, color, gender, age, sexual orientation and so on." As for the glorification or worship of war, I am actually quite blunt in explaining the consequences of combat on the body and psyche of the combatants; on the innocent who are drawn in by unfortunate proximity to the fighting, or otherwise impacted by the carnage of it; on the communities and surrounding countryside that bear the brunt of the battle. There is no glory in war. There was certainly heroism - on both sides - aplenty at Gettysburg, and we discuss and marvel at it, but that's not the main point.

The main point is that it was a fight about slavery, a mighty struggle to decide what kind of a country America would be. And it wasn't pretty. It is almost incomprehensible to believe that just over 150 years ago, in the United States of America, almost four million African-American men, women and children lived in bondage. Our past is indeed "shadowed and scarred" by this fact. Slavery was the foundational issue that caused the Civil War. As renowned historian Bruce Catton wrote in his masterful book, *This Hallowed Ground*, "At the very bottom of American life, under its highest ideals and its most dazzling hopes, lay the deep intolerable wrong of slavery... It was the one fatally limiting factor in a nation of wholly unlimited possibilities; whatever America would finally stand for, in a world painfully learning that it's most sacred possession was the infinite individual human spirit, would depend on what was done about this evil relic of the past. Abraham Lincoln had once called it 'the great Behemoth of danger'..."

I will occasionally have a program participant argue that the main question was states' rights, and that the South fought to throw off the shackles of an oppressive central government, just as our revolutionary forebears had done. Slavery was "no big deal"; I strongly disagree. The fundamental contradiction was this: how could a great nation, founded upon the principle that "all men are created equal," in good conscience allow the institution of slavery to even exist, much less expand? After decades of political wrangling, the question had to be decided once and for all, and it was, at inconceivable cost in blood, sweat, toil and treasure. The historian and author Shelby Foote said, "It was the crossroads of our being," and he is right. Sadly, I would also argue that, in a very real way, we are still fighting the Civil War to this day. As documentary filmmaker Ken Burns says, "Today, even with a century and a half between us and our greatest cataclysm, we have an eerie sense that so much of what seemed safely finished and distant about the Civil War now seems present, palpable, the underlying racial causes of the old conflict on nearly daily display." Ours is not a history entirely victorious and we are indeed, as a nation, still very much a work in progress.

In 1998, the National Park Service turned away from its traditional line of focus on the strictly military and heroic aspects of battlefield sites, including Gettysburg, to acknowledge and incorporate the painful story of the evils of slavery into the narrative. Interpretive efforts began to include an examination not just of the conduct but also the causes and context of the war. In the spirit of creating a more honest and authentic experience for visitors, in 1999, leadership at the Gettysburg National Military Park embarked on a 20-year project not only to tell the story more accurately but also, as much as possible, to restore the battlefield to its 1863 appearance. This plan sparked great controversy. Over the past almost 20 years, it has entailed the removal of more than 500 acres of non-historic woodlots (any process that requires the destruction of trees will tend to get people up in arms), the replanting of 100 acres of orchards that existed at the time, and the replacement of over 12 miles of original fence lines. I have personally had a wonderful time over the last decade watching this great endeavor unfold. For example, the trees in the farmer Joseph Sherfy's notorious Peach Orchard – where so much terrible fighting took place on July 2nd – have gone from knee-high saplings to fully mature and bearing succulent peaches. Preservation-minded private and non-profit interests from both the north and south have purchased land so that it might be restored to historic lines of sight (much of the land contained within the 10 square miles of the National Military Park is privately owned.) Buildings, including the venerable but aging and poorly placed cyclorama structure, have been torn down, and golf courses turned back into fields. In 2008, the Park Service unveiled the sparkling new, $103 million National Military Park Museum and Visitor Center. It is an amazing facility and a national treasure.

Terry Tempest Williams sums up: "In this instance, the national park has been a unifying force in bringing opposing sides together. By re-creating historical cultural landscapes through environmental manipulation, ironically, a more accurate depiction of the battle has been rendered from the restoration of the peach orchard to the view on Little Round Top... We are slowly returning to the hour of land where our human presence can take a side step and respect the integrity of the place itself – paying attention to its own historical and ecological character beyond our needs and desires. This kind of generosity of spirit requires an uncommon humility to listen to the land first."

Despite the hard-won successes achieved at Gettysburg, with its high national profile and two million visitors per year, there are dark clouds on the horizon for our environment and many of our cherished public lands. Under the shortsighted "leadership" of the ignorant, bumbling shit-show that is the Donald J. Trump administration, America has reneged on its obligations under the Paris Climate Accord and, in effect, ceded our enormous power to positively address global climate change to others. Domestically, many long-standing environmental initiatives have been overturned. An executive order called the Review of Designations under the Antiquities Act allows for the rescinding or reduction in size of national monuments. The Act will be applied to review around 30 monuments, all established by previous presidents since 1996, and totaling tens of millions of acres. The Trump administration looks to make more public lands available to drilling, mining, logging, motorized recreation, and gas and oil development.

Sadly, the list includes our most recent national monument, so designated by President Barack Obama, a spectacular place of high desert country called Bears Ears, located in Utah. Bears Ears is enormous, about 90 times bigger than Manhattan Island and one third again larger than Grand Canyon National Park. This spot contains 3,500 years of Native American history and 100,000 protected archaeological sites. Barack Obama noted that it encompasses "some of our country's most important cultural treasures, including abundant rock art, archaeological sites, and lands considered sacred by Native American tribes." President Trump, in contrast, has called the time-honored process of designating national monuments, commenced during the administration of Theodore Roosevelt, and never questioned by any president since that time, "another egregious abuse of federal power." The process of setting aside public land like Bears Ears, says Trump, constitutes a "massive federal land grab" that "should never have happened."

Writer and conservationist Shane Mahoney says, "While citizens may enjoy them for a while, and the federal government may hold them in trust forever, America's public lands essentially belong to the nation's future. If the next generation of Americans are to survive and live well, it is essential America preserve its public lands and the myriad benefits they provide. Federal custodianship of public lands remains something worth fighting for..." The fight will not be an easy one. Despite our angst and heartache at the present state of affairs, those who love the land must persevere.

←——————→

One of the things that I had always thought was a little off and even inappropriate about the whole Gettysburg experience for the typical tourist is the obsessive focus on ghost stories; taking advantage of peoples' most fundamental fears in a sacred place to make a buck seems, at the very least, a bit insensitive. At worst, it borders on un-American. As historian Jennifer M. Murray explains in her book, *On a Great Battlefield: The Making, Management, and Memory of Gettysburg National Military Park, 1933-2013*, "The rapid proliferation of ghost tours stands as a crass, commercializing enterprise, if not exploitation. Ghost touring companies arrived in Gettysburg in the mid-1990s... Today, over a dozen ghost tours are available to visitors seeking a paranormal experience..." Terry Tempest Williams concurs: "Many ghost stories fly around this town."

As I explained in my story about Venice, I am a practical man and a non-believer in paranormal phenomena. I have always felt a certain unseen energy on the battlefield, but I attribute that to the fact that I know what happened there and my senses are somehow heightened. For years I had scoffed and snickered at the whole damn ghost thing as a bunch of poppycock. But then I had a highly unusual experience.

In March of 2017, for the fourth year in a row, I presented my leadership workshop to a group of a dozen 20-year-old sophomores from my beloved alma mater, Carleton College. I take the kids through the very same program I would present to a CEO and her C-level team. Carleton picks up the tab for travel, but I donate my time as a way to give back to the school. The students are incredibly smart, very diverse in their backgrounds – many of them from foreign countries - and I get a kick out of watching their reactions and hearing their perspective on the whole event. We have to go in March, which is not the ideal time of year in Pennsylvania from a weather standpoint, because that is when they have their spring break. No other time of year works as well.

I always arrive at my events a day early, to allow time for travel snafus and to take a solitary tour of the battlefield. I rehearse each stop in my mind and strive to get my ducks in a row. I check for any adverse conditions, like standing water or mud, on the field. On the date in question, Wednesday March 22, skies were mostly cloudy and the weather was extremely chilly, with temperatures around freezing. I woke up, ate breakfast at the hotel, got in my rental car, and commenced my individual rounds. I wore the same light-weight but extremely warm down jacket that got me to the top of Mount Kilimanjaro.

When I arrived at Little Round Top, it was probably about 10 a.m. For the first time in the many dozens of times I had stood on this spot, I was absolutely alone. I could not believe my luck, for there was no one in sight when I stood near Union General Gouverneur K. Warren's statue, as he gazes westward into the sweeping valley before him and over to South Mountain in the distance. It is a beautiful place with a magical, panoramic view, and I soaked it in. I took several deep breaths of fresh, cold air, then began to do as I always do, making my way south across the undulating hilltop to the very special spot where Paddy O'Rorke and the 140th New York made their heroic stand. I always rub Paddy's nose for good luck. It can't hurt. Yes, I am a creature of routine.

As I walked across the hill, from perhaps 200 feet away, I could see, alas, that there was someone else standing near Paddy's monument. *Oh, I am not alone here anymore. Damn. It was good while it lasted.* As I got closer and the person came into better view, I realized, interestingly, that he was a Confederate reenactor. Reenactors are the guys (and sometime gals) who dress up in authentic Civil War garb and, well, reenact famous battles or otherwise make their presence known so people can appreciate what they do. At Gettysburg I had seen them many times. Sometimes they mix with the crowds in the Visitor Center, and I have seen them on numerous occasions at Little Round Top, but only when crowds are thick – Little Round Top is the most visited site on the entire battlefield, and these guys clearly love the attention. All the Gettysburg reenactors I had ever seen were dressed in Union uniforms. I had never witnessed Johnny Reb. And, to be truthful, many (but certainly not all) of the reenactors in my experience tend to be older white guys with bulging midriffs. They are not quite authentic, in my humble opinion, because the typical Civil War soldier was young, lean, rangy and usually hungry.

Which made this an atypical situation. I mulled it over as I slowly trod in Paddy's direction. *What is a Confederate reenactor doing here anyway? Never saw that before. And why is he on Little Round Top, all alone, on a freezing cold day, with no crowd to appreciate his impressive getup? Even if he was at the Visitor Center, there wouldn't be many people there to see him on a frosty Wednesday morning in March. What's he doing?*

I saw him not through a glass darkly but, rather, as clearly as I have ever seen any person. The only drug in my system was the caffeine from my usual four or five cups of morning coffee. He was a young man, perhaps 30-years-old, if I had to guess. Maybe 5'10". He wore black boots with his pants tucked inside. His pants were fancy, with perpendicular stripes of light grey and Kelly green. This is not the uniform that a Gettysburg Confederate would have worn, as basic Yankee blue and Rebel grey uniforms had come into common use by 1863. The soldiers needed to be able to tell who was who in combat. But earlier in the war, when standards were looser, a soldier from either side certainly could have donned such a colorful outfit, as part of his classiest dress uniform, for example. He might have worn it while on parade, or to impress his best girl. Or for a ceremony of some type. My friend had a grey blouse, somewhat darker than his pants, and lightweight. *He's not dressed for the weather, is he?* He was cinched up with a thick black belt outside of his blouse. On his head he wore a broad-brimmed slouch hat, almost navy in color. He sported a full beard, just like a Civil War soldier would have had. It was a real beard, black and luxuriant. He was unarmed; no sword, no pistol, no rifle. He wore no insignia of rank. *Looks like a common enlisted man.* He was not dirty or unkempt; he was neat and put together. But he looked young, lean, rangy and hungry.

As I made my way closer, walking at a snail's pace, he took no notice of me. He removed his slouch hat, placed it over his heart, and looked out across the valley. *Why would a Confederate reenactor be on Paddy's spot, honoring this sacred ground, remembering this sacrifice? Oh, I forgot, that's right, it wasn't just the New Yorkers. Many a brave Rebel from Texas and Alabama gave his life here, too. Right on that patch of jagged rock, over where he is standing.* I decided to respect his moment, not to barge in and intrude on his quiet solitude. I stopped, perhaps 20 feet away, and pretended to read a battlefield tablet that I had long ago memorized. I looked down; I did not gaze in his direction. But I became increasingly apprehensive. My foot tapped. My heart began to race. *This does not answer. Even if he is a real flesh-and-blood man, this does not make sense. The simplest and most likely theory is probably correct: he is a man, just a weird reenactor, doing a really inexplicable thing right now... but it still doesn't answer.*

I heard his boot heels clicking softly on the asphalt walkway behind me. He was leaving. I turned around. He was perhaps 15 feet distant. He looked me straight in the eye. He did not speak, but he nodded his head, in a deeply respectful and gentlemanly way, in my direction. I gave a half-wave with my left hand; I probably had a weak smile on my face. *We are both here for the same reason. I don't know you, and we may not even be from the same time dimension, but we both know what happened here. The loss of too many young lives, right here, right where we are. We are both here to pay our respects, that's all.* He turned away and I watched him saunter east, the short distance to the back of the hilltop. If he had gone poof in the air - which I half expected him to do - I would have soiled myself. But he did not. He just took a dozen or so more steps and went out of my sight.

When I have had eerie experiences in the past, or somehow gotten spooked, I get the proverbial goosebumps on the arms. You know, the hair stands up. In this case, I had a physical reaction unlike anything I have ever known. My heart pounded out of my chest. I became short of breath. A thunderbolt of electricity went from the back of my neck all the way down my spine, and then back up again. My head throbbed. I was stunned. *What did I just see?!*

I have been reluctant to share this story with many people. I don't want anyone to think I'm fucking nuts. Maybe they do anyway. But there it is. That's what happened. All I can say is this: I know what I saw; I just don't know how to explain it.

◀━━━━━━━▶

At the end of battlefield day in my seminar, I always have one of the participants read the Gettysburg Address in the National Cemetery, near the spot where Abraham Lincoln delivered it in November 1863. I feel that, as Lincoln said in his famous speech, "It is altogether fitting and proper that we should do this."

When the battle ended, the people of the tiny borough of Gettysburg faced a major catastrophe and cleanup. Bloated and rotting corpses littered the field by the thousands, and they were initially buried in shallow graves which, in many cases, with heavy rains, soon came open again. Something like 3,000 dead horses were piled together, doused with kerosene, and burned. Due to the stench, and the obvious threat to public health, the citizenry kept their windows shut all during the rest of the long, hot summer that followed. From the point of view of the victors, a need for a proper and honorable burial, at least for the Union dead, became readily apparent.

Local attorney David Wills, working closely with politicians and other supporters from several of the northern states, oversaw the acquisition of a plot of land and the construction of the National Cemetery. William Saunders designed the cemetery with the ornate and towering Soldiers National Monument at the center, and graves with simple in-ground markers, arranged in semi-circles around the monument, by state, to emphasize equality. There were approximately 3,600 Union bodies, as best they could be identified, that were disinterred and then reburied. Sadly, nearly half of them are "unknown." Countless families sent a husband, father, brother, or son to war, and never knew what happened to him. Years later, through the efforts of a number of southern women's groups that later coalesced as the Daughters of the Confederacy, a project was undertaken to disinter the Confederate dead at Gettysburg, for a proper and honorable reburial in the South. Despite this, it is said that there may still be 500-1,000 unknown Southern boys lying at rest, wherever they may be, beneath the rolling fields of Gettysburg. I cannot help but believe that, at least in a few instances, Johnny Reb is buried at the National Cemetery, too. Of the price that families on both sides paid during the Civil War, Bruce Catton said, "These are some of the coins, bloodshed and suffering and a deep sorrow in the breast, spent prodigally by folk who had not wanted to buy anything at all but who had just hoped to get along the best they could, winning a little happiness out of life if their luck was in: the total of these coins high beyond counting, the payment extracted from people who had made no bargain, the thing bought a mystic intangible dim in the great shadows."

President Lincoln, who would not be the main speaker that day, was invited to deliver "a few appropriate remarks" at the dedication ceremony, to be held on November 19, 1863. Lincoln arguably had the thinnest resume, prior to taking office, of any person in the history of the American presidency. He had less than a year of formal schooling, and limited political experience (a stint in the Illinois Assembly and one term as a U.S. congressman); but he read constantly from an early age in an effort to improve and educate himself. He developed into a master communicator whose skills as a courtroom lawyer and innate yet carefully honed abilities as a story-teller and humorist enabled him to reach and teach ordinary people in an unforgettable fashion. His deep study of the King James-version of *The Holy Bible* and the works of William Shakespeare influenced the lovely cadences of his speeches.

Lincoln's masterpiece, the Gettysburg Address – just 272 words long, which he delivered in about three minutes in his high-pitched Kentucky twang – forever changed the way Americans think of themselves. In the speech, he explained the meaning of the sacrifice of so many lives on the battlefield just a few months prior. He asserted the Declaration of Independence and its central idea, equality, as a matter of founding law. What kind of a nation would we be? Were the words, "all men are created equal" just words, or did they really mean something? The Civil War, Lincoln told us, was the great struggle around and testing of this principle. As historian Gary Wills says in his book, *Lincoln at Gettysburg: The Words That Remade America*: "By accepting the Gettysburg Address, its concept of a single people dedicated to a proposition, we have been changed. Because of it, we live in a different America."

Over the years, I have been honored to invite a number of different people to read the Gettysburg Address at the end of our day-long journey together: a young African-American man who was a store manager from Best Buy; a Jewish woman from Russia who immigrated to the United States as a teenager and finally became a citizen; an older woman of Cherokee descent who was a top college administrator; a young female college student from India who aspires to stay in the U.S. and become a medical doctor; a Chinese exchange student whose fluency in English and desire to understand America astounded us all; a white business executive whose late father forced him to memorize the Gettysburg Address; a bunch of other regular white guys and gals; a bunch of other regular people of color; a bunch of people who happen to be older; some who are younger; several people who happen to be gay. Maybe someone who was transgender, and I didn't even know it. And on and on. The Almighty Creator's great rainbow coalition of people, some Americans, some not, in all their unimaginable, gorgeous diversity, reading the Gettysburg Address, right there where it was delivered. What a thing to see.

I do believe that Mr. Lincoln, God rest his blessed soul, would have heartily approved. In fact, I'm quite sure of it.

"Four score and seven years ago our fathers brought forth on this continent, a new nation, conceived in Liberty, and dedicated to the proposition that all men are created equal. Now we are engaged in a great civil war, testing whether that nation, or any nation so conceived and so dedicated, can long endure. We are met on a great battlefield of that war. We have come to dedicate a portion of that field, as a final resting place for those who here gave their lives that that nation might live. It is altogether fitting and proper that we should do this. But, in a larger sense, we cannot dedicate - we cannot consecrate - we cannot hallow - this ground. The brave men, living and dead, who struggled here, have consecrated it, far above our poor power to add or detract. The world will little note, nor long remember what we say here, but it can never forget what they did here. It is for us the living, rather, to be dedicated here to the unfinished work which they who fought here have thus far so nobly advanced. It is rather for us to be here dedicated to the great task remaining before us - that from these honored dead we take increased devotion to that cause for which they gave the last full measure of devotion - that we here highly resolve that these dead shall not have died in vain - that this nation, under God, shall have a new birth of freedom - and that government of the people, by the people, for the people, shall not perish from the earth."

CHAPTER TEN

LAND OF FIRE & ICE

ICELAND

"One's back is vulnerable, unless one has a brother."
— *THE SAGA OF GRETTIR*, CHAPTER 82 —

The epic literary masterpiece, *Njal's Saga*, author unknown, is considered by many scholars and historians to be the finest example of the genre of incredibly compelling stories known collectively as the Sagas of the Icelanders. The setting for the sagas is generally the period from 930 to 1030 AD - known as the Saga Age - but they are not believed to have been written until the 13th and 14th centuries. The sagas relate amazing tales about heroes and events, and are regarded as one of the monumental artistic achievements of the Middle Ages. *Njal's Saga* has been described by the English critic W.P. Ker as "one of the great prose works of the world." The narrative centers on the fascinating, tumultuous lives and deep, brotherly friendship of two men, Gunnar Hamundarson and Njal Thorgeirsson, who are very different, but who both exemplify the ideal of the medieval Icelandic hero. Gunnar and Njal actually lived; they are not fictional characters. In the end, after many trials and tribulations, both men met a violent fate. Gunnar was outlawed and told he must depart the country on pain of death. But he could not leave his beloved farmstead at Hlidarendi, and a war party ambushed him in his home. He fought ferociously, killing and injuring many of his attackers, then finally succumbed to his wounds. For Njal, he was similarly trapped in his home, at a place called Bergthorshvoll, by his enemies. In an event familiar to all

Icelanders as the Burning, in the year 1011, the war party set fire to the farmstead. Njal, by then an old man, and members of his family were burned to death. Both locations, Hlidarendi and Bergthorshvoll, sitting about a dozen miles apart as the crow flies, are today regarded as sacred places by Icelanders, though neither of them is necessarily easy to find. I was honored and humbled, in the summer of 2018, to visit both hallowed sites, to ponder the wonders of the sagas, and to stand in awe of the vast expanse and magical beauty of the glorious island called Iceland.

⟵⟶

In February 1999, our family moved into a new home in a quiet cul-de-sac in the south suburban Twin Cities. One day, as I cleared snow from the base of my driveway, a man in a leather Navy flight jacket and his young daughter walked by me. It just so happened that I too was wearing a flight jacket. He said to me, "Hey, you're the new neighbor. Were you a naval pilot?" I said, "No, even better than that, I was a Marine infantry officer." He laughed, shook my hand, and introduced himself as John Magnusson. We have been a two-man band of brothers ever since that moment.

Johnny was born in Iceland. He came to the United States with his family at age three. He grew up and was educated in New Jersey, but always maintained close ties and frequently visited the special land of his origin. He remains to this day highly fluent in the Icelandic language, and has dual Icelandic and American citizenship. He served for seven years on active duty as a naval aviator, flying the Lockheed S-3, known (appropriately, in John's case) as the Viking. The Viking is a four-seat, turbofan-powered jet that specializes in anti-submarine warfare. It is a carrier-based, all-weather aircraft, which John Magnusson flew on and off of the deck of the carrier U.S.S. *Independence* approximately 180 times. About 40 percent of those missions were flown at night. Fortunately for John, the number of clear takeoffs exactly equaled the number of safe landings. In his typically understated words, "It could get a bit dicey in the North Atlantic, when wave heights were at 15-25 feet." Any person, male or female, who has the cajones to successfully land an airplane onto the rolling, pitching deck of an aircraft carrier, and especially in the dark, has my undying respect. What a feat!

John spent 13 additional years in the naval reserve, while joining then Northwest Airlines as a commercial pilot, in 1985. Northwest eventually merged with Delta, and John ended a 31-year career as the captain (manning the "left seat," as he would say) of a Boeing 757. He also served his native country for 16 years as Icelandic consul in Minneapolis. He was my neighbor and close friend for 18 years until he retired – with a nice pension from both the U.S. military and Delta - and moved to Orlando, Florida, so that he and his wife could be closer to their youngest daughter and their new grandson. John also purchased a comfortable two-bedroom condominium in the heart of Reykjavik, where he now spends four or five months out of the year, during the summer. Among other things that we have in common, John and I are both descendants of the Vikings, he of the Icelandic Vikings and me of the Swedish Vikings, although we have never once discussed or even acknowledged that fact. I guess it has just been understood for all these years.

Johnny and I palled around together a lot. One of our favorite activities was what we called "Red Meat & Violence" night or, for short, just "RM & V." We would head out and get a steak dinner (John would usually devour a filet; I would belly up to a porterhouse), have a few drinks, then go see any kind of action-oriented movie (which invariably contained violence) that we could find. War movies predominated, but the James Bond or Tom Cruise *Mission Impossible* movies were also perfect RM & V fare. Occasionally, when we had more time, we would undertake what we called "Turbo-RM & V." This entailed getting together in the afternoon and going to a local indoor gun range. John would bring a hand-me-down pistol given to him by his father, and I would tote my Springfield .45, just like the one I fired in the Marine Corps. We would purchase ammo and set ourselves up in a shooting station with a paper target. Our favorite target after 9/11 was a life-sized image of Osama Bin Laden. We would blow that thing full of holes, then go have our red meat and see the movie. Once, as I was blazing away at our nemesis, John stood behind me and, unbeknownst to me, took a video with his phone. My concentration was intense, and a small, bright-orange flame emanated from the end of the barrel each time I pulled the trigger. I hit that evil bastard squarely in the head and torso with every shot in a rapid-fire string, then turned to Johnny and commented tersely, "He's dead." (Sometimes the Viking blood lust comes to the fore.) This was in late April of 2011 and, ironically, not 10 days later, on May 2nd, a real-life Navy Seal shot the real-life Bin Laden, also in the face, bringing his sick, malevolent life to an end.

John and I had lots of fun. I missed him when he left. I was ecstatic when he invited me to come visit him in Iceland. I secured a surprisingly cheap round trip ticket (with Delta, who else?) direct from Minneapolis to Reykjavik. In August of 2018, the two-man band of Viking brothers was together again, even if just for a week.

◄────────►

An Anglo-Saxon chronicle dated 793 A.D. says, "In this year dire forewarnings came over the land of the Northumbrians, and miserably terrified the people: these were extraordinary whirlwinds and lightnings, and fiery dragons were seen flying in the air. A great famine soon followed these omens; and soon after that, in the same year, the havoc of heathen men miserably destroyed God's church on Lindisfarne..." Most modern historians consider the Viking raid on Lindisfarne – a tidal island off the northeast coast of England – to constitute the beginning of the "Viking Age." The ferocious surprise attack on the Church of St. Cuthbert at Lindisfarne, in which defenseless monks were brutally murdered, buildings burned and treasures stolen, sent shock waves throughout Britain, Ireland and beyond. In the view of many, it was the Apocalypse made real on the shores of Northumbria. The Vikings were superb sailors, and they possessed fearsome combat skills finely honed during generations of skirmishing in their home territories. Why they chose to take to the seas and go pillaging abroad is not precisely known, but they did so with a vengeance. Over three centuries, warriors from what are now Norway, Denmark and Sweden pushed west, south and east. Their raiding parties ranged as far as Russia, Constantinople, Britain and Paris. In their splendid, seaworthy longboats they traveled to Iceland, Greenland and, ultimately, North America. Wherever they ventured, they struck fear into hearts – these were bad dudes. There was a common Latin refrain during this era: "A furore nordmannorum, libera nos, domine." ("From the fury of the northmen, deliver us, O Lord.")

A Viking named Floki Vilgeroarson sailed westward from Norway in the second half of the ninth century. He ventured in search of a rumored land somewhere in the North Atlantic Ocean. Floki made landfall and set up a homestead intending to stay. But he only lasted one winter before returning home to Norway; once there, he devised a ruse to discourage further settlement in the lovely place he had discovered: he called it "Iceland." But word got out – Floki had some loose-lipped shipmates - of lush vistas, abundant fishing, and temperate seasons. In 874 A.D., a man named Ingolf Arnarson, who was allegedly escaping a blood feud in Norway, sailed within sight of the Icelandic coast. Per longstanding Viking belief in preordained fate, Ingolf threw overboard his high-seat pillars (posts that flanked his master's chair at home). The pillars came to rest on the southwest shore, near a place with steaming hot springs. Ingolf determined that this was where he would settle, and he named it Reykjavik, which translates as "Bay of Smoke" in Old Norse.

Ironically, when Norwegian settlers arrived, they discovered they were not alone. A few small bands of Irish monks had already taken up residence. The holy men had fled Ireland in flimsy boats and courageously sailed 500 miles in the open ocean to reach Iceland, in pursuit of the goal of better worshiping God in their own austere wilderness. The Vikings regarded the monks as strange hermits; the monks regarded the Vikings as coarse pagans, with whom they could not coexist. The monks were soon on their way, off to what exact locations historians are uncertain. In subsequent years the Vikings captured Irish slaves and brought them to Iceland. Historically, because of a lack of immigration over many centuries, the ethnic makeup of the Icelandic population remained quite stable. Nevertheless, there is still some proportion of Irish blood-group distribution in the general population. (It is said that, in the view of certain people anyway, to be a red-headed Icelander carries a slight stigma of being descended from slaves.) Today, despite increases in immigration, still only around seven percent of the Icelandic population is foreign.

The pattern of settlement that evolved in the country's early years remains true to this day. There was no particular need to be focused on the threat of warfare or the construction of defensive enclaves in the form of fortified towns. Indeed, there were no towns in ninth and tenth century Iceland; rather, the perimeter of the country rapidly became dotted with farmsteads.

Today, there are of course any number of bustling coastal cities and towns, but thousands of individual farms still predominate across the landscape. Interestingly, a modern Icelandic farm will frequently sit on a plot of land whose place name goes back to the country's very beginnings. The lack of any formal governmental structure in the first several decades also meant that power tended to concentrate in the hands of large property owners, who possessed significant holdings in land, animals and slaves. These proud, wealthy chieftains frequently came into conflict with one another, resulting in bloody feuds and endless reprisals (many of which are featured in the sagas.) Eventually, the need for law and order became apparent.

In the year 930, Icelanders convened the very first Althing, in a scenic valley just north of Iceland's largest lake, called Thingvallavatn. The Althing represented a remarkable experiment in democracy – at a time when the rest of Europe was feudal and ruled by kings – and the world's first attempt at a parliamentary form of government. The Althing took place for two weeks every June. Primary participants were around 40 of the most powerful priest-chieftains, collectively called godar, from all over the country, some of whom travelled as far as 400 miles to attend (they came on horseback.) The reputation of individual godi could be enhanced based upon the number of followers he brought along to the Althing; sort of like a long-ago version of Twitter. The Althing served multiple functions: it was a much-anticipated social event, in which booths established by the various parishes held elaborate feasts and distributed expensive gifts; participants traded news and gossip from all over the land; and lots of folks got very drunk. More important, members of the assembly agreed to be governed by the rule of law, which allowed the disparate domains to at least begin to come together as one country. The Althing chose a Law Speaker, who served a three-year term. He was required to memorize all the laws of Iceland, and every year he stood upon the Law Rock and recited one third of the legal code (there were no written texts to aid him.) If by chance his memory failed and he missed something, that law then passed out of existence. The primary purpose of the Althing was the attempt at peaceful resolution of disputes. Any aggrieved party could bring his complaint before the assembly for a fair hearing. It was up to the party who brought suit to pursue his claim if the Althing ruled in his favor. For this reason, judgments rendered by the Althing were mostly toothless, and opposing parties often ended up solving their conflict as they always had: by violence. Nevertheless, the Althing, which continued for more than 300 years until Iceland came under Norwegian control, represented one of the most unique and highly innovative political experiments in the annals of history.

In the year 1000, Norwegian missionaries succeeded in converting a southern Icelandic warlord to Christianity. For a short time, paganism and Christianity coexisted, until a Law Speaker named Thorgier, after much deliberation, determined that Iceland would become Christian, but that its citizens could continue to worship the old gods if they chose to do so. In 1262, Iceland submitted to the domination of the Norwegian crown. King Olaf of Norway inherited the Danish crown in 1376, and Iceland subsequently became subserviant to Denmark. It was not until 1944 that Iceland finally achieved independence from Denmark and, at long last, the Republic of Iceland came into being.

←——————→

I boarded a Saturday night flight at 10 p.m., flew five-and-one-half hours, got no sleep, and arrived in Reykjavik around 8:30 a.m. Sunday morning – the Icelanders are five hours ahead of Minnesota. I thought I would be less goofed up body-clockwise because of that relatively small time difference, but I was wrong. Johnny picked me up, let me nap for a couple of hours, and then we were on our way to Thingvellir, about 25 miles east of Reykjavik, the very valley where the Althing convened in 930. John's extended family has shared a rustic country home (built by his grandfather after the Second World War) for many decades, located on a peninsula called Kjalarness near the shore of Lake Thingvallavatn, on the valley's southern boundary. Thingvallavatn is the largest natural lake in Iceland, with 90 percent of its clear, cold water emanating from underground springs. The valley sits directly upon the continental rift; from there, the North American land mass moves west, and Europe moves east, at the rate of less than one inch per year. The entire plain is torn with craggy fissures and crevices, formed over millions of years. The valley, lake and surrounding cliffs are dazzling in their beauty, but one would need to know something of Iceland's history to surmise that this is a legendary place with enormous symbolic importance for the Icelandic people. There are no historical markers or noticeable ruins to designate the spot where the Althing met, but Icelanders know that it was here that they gained political independence, passed on stories that ultimately became the sagas, and began to achieve a sense of nationhood. On the 1,000-year anniversary of the Althing, in 1930, Thingvellir became Iceland's first national park and, in 2004, a UNESCO World Heritage site.

John has relatives in Reykjavik, a married couple named Valdi Bjornsson and Pala Bjornsdottir (Pala is John's cousin; in Iceland, if you are the son of Bjorn your last name becomes Bjornsson, if Bjorn's daughter, then Bjornsdottir; Valdi and Pala, just by coincidence, each had a father named Bjorn), whose daughter and son-in-law started what has become Iceland's most successful dive shop, a PADI (Professional Association of Dive Instructors) 5-star center called DIVE.IS. Through them, John arranged for me to snorkel at a lovely spot in the park known as Silfra. Silfra, fed by multiple springs, is a large, deep fissure that lies directly between the continental plates. The day was sunny but chilly, very windy, and with temperatures in the mid-50s. I and a small group of fellow adventurers donned dry suits – the water temperature is nearly freezing – and swam along, faces down, astounded by the limitless visibility, depths to 130 feet, and the fact that the water was so pure we could drink it; delicious, but damn cold. Someone said that even in the shallow water if you touched the rocks on either side of you, then you would simultaneously have a hand on two continents. Assuming that is so, that is what I did. Not sure how many people in the world have touched two continents at once, but I guess I must be one of them. We floated in a meandering way for probably 30 minutes but, eventually, with the team succumbing to ice-cold hands and blue lips, it was time to leave the water and head off to dinner.

We drove in John's compact Nissan SUV back to Reykjavik. Over the course of the week he did a great job of showing me all the exquisite scenes of nature, but we also had time to explore this incredible city where John was born. Reykjavik is the world's northernmost capital, with a population in the city proper of more than 120,000, and better than 215,000 in Greater Reykjavik (the overall population of Iceland in 2018 is just shy of 340,000.)

One gets a strong sense of prosperity and the good life, a population that is thriving on every level, and urban living as it should be lived, in Reykjavik. The crime rate is low, homelessness and pollution virtually nonexistent. It is an immaculately clean place. Thermal energy generates electrical power and fuels home heating systems. It is just understood in Reykjavik that development must be sustainable. The nightlife is bumping (as my daughters would say), and incredibly hip (that's what I would say) with good food, drink and music abundantly available. Upscale shopping venues are plentiful (glad my wife wasn't there; no, not really; well, yes, really – it could have gotten expensive). In short, Reykjavik is a really cool city.

We dined at a quaint venue called Thir Frakkar (Three Jackets – who knows why that name?). The appetizer consisted of roast whale – served cold – with apples, balsamic and sunflower seeds. The whale tasted like beef (whale hunting is controversial in Iceland – to the consternation of those who would protect the whales, the country does not recognize the international moratorium on commercial whaling. But whaling still has majority support among the population; about two thirds of Icelanders surveyed in 2018 support whaling.) We ordered up a bottle of *Joseph Drouhin Larforet* Pinot Noir, from Frakkland (France). It was just right, and nicely complemented John's hashed fish with black bread, which he said was almost as good as the hashed fish his mom use to make, as well as my grilled arctic char with carrots, leaks and lemongrass. It is hard not to eat healthy in Iceland. We retired to a bustling, noisy hole in the wall known as Kaldi Bar for a beer. On our way to pick up a taxi home (no Uber in Iceland, yet), we passed a cigar shop whose sign read, Varud! Tobaksvernlun. John said legend has it that the shop is so old, and has been purveying tobacco products for so long, that when Leif Erickson arrived in Iceland 1,000 years ago, he immediately went there and bought a cigar.

John chatted amiably in Icelandic with the cab driver on the way home. It's really weird to hear my buddy, with whom I can only speak English, engaging some other person fluently in some other language. I am not normally the paranoid type, but during their conversation I heard my name come up. I said, "Hey, you guys aren't calling me a dickhead in Icelandic are you?" John responded, "No, I just told him you flew in this morning and have never been to Iceland before."

"Really."

"Sure, as far as you know."

"Okay, I trust you. I guess..."

Johnny just smiled.

Apparently Monday, August 6, was the Icelandic equivalent of Labor Day. Accordingly, since neither I nor anyone else on the island had to get up for work, I slept till 10:20 a.m. John generously let me sleep in, but finally started to run the coffee grinder loudly to wake my ass up. We had places to go and people to see. Hot coffee, buttered toast and a banana for breakfast and we were on our way on a route north by northeast. We traveled through the famous Hvalfjorour Tunnel, which runs underneath the gigantic fjord of the same name, for a distance of almost 19,000 feet and to a maximum depth of more than 540 feet below sea level. This passageway significantly reduces the time required to travel to the western and northern reaches of Iceland, because one can now simply pass underneath rather than around the fjord.

Once beyond the tunnel and to the other side, John mentioned an out-of-the-way craft brewery called Stedji, and we stopped to sample some of their products. We tried a couple of dark lagers, an Easter beer, a summer beer, and one last pour that the bartender offered up, complimentary, named *Valur 2*. This is a very special beer, because it contains some level of what our barkeep described as, "the essence of whale testicles." I hesitated a bit, but then said, "What the fuck, you only live once," and knocked back a shot. John did the same. To me, it tasted just like any other really average beer. I would never have willingly purchased it, but it wasn't terrible. Johnny, ever the tactful one, commented, "Well, there is something different about it, that's for sure."

Our next stop was the community of Reykholt, which was the home of one of the most notable figures in Icelandic history, Snorri Sturluson (1179-1241). There is an impressive museum there, which highlights Snorri's eventful life: he was an author, a poet, a world traveler, a powerful chieftain, a wealthy businessman and a crafty politician. He served as the Law Speaker at the Al-thing, appointed in the year 1215. In his prolific writings, Snorri used the Old Norse language. He is thought to be the author of one of the most well-known of the sagas, called *Egil's Saga* - the only instance where scholars believe they may know who wrote a particular saga. Like any number of characters from the sagas, Snorri, tragically, also met a violent end. He was hacked to death by his enemies, who were led by his former son-in-law, and who hunted him down at Reykholt, in September 1241. Grim battles, acts of vengeance, horrific deaths: in *Godfather*esque fashion, it seems like it was just one damn thing after another with these guys.

We proceeded on to the waterfalls at Hraunfossar and Barnafoss. The Hraunfossar falls are formed by clear, roaring water, produced by countless springs, that emerges from under a lava bed and flows relentlessly across an entire kilometer downward into the river Hvita. I had never seen anything like it. The Hvita narrows at the waterfall Barnafoss (Children's Falls). Here, there are bridges and stone arches that have been carved out of the landscape by eons of violent, rushing water. Apparently, a stone arch that once spanned the river is now gone. The story is that ages ago, on Christmas day, a family that lived nearby went to attend mass, but left two young children alone at home. They returned from mass to find the children missing, but footprints led to the river. The children had fallen into the water off of a stone arch and drowned. Their mother decreed that the arch be destroyed, so that such a tragic accident would never happen again.

Johnny and I were hungry now, so motored to Husafell for a buffet lunch. The lamb soup was superb. Then we were off on a long drive east toward the Langjokull Glacier and Lake Hvitarvatn. At a point between Langjokull and the Borisjokull Glacier to the south, we bounced around in hell-for-leather fashion over more than 25 miles of unimproved roadway through what I can only describe as desolate, uninhabitable country. This part of Iceland is lonely. Even John had never in his life visited here, and we both stared in wonder. It was like exploring the terrain of a distant planet. Black and gray lava beds and enormous white glaciers abounded. The wind was unrelenting, and we almost blew over when we stepped out of the vehicle to take photos. No homesteads for sure; but also no flora or fauna to speak of. Nothing lives here. John's cousin Pala had told us that the Apollo astronauts trained in Iceland prior to their various missions. If they did, it must have been here. From the lunar surface, we went back to the Magnusson lakeside home near Thingveller, where I met the venerated Uncle John (brother of Johnny's dad) and other extended family members. Really nice people.

In the early evening, we were on our way further south to a little town on the ocean called Stokkseyri. There is a well-known restaurant there, Fjorubordid - people just call it the "lobster house." We both ordered a meal known as Seashore Langoustine. Langoustines are diminutive lobsters caught off the southern coast of Iceland. The little guys that we ate, in abundant numbers and ravenous fashion, had probably woken up in the ocean that morning; they ended up on our plates, piping hot and slathered in butter, that evening. A fresh salad with cucumbers and tomatoes, along with baby potatoes and a cold beer or two, complemented this delicious repast. We finally made our way home, after a whirlwind day. I slept well. Or at least pretty well.

The renowned British poet laureate, Ted Hughes, once observed, "The Icelandic Sagas remain one of the great marvels of world literature, a great human achievement. We can see how much of our Western modern tradition of narrative realism begins with them. But we can also see that the subsequent seven centuries have produced no other work so timelessly up-to-date, nothing with such a supreme, undistorted sense of actuality, nothing so tempered and tested by such a formidable seriousness of life." How, then, did the sagas come to be?

At the start of the second millennium, Icelanders became literate. Around the year 1000, the nation of Iceland began the conversion to Christianity. It was the Church that introduced literacy and mainstream intellectual thinking to the masses through books. The Church led the way in promoting learning and, over time, established schools in which formal education became available to all, not just men and boys but to women and girls as well. This was, needless to say, not the standard practice in Europe at the time, but was a direct reflection of the unique Icelandic culture. In Iceland, there was no exclusive elite, clerical or otherwise, that monopolized intellectualism; it was simply understood that learning was a good, empowering thing, and should be made available to everyone. Perhaps just as important, not only did people learn to read in the official language of the Church – Latin - but in the vernacular Icelandic language as well. By the early 1200s, writing in the Icelandic language had become common, and circumstances were favorable for the output of a large, significant and unique series of literary works.

The sagas were composed primarily in the 13th and 14th centuries, but generally relate tales of people and events that occurred 300 years earlier. We have surviving texts of about 40 of the sagas, and they represent what might be called in modern parlance, "historical fiction." One scholar of the sagas says, "They are not folktales, epics, romances, or chronicles, but mostly realistic stories about everyday issues confronting Icelandic farmers and their chieftains." In my own reading of them, I would describe the sagas as "stories about regular people getting really pissed off at each other, and the complications, confrontations and frequently tragic outcomes that occur as a result." ('Farmers in fisticuffs,' as one wag has characterized them.) The sagas are brutal; they contain endless descriptions of wanton violence. People kill each other on a whim, and those events are described with a matter-of-factness that undoubtedly repels some readers. Despite the fact that they were written during a Christian era, the sagas are thoroughly pagan and exceedingly Viking-like in their tone and spirit. They are a sort of Icelandic version of the classic, gritty, blood-stained American western.

Are the sagas true stories? Mostly true? Somewhat true? There is no doubt that they contain a great deal of factual information: we learn about how people lived during that era, what they ate, farming techniques, how their boats worked, what they did to survive snowstorms and famines. The professor of Old Norse Jesse Byock calls the sagas, "the most comprehensive extant portrayal of a Western medieval society." They also contain stories about people who actually lived, such as Gunnar Hamundarson and Njal Thorgeirsson in *Njal's Saga*. Many Icelanders to this day consider the sagas to be reliable history. Yet there is also a school of modern scholarly thought in Iceland asserting that the sagas represent nothing more than very effective, compelling and realistic works of fiction; they may be based in part on oral traditions that perhaps contained some element of historical veracity, but they also reflect the imaginations of their authors. We shall probably never know the precise truth.

That the authors of the sagas were almost entirely unknown is fascinating. The writer and editor Jane Smalley says, "... one of the unique characteristics of saga literature is its cohesiveness as a group of stories in which, although they are by different authors, their similarities are greater and more obvious than their differences. They are like an extended family of individuals who all look rather alike and all share basic values…. it is a literature in which individual authors seem to disappear, while the voice of an entire way of life seems to speak distinctly…. It is thus a literature of unity rather than diversity, where the inability of an individual to fit in is noticed, remarked upon, analyzed and perhaps admired, but always dealt with in the end."

Women in the sagas play important roles. While the world these stories depict is no doubt a man's world, women are not ignored or looked down upon. These are not romantic tales; there is nothing closely resembling an ongoing love story. Women get the same blunt treatment as men; they are not the equal of men, but they are present and accounted for. In a number of sagas, women are wholly involved and instrumental to the outcome. How could it be otherwise in the Iceland of that era, when women had access to education, and everyone was encouraged to speak up and be heard?

Finally, another critical component of the sagas is the emphasis on place. In the introduction of the anthology, *The Icelandic Sagas*, editor Magnus Magnusson states, "What helps to give the sagas their sense of verisimilitude is their sense of place. The sagas and the landscape are inseparable. They were written in that landscape and about that landscape; this adds immeasurably to their immediacy. And that saga landscape has scarcely changed over the centuries… farmhouses have been built and rebuilt, generation after generation, on precisely the same sites as the original settlers selected, for they had chosen well. Place names have hardly varied for a thousand years…. One can stand today at the sites where the saga events are said to have occurred, and recognize every detail of the landscape…. However lonely the landscapes, they are peopled by the constant presence of the past."

◄─────►

The next three days were an absolute blur of activity. Johnny is an all-time great, world-champion-caliber tour guide. Tuesday dawned extremely cold, with a high that never got out of the 40s; lots of wind and rain to boot. Just a raw day. I bundled up in a Patagonia fleece pullover and we were on our way.

The first stop was a gargantuan geothermal plant at a place called Hell-isheidarvirkjun (I'll give you a dollar if you can say that one in less than five seconds. Go!) I learned that as a result of its position on a volatile section of the Mid-Atlantic range, Iceland is a world leader in the use of geothermal energy. Of the six geothermal power plants in Iceland, the facility we visited, which is called Hellisheidi, is the newest and largest. According to their website, this incredible plant "provides electricity and hot water for space heating in the industrial and domestic sectors of Iceland. To access the potential energy under the surface, wells are drilled thousands of meters deep into the ground, penetrating reservoirs of pressurized water. Heated by the Earth's energy, this water can be more than 300 degrees centigrade in temperature, and when released it boils up from the well, turning partly to steam on its way. At Hellisheidi, the steam is separated from the water to power some of the plant's seven turbines, while the remaining water is further depressurized to create more steam, used to power other turbines. At its maximum output the station can produce 303 megawatts of electricity, making it one of the largest single unit power plants in the world... Renewable power sources account for more than 70 percent of the total primary energy consumption in Iceland, far higher than anywhere else in the world." Wow – so very impressive. We can all learn from Iceland's example.

We next motored to Hengilssvaedid (aren't these place names a kick? Just don't ask me to pronounce any of them; that's why I had my fluent friend Johnny at my side.) There is a steep, winding path there called Reykjadallur, where we did just a bit of hiking and saw some of the proverbial hot springs up close. From there, we toured the Bobby Fischer Chess Museum, housed in a tiny building on the main thoroughfare in the village of Selfoss. Bobby Fischer was the great American chess genius, who in 1972 defeated the Russian Boris Spassky for the world chess championship. They played their intense, controversial match in Reykjavik, and Fischer has been something of an icon in Iceland ever since. Fischer eventually forfeited his title and became a recluse. He suffered from serious mental illness which, unfortunately, sometimes manifested itself in profane, anti-Semitic tirades. He got into trouble with the U.S. government, fled to Japan, and was arrested there in 2004. Eventually, he was granted an Icelandic passport and citizenship. He lived there for the rest of his life. The guy was a piece of work, but Icelanders loved him and considered him one of their own. He died in 2008. At the museum, there is not much reference to anything other than Fischer in his glory days.

There is a place in Iceland called Geysir, where one can see what we in America would call a "geyser" (yes, our word derives from that place name.) That sucker blows on a regular basis, and John and I saw it happen. Twice. Not quite as dramatic as Old Faithful, but pretty good. Then to the most glorious waterfall I have ever laid eyes on, called Gullfloss (meaning "golden circle"). The Gulfloss waterfall is enormous, mighty, multi-tiered, and roars so loudly that one needs to shout to be heard in its proximity. We could feel the misty spray from hundreds of yards away as the earth shook beneath us. I love the primary waterfall on the Missouri River in Great Falls, Montana – the one that Meriwether Lewis first laid eyes on in June of 1805 - which is indeed spectacular and noisy too when it flows freely, but it often does not as it is, unlike Gulfloss, harnessed by a vast electrical plant. The Great Falls have nothing over on Gulfloss.

Valdi and Pala were kind enough to invite us to their lovely home back in Reykjavik for dinner that evening. Valdi is quite a gourmet chef. While we sipped cocktails with Pala and heard all about their kids and grandkids, Valdi bustled about the kitchen preparing a scrumptious meal of roast lamb, au gratin potatoes, and salad. We ate and ate some more, then were forced to consume ice cream for dessert. Shared a bottle of red. Or was it two? There is a popular non-alcoholic drink in Iceland called "Appelsin." My Swedish last name is spelled Appelquist, which I am told means apple branch or twig. One would assume that appelsin refers to apples. No. Appelsin means "orange." The drink is a version of what I have always known as orange crush. It is sweet and delicious, and would probably wreck your teeth if you drank too much. Okay, I asked them, then how do you say apple? It is "epli." I took a funny photo of Valdi, with a sort of smirk on his face, holding a large orange bottle of Appelsin.

On Wednesday, a sunny, less windy, high-50s kind of day, we ventured north to the ocean and the beach at Ytri Tunga, where the two primary types of Icelandic seals, harbour and grey seals, hang out, especially at low tide. We saw not a one of them. I told Johnny they had taken the morning off. The peninsula is named Snaefellsnes, and we located a charming, out-of-the-way hotel for lunch. We sat in the nautically-themed lobby and peered out at the shimmering blue waters. They delivered our meal, which consisted of a simple plate of cheeses, breads, nuts and fruit. Two beers. Fifty bucks! Did I mention that Iceland is not cheap?

By now we needed some exercise. There is a rugged trail on the peninsula that runs along the sea. It is jagged and in its ups and downs and iffy footholds, reminded me of some of the trails along the path to the summit of Kilimanjaro. One needed to pay attention, and footwork needed to be deft. Church Mountain and Church Falls were next, a location that reminded me a great deal of the American west, say Montana or Wyoming. Church Mountain essentially resembles a massive, steep-sided butte, albeit without the flat top. Apparently some people think it looks like a church, but I did not see that connection. At the falls, known in Icelandic as Kirkjufellsfoss, there is a legend that long ago, a woman who lived on a farm nearby lost two sons, both of whom drowned in the falls while fishing. She cast a spell that no fish would be caught and that no one would drown there ever again. Unfortunately, neither of the grieving mother's wishes has come to pass.

Finally, we took our supper at the restaurant Narfeyrarstofain (Johnny says the locals know it as the "mussel place") in the town of Stykkisholmur. John had the mussels, but I had just been reading in the American chef Anthony Bordain's classic book, *Kitchen Confidential*, that he would never eat mussels in a restaurant unless he personally knew and trusted the chef. Since I did not know the chef at Narfeyrarstofain, and discretion is the better part of valor, I opted for lightly pan-fried scallops with mashed sweet potatoes and barley milanese. Delicious, with no tummy upset. Home to John's place. Sat out in the chilly night air on the deck, had a nightcap and, in leisurely fashion, smoked a couple of Romeo y Julieta Churchills. Johhny had never had one before and told me he now has a new favorite cigar.

Thursday we spent the bulk of the day touring Reykjavik. I told John I needed to find a gift for Faith, preferably an authentic Icelandic garment, such as a scarf or a sweater. It gets frigid in Minnesota, you know. We were like two old girlfriends, shopping the various women's departments at a number of stores before we came upon a striking, colorful wool sweater with a pretty pattern and little metallic clasps instead of buttons. I knew right away that Faith would love it (and she did.) We proceeded to meander to City Hall, where we checked out an enormous relief map of Iceland in the lobby. John pointed out all the various locations we had seen, and the whole thing gave me a different perspective on the vastness of the island. We had lunch at a fancy hotel; two burgers and three *Einstock Toasted Porters* (I had two, John had one; turns out they were around 18 bucks a piece.) I had not thought to look at the prices before I told John I would pick up the tab since he had been such a gracious and generous host. It was $111! *Shit man. This place is expensive.*

I needed to say a prayer that my money would hold out, so we wandered to a magnificent Lutheran church, called Hallgrimskirkja, which is the largest church in Iceland at nearly 250-feet tall. There is an imposing monument in front of the church depicting Leif Eriksson, which was a gift to the Icelandic people from the United States, bestowed in 1930, on the 1000-year anniversary of the Althing. John and I took the elevator to the observation deck at the top of the church, and enjoyed panoramic views of the city in all four directions.

A number of years ago, during a construction project in the middle of Reykjavik, workers unearthed the remains of a 10th-century Viking hall. Archaeologists were called in, and determined that people had lived in the hall from approximately the time of the Althing in 930 to the year 1000. A small museum, which was our final stop of the day, has been constructed around the site so that it can be preserved and enjoyed. It provides a fascinating glimpse into what life was like for Icelanders long ago.

John has a buddy who is a captain for Icelandic Airlines. That fellow's family owns a fishing boat, and although he was out of town flying at the time, he enlisted his brother to take John and me out angling on Thursday evening. We motored to the seaside village of Grendavik to meet our guide, a robust, outgoing, charismatic guy, also named Jon (pronounced "yun"). Definitely Viking stock. Jon Gauti Dagbjartsson was trained as a fishing boat captain, but decided as a young man that that was not the life for him. He went into sales – no surprise with his big personality – and has done well for himself. He met us after his work day was over, and generously spent time taking us out to sea and teaching us all about fishing in the North Atlantic Ocean. Jon's deceased father had owned a very successful fish processing business, long since sold to a larger competitor. Jon explained that commercial cod fishing is extremely closely managed in Iceland, with a strict quota system that preserves fish populations. We threw a couple of lines into the water and succeeded over the course of an hour or so in catching five cod – they put up a nice fight, which makes it fun - and several smaller species such as paddock. We threw the little guys back but kept the cod. Jon cleaned them up for us so that Johnny and I could feast on our own harvest the next evening. We got back to Reykjavik late and, bone tired, decided to keep things simple for dinner. We hit the nearby Ruby Tuesday (yes, Ruby Tuesday) and I supped on a baked potato and some broccoli. I could hear the folks back home in a few days as I regaled them on my trip to Iceland.

"Gee Jeff, you must have experienced some amazing restaurants with authentic Icelandic fare during your trip. Where did you go?"

"Ruby Tuesday."

"Wow. Wait. What?"

"I said Ruby Tuesday."

"Hmmm, okay. Must have been really special."

While Iceland undoubtedly serves as a model in terms of clean energy and sustainable practices, like every other place in the world, there are environmental challenges as well. In 2017, a University of Minnesota team called "Changing Earth" traversed 137 miles across Iceland on skis and snowshoes, while pulling heavy sleds that carried high-tech gear such as drones. Their goal was to learn more about the impact of climate change on Iceland. Their scientific conclusion, supported by the observations of long-time Icelanders, is that the island has indeed been seriously impacted by global warming. The expedition's leader, U of M professor Aaron Doering, likened Iceland to the proverbial "canary in the coal mine." He said, "The people of the north constantly ask, 'Why aren't people listening to us? Things are changing.'"

Specifically, Iceland's many glaciers are rapidly receding. As a result, the pristine island nation has experienced rising seas around the island, increased volcanic activity (because of underground melting), more frequent flooding from rising rivers, a diminishing of freshwater sources, and decreasing hydro-power capabilities. In March of 2017, Icelandic glaciologist Helgi Bjornsson said in an interview, "There has been a dramatic change in our glaciers – especially after 1995. Then they started to lose mass at a very rapid rate... The retreat of glaciers is not linear. It's going to be faster and faster as they are shrinking more and more."

In March 2018, Iceland's President Gudni Johannesson recognized the seriousness of a situation that had in the past been treated in a lighthearted way by some Icelanders: "The common joke in Iceland is to say that on this cold and windy, rain-swept island, global warming is something we should cheer for – but it's no longer funny... Climate change affects us all on this globe, but you can see the effects in particular in the northern regions – the icecap around the North Pole is melting at record rates, and the oceans are getting warmer."

⬅━━━━➡

Njal's Saga is the longest of the sagas, weighing in at approximately 100,000 words and 59 chapters. The narrative is grand, episodic and sweeping in its scope. It is the only saga set in the south of Iceland, which was the last region in the country to be settled, and it covers real people and events over 65 years in time, from 950 to 1015 A.D. The two main protagonists, Gunnar the hero and Njal, his wise friend, actually lived and are believed to have been born between 930 and 945. Numerous events depicted in the saga are recorded elsewhere or otherwise known to have happened: descriptions of facts concerning Law Speakers; the adoption of Christianity in Iceland in the year 1000; various battles and skirmishes; and the burning of Njal's farm in 1011. This epic tale was written by an unknown author around 1280 A.D., during the peak of the Saga Age.

Gunnar is not contemplative but, rather, an intense man of action. He is revered as a great fighter, yet he sometimes displays a reluctance to resort to violence. Over time, he succeeds in making many enemies. He is finally banished from the country but refuses to leave. In the end, with only his wife and mother alongside him, holed up together in his homestead at Hlidarendi, he is ambushed. He fights desperately with all his strength, singlehandedly holding off his attackers. He kills two and wounds 16, but then his bowstring breaks. Finally, unarmed, exhausted and mortally wounded, he dies. The saga says that, "The killing of Gunnar was condemned throughout the land, and many people mourned him deeply." The year was 990, and he was probably about 55 years old.

Gunnar's devoted friend, Njal, received the gift of a longer life. Njal strove to be a man of peace and integrity, and was deeply learned in the ways of Icelandic law. Njal is also supposed to have had the skill of "second sight"; that is, he could predict the future. But like Gunnar, unfortunately and despite his best efforts, Njal made enemies too. And he foresaw his own death. In the early autumn of 1011 a war party – 100 men strong - came to find him. Just like Gunnar, Njal was ensconced with his family at his beloved homestead. His foes surrounded him at the place called Bergthorshvoll, and perhaps the most famous incident in all of the sagas ensued: the Burning. The warriors set fire to the farmhouse. In an eerie and moving scene, as the flames rage about them, Njal and his wife stoically accept their fate, climb into bed, cross themselves, commend their souls unto God, and wait to die. Njal was an old man by this time, around 70 years old; he had once presciently said, in defending the concept of the Althing, "With laws shall our land be built up but with lawlessness laid waste."

<hr>

Johnny and I made it our mission on Friday, our last full day together, to find the holy ground of Hlidarendi and Bergthorshvoll. John had never been to either venue, but surely these two incredibly historic locations would be easy to find. We started the day in a museum called the Saga Centre and studied an exhibition entitled *In the Njala Region*. We learned more about the world of the Vikings, weapons and clothing, Paganism and Christianity, the writing of the sagas, and on and on. We had an understanding that we were somewhere near the sites of the two fatal ambushes from long ago but, somehow, no one seemed to be able to tell us exactly where they were. We checked Wiki, but no luck. Our phones and GPS were of no use. Even people who worked at the museum had a tough time pinpointing exactly where it was we needed to go. We got ahold of a very basic paper map of the area and someone pointed to a general location in Fljotshlid County. They said if we stayed on that road and kept our eyes peeled, we would eventually find Hlidarendi.

We hit the road and kept our eyes peeled. I was flabbergasted that there were no signs anywhere along the way indicating an upcoming historical spot, especially such an important one. In America, those markers are everywhere. Finally, we saw a tiny sign that said "Hlidarendi" which also depicted a small black and white graphic of a church. We were able to ascertain that the quaint, tidy, red-and-white church building on the hillside above us stood somewhere near where Gunnar had fought his final battle. It is said that Gunnar is supposed to be buried somewhere on that hillside, but many historians are skeptical. We drove on up the winding path and parked. The scene as we looked down from the grassy, windy slope into the majestic valley below, even though the day was mostly overcast, took our breath away. Now I know why Gunnar never wanted to leave this place.

Our visit complete, we ventured forth in search of Bergthorshvoll. We used the same simple map, but again we struggled to find our destination. We had been told it was about a dozen miles as the crow flies from Hlidarendi, but it seems like it took us an hour to get there. We finally thought we were in the right spot, that the sacred ground would be just at the end of a long unimproved road, but we were unsure. At that precise moment, a young Icelandic man of perhaps 20 years old, who happened to have Down syndrome, drove by us on a four-wheeler. Johnny flagged the kid down and asked him in Icelandic, "Where is the famous Njal's farm?" He smiled, pointed down the roadway, and told us we were headed in the right direction. John smiled right back; his eldest daughter, Heide, also has Down. Just like the fellow we met, she is fortunately very high-functioning, and a sweetheart to boot. She is a wonderful young woman. As we made our way ahead, John laughed and said, "I will have to tell Heidi about the guy we met on a four-wheeler, who gave us directions. We might not have found the site without him. She will get a kick out of that."

Njal's place – the location of the Burning, the most notorious event in all of the sagas, and a story that echoes in the memory of every Icelander with a sense of history - is even less imposing than Gunnar's. At least Gunnar has a church. Njal has, well, nothing. A grassy, diminutive knoll and that's it. Plus a completely cracked, weathered sign that looks like it has not been replaced or repaired in 30 years. The sign reads in part, "This is one of the main scenes of the action of Njal's saga. It is here that Njal and his family are burned in their house.... The burning of Njal's farm took place in the autumn of 1011. Eleven people were killed in the attack that was carried out by about a hundred men... The burning is one of the most famous events related in the Icelandic sagas... Kari Solmundarson, Njal's son-in-law, escaped alive and avenged the victims ruthlessly after which full reconciliation was reached." A pretty dramatic tale for such a humble spot. By this time, though, I had learned, such is the wonderful humility and almost comical understatedness of the Icelandic people. Njal's hallowed venue is good enough for them, just the way it is.

That evening, John and I cooked up the cod we had caught the night before. We breaded and fried the fillets in a pan, and enjoyed their delicious freshness and flavor with some boiled potatoes and a salad. A nice bottle of white wine. It was a great way to end my visit to one of the most exceptional places on the entire Planet Earth, Iceland, the land of fire and ice.

⟵⟶

The importance of place. Gunnar captured it beautifully when he became mired in legal difficulties and was outlawed by the authorities. He was told in no uncertain terms to depart the country on pain of death. But he could not go, even if to stay was the last decision he would ever make. He started to leave, but as he rode away from his cherished farmstead, his horse stumbled. Gunnar fell off and when he hit the earth, he turned and looked back. In lines that are held dearly in the heart of every Icelander, he said, "How lovely the slopes are, more lovely than they ever seemed to me before, golden cornfields and new-mown hay. I am going back home, and I will not go away."

CHAPTER ELEVEN

PARADISE OF THE PACIFIC

THE HAWAIIAN ISLANDS

"Hawaii is not a state of mind, but a state of grace."

— PAUL THEROUX —

He was a little guy, only 5'3" and about 130 pounds. As a young sailor, while fighting for Japan in the 1904-5 war against the Russians, he had been wounded in battle, losing his left middle and index fingers. Ever afterward, the geishas who manicured his nails called him "80 Sen," because they were paid 10 sen per finger and he only had eight. He was an inveterate gambler who was not truly happy unless he was involved in some game of chance. "Boy, he was a good bridge player..." marveled one American naval officer who had lost money, "... He played for blood." He was a moderate drinker but a compulsive betting man. He played and could consistently defeat good players in poker and bridge. He excelled at Go, the Asian game of strategy, as well as chess. He triumphed in roulette, pool, mahjong and shogi. He would bet on bowling, and then win. He did handstands - a dicey stunt for a man with only eight fingers - just to show off. A Japanese admiral said of him, "Few men could have been as fond of gambling and games of chance as he. Anything would do." Another officer declared, "He had a gambler's heart."

But he was also a person of great professional competence and shrewd, even ruthless, intelligence. He had risen steadily in the ranks of the Imperial Japanese Navy. He had acted as naval vice minister, and been involved in naval arms-limitation negotiations. He had served two tours of duty in the United

States and studied at Harvard University. One American admiral called him, "smart and dangerous." A formal American intelligence report characterized him as "exceptionally able, forceful, and quick thinking." In a future war with the U.S., the report went on to speculate, he "may be expected to adopt a bold and positive course of action." He rose to become commander of the Japanese Combined Fleet in 1939. Though he deeply respected the economic power and armed might of the United States, and he believed that to fight and win a war against America would probably be an impossible task, he nevertheless conjured up a supremely risky plan that he believed represented Japan's only chance for victory. He would destroy the U.S. Pacific fleet that sat anchored at Pearl Harbor, in the city of Honolulu, on the island of Oahu, in the Hawaiian chain of islands, with a surprise attack using warplanes that had been launched from aircraft carriers. Nothing like it had ever been attempted before in the history of warfare and it would represent the most dangerous toss of the dice of them all. This bold, high-stakes gambler's name was Isoroku Yamamoto.

⟵⟶

FRIDAY, MARCH 31, 2017

Paul Theroux hates air travel. He says, "There is not much to say about airplane journeys. Anything remarkable must be disastrous, so you define a good flight by negatives: you didn't get hijacked, you didn't crash, you didn't throw up, you weren't late, and you weren't nauseated by the food. So you are grateful..." And he says, "Airplanes have dulled and desensitized us; we are encumbered, like lovers in a suit of armor." He also says, "Airplanes are a distortion of time and space. And you get frisked." Finally, he says, "Air travel is very simple and annoying and a cause of anxiety. It is like being at the dentist's, even to the chairs." Indeed.

On Friday, March 31, 2017, I boarded a plane for what would be my third extremely long haul in just the past 60 days; I had gone back and forth to Africa, and I was now on my way from Minneapolis half-way across the Pacific to Hawaii. When I began planning the Kilimanjaro trip, I had asked Faith if she wanted to go with me, if not for the climb then perhaps for a post-climb safa-ri. She thought about it, briefly, and said 'No.' Probably a good thing for both of us that she did - one of my Kilimanjaro buddies had speculated that if his wife had accompanied him they would have soon thereafter been divorced, and I could see what he meant. For a variety of reasons, it was not a scenario that was conducive to marital solidarity or bliss. Then I asked Faith where she would like to go instead, and Hawaii came up. Neither of us had ever been there, we had of course heard wonderful things and, for me, it would repre-sent my 50th state. I had been, primarily as a result of family auto trips as a kid and then, later, many years of business travel, to each of the other 49 states, but never to Paradise. We arranged the logistics and were underway on a di-rect route to Honolulu, with plans to stay there for two days, then take the little Hawaiian Air hop over to Maui for the balance of the week.

I am a terrible airplane sleeper, even on long, overnight flights. I can think of only a small handful of occasions when I have ever fallen fast asleep on a plane. I just can't do it. Faith has a better time than I do; she can gener-ally get at least a few hours of rest. So, being the bookworm that I am, I pass the time with my face buried in either a cloth-covered book or a paperback; no e-reader for me, being an old-fashioned guy, thank you anyway. On this particular flight, I immersed myself in a book by Jim Harrison, long one of my favorite writers, who had just passed away the previous year after a fascinat-ing, productive and iconoclastic life. The book, *A Really Big Lunch: The Roving Gourmand on Food and Life*, is a collection of essays written over many years on two of his favorite topics – and mine as well – food and wine. From the book jacket: "...Harrison muses on the relationship between hunter and prey, interrogates the obscure language of wine reviews, and delivers a manifesto against the bland, mass-produced food of our time, proposing instead what he calls the Vivid Diet. He delights in food from tete (de veau) to nose (baby pigs') to feet (calves'); from the most outre indulgence (a French lunch that went to thirty seven courses) to a simple bowl of menudo. Harrison's food writing is a program for living..."

The book caused me to ponder, deeply, if I hadn't thought about it much before, what an incredible amount of time those of us who are lucky enough in the world to have a plentiful food supply actually spend thinking about, shopping for, preparing for consumption, and then finally eating our food. We clean up after ourselves and then do the whole damn thing over again, right away, typically three times a day. It is a major and necessary human undertaking that sustains us as a race. Harrison speaks the truth when he observes, "How feebly the arts compete with the idea of what we are going to eat next."

I even genuinely enjoyed, with a new perspective as I read, several glasses of the fairly atrocious Merlot that Delta serves in its economy class (remember the Paul Giamatti character, the insufferable wine snob Miles, in the hilarious movie *Sideways*? "I am NOT drinking any fuckin' Merlot!") I can't complain; it's free on long distance flights and, after all, as Harrison argues, "Any fool knows that red wine is the best energy drink if you keep it within two bottles."

So if my recitation of the details of our Hawaiian trip seems a bit more focused on food and wine than usual, you will know from whence I received my inspiration. Faith and I did in fact have dinners scheduled, starting Saturday evening, at a number of much-acclaimed restaurants, and we enthusiastically looked forward to the gastronomical and oenological aspects of our adventure. Jim Harrison, God rest his soul, has the final word: "Your meals in life are numbered and the number is diminishing. Get at it."

We landed in Honolulu at 3 pm local time, which equated to about five hours behind where our biological clocks told us we were. We determined to stay awake until a normal bedtime. We got into bumper-to-bumper traffic right away as we Ubered from the airport. What friends had told us, that Honolulu is as crowded, noisy and traffic-jam-prone as any other large American city, proved immediately to be true. We settled into the Marriott Courtyard Waikiki Beach at a busy intersection downtown, and the concierge pointed us to a small, hole-in-the-wall place, called Mahina & Suns, right next door, for dinner. Faith had as her main meal the grilled He'h and watercress salad with roasted carrots, potato, green olives, cilantro, ricotta and dill. I stole a bite. Lovely. I started with a Portuguese bean soup with watercress, smoked hock, and a soft boiled egg in a kind of delicate, crispy coating, much like the coating of the fried mini-donuts that I snarf down at the Minnesota State Fair every fall. It was terrific, and our server told us it was the chef's grandmother's recipe. Tasted a lot like home cooking. The main entrée for me was

Opha (Moonfish) with savoy cabbage, purplettes and u'ala mustard, in a bacon broth. Quite good but the fish was slightly bland and too soft in texture for my taste. We ordered a French red from the Rhone Valley called *Delas Ventoux*, a Grenache and Syrah blend – it had a bouquet of berries and pepper, with a silky smooth finish; it beat Delta's Merlot by a good margin.

MONDAY, DECEMBER 1, 1941

Isoroku Yamamoto staunchly believed that any long, drawn-out war between the United States and Japan would almost certainly end in American victory. He wrote, "Japan's resources will be depleted, battleships and weaponry will be damaged, replenishing materials will be impossible," and, therefore, that any such war "with so little chance of success should not be fought." But he was also a realist. His superiors, who now controlled Japan's aggressive, militaristic government, had determined to entirely rid the southwest Pacific of European and American influence and to establish complete Japanese domination of the region. The goal was to create an all-Asian "co-prosperity sphere," under Japanese rule, whose members would participate whether they liked it or not. Japan invaded China in 1937 and occupied French Indochina in 1940, moves that resulted in economic sanctions from the Western powers – in particular a shutting off of the critical flow of oil from the U.S. – that soon became painful. Japan responded with a plan to seize the oil and other materials it needed to fuel its war machine from the British and Dutch colonies in Malaya, Singapore, and the Netherlands East Indies, as well as the American-owned Philippines. Yamamoto said that, "My present situation is very strange," because he would be required to lead the Imperial Navy in a war that went "entirely against my private opinion." In the end, nevertheless, he knew he would be "expected to do my best." And this obligation he would carry out to the fullest.

In Yamamoto's mind, his plan to destroy the American Pacific Fleet at Pearl Harbor represented the only chance for success – to leave the Pacific Fleet untouched while attempting to carry out a vast and complex attack throughout the southwest Pacific would be to concede the initiative and invite the mighty, fully intact American armada to respond. He faced significant internal opposition to his plan, but he would not give in. To another skeptical admiral he said, "I like speculative games. You have told me the operation is speculation, so I shall carry it out."

Yamamoto handed detailed planning of the operation over to a strange, gifted, driven young officer named Minoru Genda. He was a pilot who fervently believed in the potential of air power, specifically the power of warplanes delivered to their target by aircraft carriers. In an age when conventional thinking held that the battleship was still the preeminent weapon of naval warfare – just as in the days of Admiral Nelson in the Napoleonic wars - Genda thought differently, characterizing war games based on an exchange of heavy gunfire between battleships as "exercises in masturbation" that did not reflect the advances of modern military technology. Some of his professional colleagues whispered that "Mr. Genda is insane." But Genda shrugged off the criticism, and Yamamoto recognized his talent. Genda loved the audaciousness of Yamamoto's strategy; Genda said what they were about to do was "like going into the enemy's chest and counting his heartbeat." So he set about working feverishly to settle all the myriad details of the operation: How many carriers would there be? How many planes and of what type? What ordnance would be needed and in what quantities? What ships would accompany the carriers and what should the sailing formation be? What route will we take? How do we overcome the problem of refueling at sea over vast distances? Most importantly, how do we keep our plan secret and escape detection once underway?

Genda did his work well. On Wednesday November 26, a force consisting of almost 400 fighter planes and bombers of various types, aboard the carriers *Akagi, Hiryu, Kaga, Shokaku, Soryu* and *Zuikaku*, along with 24 support vessels, set sail from Hitokappu Bay, Japan, for the Hawaiian Islands, 3,150 miles distant.

By Monday December 1st, with the Pearl Harbor-bound Japanese fleet well underway and, so far, undetected, it was readily apparent to top officials of the American government – up to and including President Franklin D. Roosevelt - that some type of Japanese military action was imminent. Relations between the two nations had been deteriorating for some time. On this un-characteristically warm first day of December, the Japanese ambassador to the U.S., Kichisaburo Nomura, met American Secretary of State Cordell Hull in Hull's office at the State Department building. Hull had delivered a 10-point memorandum to Nomura on November 26 demanding, among other things, that the Japanese pull out of China and Indochina and withhold military aid to Nazi Germany, in exchange for a release of frozen Japanese assets and a re-sumption of trade. The American people waited anxiously to see what Nomura's response might be; would there be peace between Japan and America, or war?

Nomura had no knowledge of the impending attack on Pearl Harbor. He knew that conflict was brewing, but not the specifics. He had been tasked by his government to procrastinate and obfuscate; in essence, to buy time. Upon departing his unproductive meeting with Hull, Nomura told reporters, "There must be wise statesmanship to save the situation." For his part, Hull was not surprised at the meeting's disappointing result. American intelligence had developed the capability of intercepting Japanese communications through a program known as Magic. Hull was well aware that Nomura would not come to him with proposed solutions, only bluster. But the Japanese were smart, and they had not revealed through any of the intercepted communications exactly what their course of action would be. Yamamoto's ships maintained strict radio silence throughout their entire journey. The strike force sailed qui-etly onward. The Americans' best guess, at this point, was that Japan would strike a blow somewhere in the southwest Pacific. But where? Pearl Harbor sat smack dab in the middle of the Pacific, more than 3,000 miles from the Japa-nese mainland. The commanders at Pearl had been put on notice, along with all other Pacific commands, to remain vigilant because, of course, anything was possible in warfare. But the truth was, the likelihood of an unprovoked attack on the Fleet at Pearl seemed miniscule, if not nonexistent.

◄─────►

SATURDAY, APRIL 1, 2017

We slept terribly; even with windows tightly shut on the sixth floor, the combination of jet lag, traffic noise and a street person who shouted random profanities for most of the night caused our unrest. But for breakfast we said, what the heck, let's go back to Mahina & Suns. We had briefly perused their breakfast menu the night before, and it looked damn good. Faith had wholegrain avocado toast with tomato jam, dukkah, aleppo pepper and pea shoots. For me it was the pork adobo fried rice bowl (I had never had fried rice, or rice of any kind, for breakfast before), with avocado, pickled mushrooms, sesame kale and kimchi. Kimchi is a spicy, pickled, fermented-vegetable mix, primarily cabbage and sometimes radishes; one of my favorite dishes when I was a young Marine serving in South Korea. I believe I was the only man in the entire battalion who could stand to get anywhere near kimchi, primarily because it stinks and, occasionally, just the smell of it makes some people throw up. One time, before we deployed to Korea, I had overheard my company commander tell another lieutenant that if he continued on his present wrong-headed course, he would soon be in "very, very deep kimchi" – so I just assumed the word translated from the Korean as 'shit' until I found out otherwise. At Mahina, I had a couple of eggs, over easy, on top of the rice. What a wonderful and unexpected medley of flavors. Lots of hot coffee perked us up quickly.

We spent the entire day touring various sites in Honolulu, the Pearl Harbor Visitor Center and the U.S.S. Arizona Memorial. I will describe that unforgettable experience at the end of this chapter.

For dinner that evening, it was the well-regarded Alan Wong's Restaurant on South King Street in Honolulu. A member of the hotel staff asked us on the elevator where we were heading for dinner. We said, "Alan Wong's, what's good there?" The reply: "Uh, gee, everything." How true. For Faith it was the ginger crusted Onaga: Long-tail Red Snapper with a miso sesame vinaigrette, mushrooms and corn. I enjoyed the seafood Cioppino. I love any kind of seafood stew, especially in a tomato-based sauce. There was lots of lobster, shrimp, clams, mussels and tilapia in a steamy tomato broth.

Faith and I had met in a bar called the Pink Flamingo, on State Street in Madison, Wisconsin, exactly 33 years ago on April Fool's Day, 1984. On that enchanted evening, I spied her pretty face from across a crowded room and waved her on over to sit with me. We have been in love ever since, and cele-brated our "anniversary" of sorts with a red wine, a California blend, which was just okay. The marriage has aged better than that particular wine, but we have no cause to complain about anything – we have been very fortunate and we know it.

←———————→

TUESDAY, DECEMBER 2, 1941

The commander of the U.S. Pacific Fleet, Husband E. Kimmel, was the embod-iment of long experience, exacting standards and professional competence. He was the very ideal of the career Navy man. Fifty-nine years old, he was confident, fit and dynamic. Like Yamamoto, he had been wounded early in his career - he was struck in the arm and both legs by bullet fragments as he stood on the deck of a warship sent to protect American citizens during the Mexican Revolution, in 1914. In his nearly 40 years in the Navy, Kimmel had commanded individual destroyers, cruisers and battleships, as well as squad-rons of destroyers and divisions of cruisers. He had served as the head of the Ordnance and Budget bureaus of the Navy Department. One admiring cap-tain said of Kimmel, "He's the most honest, conscientious, dedicated man I ever served with." As Pacific commander, Kimmel worked his sailors night and day to prepare them and their ships for the combat he was sure would soon come with the Japanese. He dedicated every ounce of his considerable energy to the idea of taking offensive action against the Japanese fleet, whenever that moment may come to pass.

Kimmel had received a "war warning" from the office of the Chief of Naval Operations on November 27 advising that diplomatic negotiations between the U.S. and Japan had ceased, and that the Japanese would strike somewhere within the next few days. The most likely targets for attack, the warning speculated, were locations in the south: Malaya, the Dutch Indies and the Philippines. The thought that the U.S. Fleet might be vulnerable to a preemptive surprise attack as it sat moored in Pearl Harbor did not preoc-cupy or even particularly concern Kimmel. He simply believed the odds were too long, and he had not seen evidence sufficient to persuade him otherwise. During a meeting on the same day Kimmel received the war warning, as the Japanese strike force drew ever closer, an Army officer raised a concern about protecting the Fleet at Pearl.

"Why are you worried about this?" queried Kimmel. "Do you think we are in danger of attack?"

"The Japanese have such a capability," came the reply.

"Capability, yes, but possibility?"

Kimmel turned to his highly intelligent and well-regarded war plans officer, Captain Socrates McMorris. Kimmel insisted on knowing whether there was any chance the Japanese would hit Oahu.

"None," responded McMorris. And that was that; the discussion moved forward to the next item on the agenda.

On the morning of Tuesday, December 2, Kimmel's fleet intelligence officer, Lieutenant Commander Edwin Layton, showed him a report indicating that the Japanese Navy had done something unusual; they had just changed radio call signs for each of their many warships, for the second time in a month. The report stated, "It appears that the Japanese Navy is adopting more and more security provisions." For obvious reasons, the Japanese were undertaking to defeat American radio intelligence. Kimmel paid close attention, wondering exactly how to interpret the information.

Layton presented Kimmel with another report that morning, taking a strategic, ocean-wide view, and detailing current assumptions about the whereabouts of specific Japanese warships. The report began inauspiciously, with the words, "From best available information, units of ORANGE [Japanese] fleet are *thought* to be located as listed below." The report estimated that 80 Japanese ships were headed south, thus confirming the notion that an attack in that direction was imminent. Other ships were likely in waters near the Marshall Islands, or French Indochina, or the Japanese mainland. Notably, the report placed only six of Japan's 10 aircraft carriers. Four of the Imperial Navy's largest carriers, with capacity to transport hundreds of warplanes, were not listed in the report, an omission that did not escape the notice of Admiral Kimmel. When Kimmel inquired, Layton posited that because no radio transmissions or updates of any kind were being sent to those carriers, they must therefore be moored somewhere, not moving at all. Apparently, that explanation seemed logical. Kimmel was satisfied.

◀━━━━━▶

SUNDAY, APRIL 2, 2017

Would you think us extremely unoriginal creatures of habit if I told you that we went back to Mahina & Suns for breakfast, our third visit in 36 hours? Look, our options within walking distance of the hotel were limited to the IHOP across the street or Mahina. I can get a mediocre breakfast at an IHOP in any town in America, anytime, for goodness sake. So Mahina was a slam dunk. When a place is good, it's good. For Faith, the Eggs Sammie, a pressed sandwich of eggs, kale, tomato, avocado and fontina. I had the Surfjack Breakfast: eggs over easy, Portuguese sausage, hapa rice (two days in a row with rice for breakfast) and a lettuce salad. I've never had a lettuce salad for breakfast, either; my circuits almost became overloaded with all the new culinary experiences. A tall glass of chilled Pomegranate juice. Many cups of coffee.

We hopped on the little Hawaiian Air prop plane that ferries people back and forth between the islands and said farewell to Honolulu. Very interesting to see the southern coast of Oahu, and then the islands of Molokai and Lanai from above but at low altitude. The contrast in density of population between Honolulu and the other islands was striking. In 25 minutes, we were on the ground at Kapalua Airport in West Maui, rented a small vehicle, and then were off to our hotel, Marriott's Maui Ocean Club, on the beach.

We were feeling the effects of a number of large meals in a row, which is not typically our style, and so I had a cup of almonds for lunch and a cold beer by the pool - I came to like a local beer called *Longboard Island Lager*, brewed by the Kona Brewing Company; it had a nice combination of hoppiness and maltiness; this was the first of several that I would consume over the next five days (just several, not many). We spent the afternoon lounging at the pool, consulting our various guidebooks, and planning our week in detail.

Each year during the first week in January, the PGA tour puts on the Tournament of Champions, featuring all of the golfers who won victories during the previous season, at the Plantation Course at the Kapalua Resort, near Lahaina. The tournament has been played there since 1999. On Sunday night, we ate at the clubhouse, which is open to the public, on this magnificent golf course. It is funny and ironic; Faith and I used to play a lot of golf together, but we got so damn frustrated with the game that we quit and have not played in years: too time-consuming, too expensive, too rules-oriented - we both cheated shamelessly - and, most of all, too frustrating. We both pretty much stunk, although she was better than I was - she had a nice, easy swing and almost always hit the ball straight, if not far; I hit it further, but never straight.

But we were more than happy to enjoy a beautiful sunset at a golf venue, with the windows of the clubhouse thrown wide open to let in the fresh, early evening air, as long as no one forced us to get out there and whack a little white ball around. Faith went lighter with just a beet salad, consisting of roasted beets, spinach, feta cheese, red wine vinaigrette, and quinoa pilaf. My choice, because I was hungry again, was a classic Caesar salad and a slab of meat they called the Duroc Pork Tomahawk. When I inquired, the server explained simply, "It's a man's meal." This gigantic pork chop featured a seven-inch-long protruding bone/handle. I could have easily defended myself with it in a barroom brawl – it was a mighty club. The Tomahawk came with Brussels sprouts fricassee, aged Cheddar, and oyster mushroom demi. I was proud (or not?) to finish it off and gnaw on the bone, Neanderthal-like. Our wine choice was an exquisite, very reasonably priced *Bodegas Breca Garnacha*, I believe a 2013, from Spain. The tasting notes we put together described flavors of blackberry and pepper, with great mouthfeel and balance, culminating in a nice long finish.

For the first time in a couple of days, we slept very well that night.

◄———————►

WEDNESDAY, DECEMBER 3, 1941

On a warm and partly cloudy Wednesday, December 3, U.S. Army Intelligence intercepted a Japanese message instructing Ambassador Nomura to immediately destroy one of the two code machine units currently in use at the Japanese Embassy in Washington D.C. The Japanese Foreign Office further told Nomura, "At the time and in the manner you most deem proper, dispose of all files of messages coming and going and all other secret documents." Nomura reluctantly complied. Anyone observing the Embassy on Massachusetts Avenue could see smoke from the fire that engulfed reams of paperwork drift gently into the sky above the compound. Nomura nervously pestered the Foreign Office with increasingly frantic messages, imploring a reconsideration of whatever action might be underway. He did not know what was coming, but he knew it would be bad. Tokyo paid no heed, and additionally instructed diplomatic outposts in London and the Far East, as well as it's consulates in Manila, Hong Kong, Singapore and Batavia to take similar actions. At headquarters for the U.S. Naval high command in Washington (known as Main Navy), the intercepted communications made a deep impression. In the words of the Chief of Naval Operations, Admiral Harold Stark, the comprehensive Japanese order to get rid of messages and machines "pointed right toward war."

Within hours, a message from Main Navy reached the Pacific fleets, warning that the purging of Japanese codes, ciphers and documents was underway. But just as with the war warning of November 27, the Main Navy dispatch failed to provide any kind of in-depth analysis, and gave Admiral Kimmel no specific reason to expect that Hawaii would be targeted. Kimmel envisioned the Japanese actions not as a prelude to an audacious surprise attack on the U.S., either in Hawaii, the Philippines, or anywhere else. Japan would never be so bold and reckless. He reasoned instead that the destruction of machines and messages reflected Tokyo's concern that the U.S. might attack first, in response to aggressive Japanese maneuvering against any American ally in the southwest Pacific. In this belief, of course, Kimmel was tragically mistaken. He lamented later, "The Department sent me a message that these codes were being burned, and I feel, while that was good information, that they might very well have enlarged somewhat on what they believed it meant. I didn't draw the proper answer. I admit that. I admit that I was wrong."

MONDAY, APRIL 3, 2017

After our refreshing night's rest, we ate breakfast at the little cabana at the hotel. Faith kept it simple with scrambled eggs and fruit, while I had something called the "Local Boy Breakfast": scrambled eggs with Tabasco sauce, Portuguese sausage, Spam and white rice. Let me tell you something about Spam, which is that I love it. When Faith met me, it was a main staple of my diet, along with such impoverished-student standards as canned Hormel Chili and Chung King Chop Suey. Even then I knew Spam was bad for you but, damn, the flavor: salty, greasy, fatty; all the main food groups. I ate it with Kraft macaroni and cheese (also a man-killer), which was a special favorite. She of the degrees in food science and nutrition – who loves me and wants me to live a long life - finally convinced me to stop eating it, which I have not done for many years; but she allowed me to splurge and relive my glorious culinary past in Maui. Turns out Hawaiians really love Spam too. I have a Hawaiian business colleague named Palani Smith, and he explained this concept to me. Apparently Hawaiians consume more Spam than any other state in the union, something like seven million cans a year. During WWII, G.I.s stationed in Hawaii really took to Spam, because it is delicious and it does not need to be refrigerated and it will last for about a century on the shelf, in the can. Our fighting men knew a good product when they ate it. And the Spam tradition continues to this day in the Land of Paradise.

I'll tell you what I didn't like, which was the price of the breakfast: $34! *What the... not doing that again, Spam or no Spam.* We determined to do a little grocery shopping and eat breakfast and lunch on the cheap going forward. We would continue to spend a touch more freely at dinner.

After breakfast we put on our swim suits and took a walk on the beach. We sat in the shallow surf and had fun as the surprisingly warm Pacific waves rolled over us. My wife is a pixie at 5'2" and 110 pounds, and it was a kick to watch her get pummeled by the occasional rogue wave. I laughed at her as she got soaked and battered, twisted and turned around, but then she laughed at me when I stood up. Unbeknownst to me, I had accumulated approximately ten pounds of wet sand in my swim trunks. I looked like a tiny child with a giant turd in his pants. Every parent has been there with that kid. I said to

Faith, "Mommy, I got somethin' for you Mommy. Need your help Mommy. Please Mommy." She responded, "I have not changed a diaper in 20-plus years, and I'm not doing it now." And so I figured out how to wade into the ocean just far enough, maintain my balance in the surging surf, and dump a load of sand out of my shorts without losing all dignity completely, but it was difficult. There was some serious, detailed crevice-cleaning work required in the shower afterward.

Our goal for the afternoon was to drive the celebrated Hana Highway to the village of Hana, ending up by then backtracking to the most-recommended-by-our-friends-restaurant-in-all-of-Hawaii, known as Mama's Fish House, in North Maui. We headed on our way, ate some almonds as we drove, and then stopped at a roadside fruit stand to pick up a few pineapples, mangos and pomegranates. A gargantuan juicy apple was all I needed to stave off hunger until Mama's. We soon reached the little town of Paia, on Maui's North Shore, and did some leisurely window shopping. We paused at a joint called the Mambo Café to refresh with an iced tea (Faith) and an IPA (Jeff). Paia used to be a bustling sugar plantation town, but the sugar industry waned and a bunch of hippies and, eventually, surfer dudes moved in during the 1970s. Now there are upscale restaurants, surf and swim shops, and trendy art galleries. It is a village that is both cool and quaint.

Back on the road, the thrill of twists and turns was offset by nature's incredible beauty. The Hana Highway, which ultimately lands a traveler in the blissfully charming village of Hana (I can only describe it based on what I've read; we never actually got that far), is 52 miles of winding, occasionally perilous roadway that apparently has 600 curves and crosses something like 50 one-lane bridges on the road from Kahului. Along the way, we saw magnificent views of the ocean, waterfalls, botanical gardens, and wildly abundant rainforests. My journal entry for that day says that the Hana road was "a bit treacherous, but the lushness and variety of the flora was like nothing we have ever seen." Faith loved the nature and took photos as we slowed down from time to time. She also generally trusts my driving, and I tried extra hard to be careful, but she admitted later that it was a bit of a white-knuckle affair for her.

Eventually, we realized if we went all the way to Hana, spent some time wandering, and then came back again, that we would be way late for our 7:00 p.m. Mama's reservations. I was reminded of the quote from Andre Gide, "The drawback to a journey that has been too well planned is that it does not leave enough room for adventure." We had fucked up, planned poorly, and didn't get to see the village of Hana, but our journey turned out okay nonetheless. We backtracked on that winding trail, got to the restaurant around 4:45, and we were hungry. Luckily, someone had cancelled – this is a months-in-advance kind of reservation - and they whisked us in. Apparently, Mama's was at some point voted the second-most popular restaurant in the United States by Open Table. The setting and Polynesian-style decor are remarkable, with everything wide open to let in the sea breezes, and views of the beach and the great Pacific beyond for everyone.

Our meal was quite simply the best that we had during the entire Hawaiian sojourn. Faith ate the macadamia nut crab cakes with fire and ice relish and Mama's special salad. For me, the splurge started with the Kula baby romaine salad with blue cheese, grilled focaccia toast and onion ranch dressing, and then two Tristan Island lobster tails. They say that Tristan Island is the most remote inhabited island in the world; I thought Hawaii was the most remote inhabited island in the world; which is right? I don't know because, frankly, I don't give a shit on that point and have been too lazy to Google it; for now, I'll trust that the info on Mama's menu regarding Tristan Island is correct. The lobster was exquisite. Delicate, flavorful, slathered in butter. Come on, man. Our wine was an inexpensive and superb 2015 French Sauvignon Blanc from Loire called *Michel Redde Sancerre Las Tuilieres*. Our notes mentioned vanilla, citrus, turpentine (in a good way); the wine was refreshing, well-balanced, and complemented the meal perfectly. We loved Mama's.

←——→

THURSDAY, DECEMBER 4, 1941

By the time Thursday, December 4, rolled around, Captain Arthur H. McCollum, chief of the Far Eastern Section of the Office of Naval Intelligence, based in Washington D.C., had an uneasy feeling. He was an experienced Japan hand, having been born in 1898, the son of missionaries, in the city of Nagasaki, Japan, which would be obliterated by an American atomic bomb in August of 1945. In subsequent years, McCollum had lived in Japan twice, first to learn the language and, later, to serve as assistant naval attache. As well as any man in the U.S. Navy, McCollum understood the Japanese. He had met several days earlier with CNO Admiral Stark and other top naval commanders and been assured that the war warning of November 27 - which McCollum had not seen - had sufficiently alerted the fleet to be wary and prepare for imminent action. But McCollum could not help but believe that the war warning, whatever it may have said, was not good enough. He was not necessarily worried about Pearl Harbor per se, but rather the status of Kimmel's warships. McCollum strongly suspected that the Japanese, knowing them as intimately as he did, "would make a very definite attempt to strike the Fleet at or near commencement time." This would be true whether the Fleet was moored at Pearl or out to sea. Kimmel needed to be ready. The Japanese were coming, and the Fleet was the target.

McCollum therefore prepared another warning. In it, he provided relevant snippets of the latest intelligence, including information on Japanese ship movements, and concluded with his analysis, as he recalled later, that "The Japanese were definitely bent on war, and we should expect the opening of hostilities almost any time." His view was clear: "Japan would strike." What impact this additional, crystal-clear warning may have had on Admiral Kimmel's view of the vulnerability of the fleet at Pearl we will never know. Admiral Richmond Kelly Tuner, the head of war planning for the Navy Department, took one look at McCollum's message and proceeded to delete the language regarding the imminence of war. Turner – who was described by another officer as a "son-of-a-bitch from a long line of bachelors," and someone who "was a regular bull in a china shop. He was rigid, narrow, intolerant and had no use for intelligence in 1941" – felt that the November 27 war warning had been sufficient. He could not be convinced otherwise. McCollum's clarion call for all hands to prepare immediately for a Japanese attack was never sent.

TUESDAY, APRIL 4, 2017

Tuesday morning it was sleep in, eat toast and fresh fruit for breakfast in our room, then sit outside with a cup of coffee and read the morning papers, which were the *New York Times* and the *Wall Street Journal*, but a day behind the mainland; that's okay, I could always count on some form of surreal dysfunction from the Trump White House on a daily basis; whether 24 hours late or not, it did not matter, because with those guys we now live in a world turned upside down; yesterday is the same as today but not really, incompetence is someone else's fault, narcissism is confidence, the opposition is not only all wrong but evil too, Russia is good, NATO is bad, the climate is not changing and, finally, lies are now truth and truth is 'fake news.' I then took a much-needed run on the beach and a swim in the ocean.

We got in the car and made our way to the Maui Ocean Center in Wailuku. What a wonderful venue, with one of the world's largest collections of live Pacific corals and dozens of tanks with thousands of kaleidoscopic tropical fish. The Ocean Center features a combination of indoor and outdoor displays, and we lost ourselves for several hours in the complex and colorful world of Hawaii's marine life. We especially appreciated the fact that, based on a County of Maui ordinance protecting these species, there are no whales or dolphins on display at the Center. I also noticed in the men's room that the urinals are waterless, which apparently saves about 45,000 gallons of water a year. I think it is true to say that most native Hawaiians are in tune with their environment and especially keen on preserving the delicate ecosystem of their sublime islands. We saw that spirit in abundance at the Ocean Center.

One of the other things that we noticed during our stay was the astonishing variety of bird life. I am no bird watcher, but I could not help but notice two birds in particular: the first was the seemingly red, white and blue (it's probably more of a grey, actually) Red-Crested Cardinal; I have never seen such a patriotically decorated bird before, and so I was particularly inclined to like that species; the second was a mid-sized, partridge-like bird, also cute, but annoying, like most little kids. It took me about 20 minutes of Internet research once I got home to find this unique creature. It is called the Grey Francolin. This bird is a wack job, there is no other way to say it. Every morning, two Francolins (husband and wife? brothers? drinking buddies? who knows?) would waddle from sliding-door-to-sliding-door, unit-by-unit, on the ground level of our hotel and peck furiously at their own image in the glass. Why? I have no idea. Maybe it was some form of combat with a perceived rival, but it really looked like it just must have hurt to keep banging that beak into the glass. You would think even an animal with, well, a bird brain would learn. Over and over, like two diminutive, feathered, jackhammer operators: wham, wham, wham! Then they would look for food on the ground. At first, we put out a few bread crumbs for them; bad move, we soon learned. And then, the piece de resistance, they would simultaneously coo, coo, coo, which soon erupted into a loud, screeching call that nearly pierced the eardrum. It went on and on with these two. Faith recorded the god-awful noise of it on her phone. These birds were bothersome. Finally, on the third morning, as I saw Frick and Frack approaching while I sat reading on the patio, and knowing their demented routine as I now did, I said gently but firmly to them, "Move along citizens, nothing to see here." I waved my paper in their direction, "Go on, fellas; trundle on over to the neighbor's unit, please. He's got lots of food over there." With just a hint of indignation, they fluffed themselves up and went on their way.

Sadly, many Hawaiian birds are dying off and even face extinction. According to a 2016 study published in the journal *Science Advances*, climate change has heated up the habitat of native forest birds in Hawaii, especial-ly on the island of Kauai, thus allowing mosquito-borne diseases to thrive. Such diseases as avian malaria now spread in wooded areas once cool enough to control them. In the upper-elevation forests of Kauai's Alakai Plateau - an eroded crater of an extinct volcano - disease has increased sharply in the last 15 years. Two varieties of a bird called the Hawaiian Honeycreeper are espe-cially at risk. The study states: "If native species linearly decline at a rate sim-ilar to or greater than that of the past decade, then multiple extinctions are likely in the next decade." The study acknowledges global warming as a "prime suspect" for the diminishing of bird populations, but also explains that non-native plants and predatory animals play a role as well. The Hawaiian ecosys-tem is indeed finely balanced. Sam Ohu Gon is a senior scientist and serves as an advisor to the Nature Conservancy of Hawaii. In referencing the study, he explained the importance to the Hawaiian belief system of birds, plants and animals as ancestors: "...we need to do something about global warming and mosquitos.... If we lose these forest birds, we lose our connection to our past." But he holds out hope: "Even though the situation is dire, it's not too late. It's not hopeless." Would that I had his confidence.

We enjoyed dinner that evening at Gerard's in Lahaina. We both started with a baby spinach salad, with Parmigiano-Reggiano shavings, bacon, egg mimosa and balsamic vinaigrette, then followed up with the catch of the day, good-old Mahi Mahi. Of particular note was our wine, an Oregon Pinot Noir - they certainly know how to produce this grape in the Pacific Northwest. It was a 2014 called Planet Oregon, and was the only organic wine that we consumed on our trip. Just as we had experienced in the Napa Valley, this was a delectable wine, organic or not. Faith noted that it tasted of cherry, and was a slightly heavier Pinot than we are used to; it was delightful.

➡

FRIDAY, DECEMBER 5, 1941

On the afternoon of Friday, December 5, President Roosevelt convened a meeting of his cabinet. Editorial and news reports throughout the country predicted imminent American involvement in a Pacific war. As a result of the present anxiety, the administration had requested that Congress remain in session rather than go home for the holidays. Roosevelt led a discussion of possible targets for a Japanese attack. Singapore seemed likely, American territory probably not. Secretary of State Cordell Hull had just met with Japanese ambassador Nomura and a special envoy named Saburo Kurusu. Hull summarized, "With every hour that passes, I become more convinced that they are not playing in the open." The cabinet came to a clear consensus in response to Roosevelt's question regarding any attack on America's allies the British and the Dutch: if that happens, the civilian leadership agreed, we must go to war. Labor Secretary Frances Perkins noted later that, with respect to the Pacific Fleet, "Nobody asked where or how it was dispersed. It would have been extraordinarily bad form to have asked. We would have been promptly told that the admirals had charge of that."

In Honolulu on that same Friday, a Japanese spy took note of the absence from Pearl Harbor of the aircraft carrier *Lexington* – which had sailed early that morning - along with several cruisers. Her sister carriers *Saratoga* and *Enterprise* and their escorts had previously departed Pearl, the *Saratoga* on a mission to deliver her air group back to the west coast of the United States, and *Enterprise* to shuttle Marine dive-bombers to Wake Island. *Lexington* had been dispatched to deliver Marine warplanes to Midway Island. In a major stroke of good fortune for America out of the mayhem that was soon to follow, the Pacific carrier fleet lived to fight another day.

Others were not so lucky. The Japanese spy further observed that day a number of warships – six destroyers, a cruiser, and three battleships – returning to the channel after a week of exercises on the open sea. The battleships joined their sister ships in line, some by themselves and others side-by-side, along the eastern side of Ford Island. They were the *California, Oklahoma, Maryland, West Virginia, Tennessee, Arizona* and *Nevada. Pennsylvania* was in dry dock. As a result, it just so happened that all eight of the battleships under Admiral Husband E. Kimmel's immediate command were home together for the weekend to come.

◄———————►

WEDNESDAY, APRIL 5, 2017

After breakfast on Wednesday, Faith took a walk on the beach and I worked out in the hotel weight room. Then it was in the car and off to the Haleakala Summit. Faith had made a couple of sandwiches for our lunch on the go: a thin, low-cal version for herself with one slice of turkey and one slice of Swiss cheese; and a huge sandwich for me, with multiple layers of salami, ham and Swiss, slathered in mayo and mustard. Couldn't wait to dive into that thing. We aimed to have our lunch at the park entrance to the summit, but Faith was starving and had to eat before we arrived. She sure did enjoy her sandwich. As I drove, I peeked over at her, jealously. "Boy this is good," she said. She licked her fingers when she was done. When we arrived at the designated spot I unwrapped my sandwich; it was the wimpy, extremely sad turkey and Swiss. No wonder she had enjoyed her meal so much. "Hey, what? That was... hey. Come on!" I said. "Sorry, I guess I wasn't paying attention," she responded with a smile, as she nibbled on some carrots and handed me one. She had made an honest mistake, or so she said, but I really don't think she was sorry at all. I pouted for seven minutes.

The summit of Haleakala is known as the House of the Sun. It is an enormous dormant volcano at 10,023 feet, and while it has not erupted for a century or more, it is still considered active. The landscape is gorgeous and eerily quiet, but stark. The drive to get there is fully as interesting as the volcano itself. The Haleakala Crater Road has 33 switchbacks, passes through multiple climate zones, and is said to be one of the most rapidly ascending roads on the planet. We were above the clouds and our ears popped as we drove to within half-a-mile of the summit, then got out to walk the remaining distance to the Pu'u Ula'ula Overlook, where one can see just about forever. Many of the more than one million visitors per year to this spot get to the top at either sunrise or sunset, which is supposed to be an unforgettable sight, but that timing did not work for us. On the way back down, it rained, and we saw a number of crazy (suicidal?) people on bicycles, cruising at warp speed, barely under control, as they raced to sea level.

Dinner was at the Lahaina Grill. Faith mostly liked her wild Pacific salmon filet, with spinach and mashed potatoes. I was just about up to here with seafood, and looking for a good steak. But there was no such possibility on the menu, with the closest option being a lamb shank. It was just alright, with too much chewy fat. The other thing that was just alright was a $60 bottle of Kendall-Jackson *Grand Reserve*, a California Cab from 2013. We normally have had good luck with Kendall-Jackson, and I love the Jess Jackson life story, but this wine was far too minerally, tasting of soil, and not especially well-balanced. We probably should have sent it back. *Not the best we have had,* Faith and I agreed. But, again, who are we to complain? So my sandwich – and a really fine one it would have been - got brazenly stolen at lunch time, so that I practically went starving, with nary a repercussion for the thief? And she was my wife! So what? So our dinner and wine wasn't the best ever, so what?

Quit yer bitchin' Jeff and Faith, get some perspective, ya spoiled-rotten so-and sos, and get on with the vacation!

$$\longleftrightarrow$$

SATURDAY, DECEMBER 6, 1941

President Roosevelt spent much of Saturday, December 6, drafting a five-page letter to Emperor Hirohito of Japan. Roosevelt had long contemplated the appropriateness of sending just such a missive, and decided that now was the time. He and the divine Hirohito had communicated periodically throughout 1941, offering birthday greetings and exchanging other cursory, polite and non-substantive notes. Roosevelt began his letter, "Only in situations of extraordinary importance to our two countries need I address to Your Majesty messages on matters of state. I feel I should now so address you because of the deep and far-reaching emergency which appears to be in formation." Roosevelt had received intelligence that very day from his sources in Indochina indicating a massive Japanese buildup of arms and supplies in the region: thousands of trucks, tractors, packhorses and machine guns, hundreds of automobiles, motorcycles, tanks and cannon. Roosevelt beseeched Hirohito, in behalf of the people of the Philippines, East Indies, Malaya and Thailand "that Your Majesty may, as I am doing, give thought in this definite emergency to ways of dispelling the dark clouds" so as to "prevent further death and destruction in the world." Roosevelt directed that the letter be passed along via simple encryption (he did not care whether Japanese intelligence read his communique or not) and hand-delivered to the Emperor by American Ambassador Joe Grew.

Later that evening, in his study, Roosevelt received a 13-part Magic intercept of an encrypted Japanese response to the 10-point memorandum that Secretary of State Hull had delivered to Ambassador Nomura on November 26, laying out conditions that the Japanese must meet in order to ensure the peace. Roosevelt scanned the document and quickly realized that the Japanese had no intention of meeting any of the American demands. The Japanese, feigning indignation, accused the U.S. and Britain of endangering the

ELEVEN | PARADISE OF THE PACIFIC

empire: "The Japanese government cannot tolerate the perpetuation of such a situation." In other words, *Up yours, Uncle Sam*. An eyewitness later recalled that Roosevelt, as he finished reading the document, turned to his trusted aide Harry Hopkins and said, in so many words, "This means war."

◆━━━━━◆

In his excellent book, *Countdown to Pearl Harbor*, author Steve Twomey describes the journey of the Japanese strike force as it neared its target: "After all the prognostications back home about inevitable discovery and naval doom, the Japanese had sailed the North Pacific for three thousand miles and twelve days, and encountered only water. The skies had been free of enemy patrols. The seas had been mostly tranquil, despite the late season. Though challenging, the oil tankers had refueled the warships over and over without mayhem... Then, too plodding to keep up, they peeled away, to a point of rendezvous, and the rest of the fleet – the destroyers, the cruisers, the battleships, and the six carriers – had revved off at twenty-four knots, straight south. With each passing mile of the vacant sea, the odds had risen they would win Isoroku Yamamoto's bet."

◆━━━━━◆

THURSDAY, APRIL 6, 2017

The alarm went off at 4:30 a.m. on Thursday. Faith drove me down to Lahaina Harbor, where I boarded a 42-foot vessel, along with five other hopeful anglers, to go after deep-sea prey. Our captain, Ben, and talkative guide, Lance, told us that blue marlin was the primary target for the morning, but that we might also hope to catch yellowfin tuna, wahoo, dolphin fish or skipjack tuna, among many other species. They gave us the name of the boat, which I don't recall, but apparently it translated as "Rock Paper Scissors" from the Japanese. Lance bragged that five "granders," which are fish that exceed 1,000 pounds, had been caught from *Rock Paper Scissors*. The boat sported one sturdy fighting chair at its stern. As we motored out to sea, Lance prepared and threw six lines into the water, and I realized one could do the math two ways: either we had six times better odds of catching fish than if we had only one line in; or, in the alternative, each of us had only a one-in-six chance of being the lucky fisherperson to be the first to land a big whopper and sit in the coveted fighting chair. Our tackle was solid (150-lb. line with a 500-lb. leader) and Lance gave us detailed instruction as to how to handle ourselves with a fish on the line. Weather conditions were warm and clear.

Alas, we were skunked. Not even a nibble in the entire six-hour circuit of the waters off Maui and Lanai. It dawned on me that six fishermen is about four too many; I understand the charter captain wants to cram as many people on board as possible - he's a businessman too, and his margins are no doubt thin – but for his customers it ended up being nothing more than a frustrating, almost $300-per-person boat ride. We were told there were six other boats in the fleet, all of them out that morning, with only a handful of smaller species caught. I know well from years of personal experience that when hunting or fishing there is absolutely no guarantee of encountering wildlife or sea creatures. Some days you get the bear; some days the bear gets you; and some days you don't even get to go into the woods. That is a given, so we must make the best of things. We had some nice conversation. We saw a huge black whale in the distance send a mighty spout of water sky high and slap his tail with gusto as he reentered the water. It was a beautiful day. I learned a lot more than I knew before about saltwater fishing just by watching and listening to the guide. Nevertheless, I couldn't help but feel that it was something of a rip-off. I gave the fellas a nice tip anyway. I'm a sucker. Oh well. I do want to deep sea fish again, and I'll know better next time what to look for in a charter operator.

We walked down the pathway along the shore from our hotel to dinner that evening at Leilani's On the Beach. Our server, Mark, was a bald, fit, deeply-tanned young man who introduced himself politely and began to speak about the menu and the specials – he was the kind of server who, the minute he opens his mouth, you know is extremely bright, probably a PhD student somewhere, who is only waiting tables to make ends meet until his extremely bright future happens – when all of a sudden he had a brain fart, froze, and could not remember what he was supposed to say next. We all laughed and he apologized, explaining that he is a scuba instructor who spent the entire day on the water, teaching. "I'm exhausted folks, sorry. Let me try again." Both of our daughters have worked long hours as servers in the restaurant industry - so did Faith when she was their age - and so we are highly sympathetic. We had a good time with Mark.

This was our final dinner out and, by golly, I needed some red meat. The lamb the night before had not cut it. Leilani's serves a thick, juicy prime rib, and the carnivore in me was finally satiated. Our wine was a Jim Barry called *Lodge Hill*, a hearty Shiraz from the Clare Valley in Australia. Faith's notes recorded pepper, plum and berries, with a hint of chocolate undertones. We watched the sun go down over the ocean. Mark delivered the check; he had forgotten to charge us for the wine. I called him over, advised "Dude, you need to get some rest," and asked him to recalculate our total. "Want to make sure you get your full tip, Scuba Man!"

Tomorrow we would finally fly home. For us, Hawaii had indeed been "not a state of mind, but a state of grace." We can't wait to come back.

SUNDAY, DECEMBER 7, 1941

When the Japanese strike force arrived at its launch point – 230 miles north of Pearl Harbor – the ships maneuvered to face into the trade winds, so as to make takeoff from the carrier decks as easy as possible for the hundreds of warplanes that would soon be on their way. Blustery winds and crashing swells caused the carriers to rock. Aircraft engines roared to life. Blazing flames spewed from exhaust systems. The first grouping of 183 planes, heavy with ammunition and fuel, carefully timed their takeoffs as the carrier decks dipped down low and then rose upward again on the waves. Once the aircraft were launched successfully they thundered due south together in a tight formation. It was 6:15 a.m., and the sky was still dark. The morning would soon dawn warm and clear. A second wave of 171 planes followed shortly thereafter. A Japanese officer aboard one of the destroyers wrote excitedly in his diary, "We are in the very day to which we have been looking forward so eagerly."

In conjunction with its overall plan of attack, Japan had also developed a scheme to sneak a number of small submarines into Pearl Harbor. At 6:37 a.m., lookouts aboard the patrolling U.S. destroyer *Ward* sighted a conning tower near the entrance to the harbor. They summoned their captain, Billy Outerbridge, who recognized the vessel as a Japanese submarine. He ordered his sailors to blaze away. The Japanese sub was hit by the very first shots of the Pacific war and it appeared to sink. For good measure, the *Ward* released four depth charges, all of which detonated. An oil slick soon appeared on the surface of the water. At 6:54, Outerbridge radioed an encoded message to Pearl: "We have attacked, fired upon and dropped depth charges on a submarine operating in a defensive sea area." And then moments later, "Did you get that last message?"

Virtually simultaneously, on the northern coast of Oahu at an elevated observation point called Opana, two privates, George Elliott and Joseph Lockard, manned their duty station as members of the army's mobile radar unit. Radar was in its infancy, primitive and lacking in precision, but it still beat scanning the horizon with binoculars. At 7:02 a.m., the two young men spotted a huge mass of inbound aircraft. They were hard pressed to explain a blob this large, something they had never witnessed before. After a brief debate, they alerted the Fort Shafter information center. The operator referred their call to Lieutenant Kermit Tyler, an army pilot, who calmly reassured Private Lockard: "Well, don't worry about it. You see, I had a friend who was a bomber pilot, and he told me any time that they play this Hawaiian music all night long [the Japanese fleet had also picked up the sounds of Hawaiian music loud and clear on its radios as it came nearer to Oahu, a further sign that the strike force remained undiscovered], it is a very good indication that our B-17s were coming over from the mainland, because they use it for homing." There was in fact a formation of B-17s flying into Pearl from California, but it would not arrive until after the attack – Tyler's logic was not all wrong. But unfortunately, in essence, Tyler told Lockard and Elliott, "Forget it. Don't worry. Be happy."

◄————►

In the first wave, Japanese torpedo bombers passed directly over the headquarters building of the U.S. Pacific Fleet and raced toward their sitting-duck targets on Battleship Row. Gargantuan torpedoes, weighing nearly one ton each, splashed into the water, came level, armed themselves, and found their victims. Bombs released from above also unleashed incredible damage. The *California* was hit, as was the *West Virginia*, which began to list to port. The *Oklahoma* was riddled and turned completely upside down, trapping hundreds of sailors inside. The *Nevada* was torpedoed. Among the battleships, only the *Maryland* escaped harm.

At shortly after 8 a.m., a Japanese bomb penetrated the forward magazine of the *Arizona*, causing an explosion of such magnitude that a plume of smoke reached 1,000 feet into the sky. Countless jagged pieces rained down to earth in a wide radius. The ship sank in less than 10 minutes, settling upright in about 40 feet of water. She never fired a shot. Out of 1,512 crewmen on board, 1,177 died – nearly half the overall number of American fatalities at Pearl - in the catastrophic bombing and subsequent ear-shattering explosion. Twenty-six pairs of brothers were among the dead.

Admiral Kimmel watched the tragedy unfold, first, from the front yard of his opulent home overlooking the harbor and then, after a staff car picked him up and raced to deliver him, from the second deck of the Submarine Building. He could not believe how badly he had underestimated the Japanese enemy, and how naïve he had been to assume that Pearl was invulnerable to attack. Eyewitnesses who observed him that morning described him as "calm and collected," but also "utterly shocked and crushed." One of Kimmel's officers said about him, "The world had exploded in his face." Husband E. Kimmel's heretofore brilliant naval career was, in effect, over.

American soldiers, sailors and Marines did not go down without a fight on that terrible day. From the decks of ships of all types, including some of those that had been damaged, and from many other locations on the ground, American personnel furiously unloaded almost 285,000 rounds of ammunition of all calibers at the dastardly enemy. A small contingent of American fighter planes took off and entered the fray. The Japanese lost 29 aircraft and suffered 55 fatalities. Fifteen American military personnel won the Medal of Honor for gallantry above and beyond the call of duty at Pearl; 60 more received the Navy Cross. Total American losses for December 7, 1941, were 2,403 dead, including 68 civilians, and 1,143 wounded.

←———————→

If the Japanese believed that they had struck a crippling blow at Pearl Harbor, they had not. The Pacific Fleet quickly became a formidable fighting force again and, more importantly, the overwhelming anger and desire for revenge of the entire American population had been mightily aroused. Isoroku Yamamoto knew as much, and he was reportedly depressed in the immediate aftermath of the attack. In early June 1942, America decisively defeated the Japanese fleet at a tiny island called Midway. Magic intercepts of coded Japanese messaging enabled America's carriers to launch coordinated aerial assaults that wreaked devastating havoc on the enemy fleet. In the action, the carriers *Akagi, Kaga, Soryu* and *Hiryu* - all of which had participated in the Pearl Harbor assault - were sunk. Midway represented the critical turning point in the Pacific contest; the Japanese war effort never recovered. In April 1943, again as a result of Magic intelligence, Yamamoto's flight plans during an inspection tour of the South Pacific became known. American fighter aircraft ambushed Yamamoto's plane and shot it down over the island of Bougainville, permanently ending the great gambler's run of luck. In August 1945, after almost four years of hard fighting, American atomic bombs leveled the Japanese cities of Hiroshima and Nagasaki, and the war in the Pacific was over.

My father, Carl Appelquist, was an 18-year-old army infantryman in early August 1945, training intensively with millions of other American soldiers to invade the Japanese mainland. Some experts put anticipated fatalities in such a horrific campaign at one million people. To this day, my now 90-year-old father, who knows that he has been truly blessed in receiving the gift of a very long and fulfilling life, thanks Harry Truman for the terrible decision he had to make. Ironically, countless lives – both Japanese and American – were saved as a result. Dad has said to me many times over the years, "Jeff, if Harry had not dropped those bombs, I would be pushing up a white cross somewhere on the Japanese mainland. And you, my boy, would never have been born."

In May 1962, a memorial designed by Austrian architect Alfred Preis opened in the form of a 184-foot white bridge that straddles the width of the 608-foot wreck of the *Arizona*. The superstructure of the ship has long since been removed, and her deck lies six feet below the surface of Pearl Harbor, exactly where she settled on judgment day. *Arizona* remains the underwater resting place for 1,102 of the 1,177 sailors and Marines who were onboard and gave their lives in the attack. The monument is simple yet elegant, with a roof that peaks at either end but slopes downward in the middle, symbolic of America's initial defeat but eventual rise, culminating in ultimate victory. The site can only be accessed by boat and accommodate 200 people at a time. There is an entryway, an airy assembly room, and a dramatic shrine room featuring the names of all those who perished, carved in stone. A miniscule amount of oil continues to ooze from the *Arizona* to the surface of the sea on a daily basis; some people say the ship still weeps for her honored dead.

Whenever we visit such a sacred place, Faith knows to just let me have some quiet time by myself. She leaves me alone, doesn't talk. She knows me well, and I appreciate her wonderful thoughtfulness in giving me those few precious moments of time and space. My mind raced during our all-too brief stay at the memorial. I will never forget it as long as I live. I had a little cry for our boys, their supreme sacrifice in the flower of youth. The notes from my journal, penned at the end of the day, probably say it best: "1,102 brave sailors and Marines, entombed beneath our feet; magnificent, somber and sad, all at once..."

CHAPTER TWELVE

AWE

VATICAN CITY, ROME

"If people knew how hard I had to work to gain my mastery, it would not seem so wonderful at all."

— MICHELANGELO —

"I record how on this day, the 10th of May, 1508, I, Michelangelo, sculptor, have received from the Holiness of our Lord Pope Julius II, 500 ducats of the Camera... on account of the painting of the vault of the Sistine Chapel, on which I now begin to work."

With those words, Michelangelo Buonarroti (1475-1564) reluctantly accepted the Pope's commission to fresco the ceiling of the Sistine Chapel, at the Vatican City, in Rome, Italy. Michelangelo considered himself to be, first and foremost, a sculptor. He had been enthusiastically at work in the early stages of sculpting a tomb for Julius II when he was called upon to divert his attention to the new project. There is some evidence that a jealous artistic rival may have promoted Michelangelo for the task, in the hopes that he would fail miserably. But he did not. The effort took four years; in the end, according to eminent art historian H. W. Janson, "He produced a masterpiece of epochal importance. The ceiling is a huge organism with hundreds of figures rhythmically distributed within the painted architectural framework, dwarfing the earlier murals by its size, and still more by its compelling inner unity."

Unlike many artists whose output is never fully appreciated during their life-times, as art scholar Dr. Maddalena Spagnolo tells us, "Michelangelo's titanic career lasted virtually three-quarters of a century and for most of that time he was unchallenged as the greatest artist in Europe, his contemporaries look-ing on him with awe." He was not only a supremely talented sculptor; he was a painter, a draftsman, and the architect who created the design for the re-building of St. Peter's Basilica; finally, he was also an excellent poet. He was the "beau ideal" of a Renaissance man. During the course of his long career, Michelangelo divided his time between Florence, where he was employed by the all-powerful Medici family, and Rome, where his artistic genius truly flourished. Despite his fame, he was in his personal life a profoundly devout ascetic. He lived modestly, worshipped deeply, and labored constantly at his craft; today he would be labeled a "workaholic." It is said that in order to most efficiently maximize his time, he sometimes slept with his boots on. He ate little, was rather grubby in his person, and cared not a whit about fashion, comfort or appearances.

When confronted with the enormity of painting the Sistine Chapel, Mi-chelangelo, age 33, lamented, "The place is wrong, and no painter I." As the project began in January of 1509, the room measured 132 by 44 feet, with a ceiling that depicted stars in the sky, more than 65 feet above a marble mosaic floor. The Sistine Chapel was built in 1473 for Pope Sixtus IV, and had original-ly been intended as both a place of worship and a fortress for defense. There were thick brick walls high above, with quarters for soldiers, and battlements. In the event of war, the place could serve as a defensive refuge. Prior to 1509, the interior walls had been frescoed with various religious scenes, done by different painters. Michelangelo worked entirely alone and from scaffolding, not on his back as legend would have it, but standing up, his neck craned to focus on what he was doing. His face was continually splattered with paint, and his eyes developed a condition such that subsequently, when he received letters from his family and friends, he could only read them by holding them above his head. He complained, but with quiet determination that, "I strain more than any man who ever lived... and with great exhaustion; and yet I have the patience to arrive at the desired goal." When he was done, he had covered 5,800 square feet with more than 300 gigantic figures - those figures started to get bigger as the work progressed and the artist's confidence grew.

Five pairs of girders subdivide the central area of the ceiling, which depicts nine scenes from the *Book of Genesis*, including the *Creation of the World* and the *Drunkenness of Noah*. In perhaps the most dramatic and unforgettable scene, the *Creation of Adam*, at a distance of precisely 65 feet and six inches from the floor below, God reaches out to Adam to impart within him the holy light of life. An as yet unborn Eve sits protected in the crook of God's left arm as he rushes through the sky, the wind in his hair and beard. Adam, earthbound, well-muscled and naked, appears to lounge casually as he extends his hand toward God. Little did Adam suspect what the Almighty Creator would have in store for the human race. H.W. Hanson observes, "... the *Creation of Adam* must have stirred Michelangelo's imagination most deeply; it shows not the physical molding of Adam's body but the passage of the Divine spark – the soul – and thus achieves a dramatic juxtaposition of Man and God unrivaled by any other artist."

Nearly a quarter of a century later, in 1534, Michelangelo returned to the Sistine Chapel to paint upon the altar wall the *Last Judgment*, an enormous fresco (48-by-44 feet) which depicted the wrath of Christ the Judge. This project took six years of difficult labor; during the process Michelangelo once fell from the scaffolding, seriously injuring himself. The central figure in the composition, a beardless Christ, sweeps down with his right arm raised in a gesture of damnation. His mother, the Virgin Mary, sits next to him as various saints and martyrs jostle their way in his direction. Smaller souls beneath Christ, assisted by angels or escorted by demons, either ascend to heaven or not. At the bottom of the fresco, the artist painted the dead emerging from their graves and the gaping mouth of hell itself. It is a somber message which reflects the times in which it was painted: Rome had been sacked nine years earlier and all of Europe wrestled with the conflict and uncertainty of religious reformation and counter-reformation. Michelangelo himself revealed the darkness and angst of these days when he implored God, "I live in sin, I live dying within myself... Oh send the light, so long foretold for all." Yet, the *Last Judgment*, like the ceiling of the Sistine Chapel, was a monumental artistic achievement. When the painting was unveiled, those who were present gaped in awe – even Pope Paul III dropped to his knees in prayer. We have gaped in awe ever since; the reverberations of Michelangelo's legacy have echoed for more than 500 years.

———————→

The *Oxford Living Dictionary* defines the word "awe" as "A feeling of reverential respect mixed with fear or wonder." Faith and I visited Rome in the fall of 2015, and awe is precisely the emotion that I experienced when I lifted my eyes to see the ceiling of the Sistine Chapel. We were only two of hundreds of tourists, smashed into the Chapel chamber like sardines. Impatient and irritated Vatican museum personnel continually reminded the noisy, excited throng that we were in a holy place and must, therefore, be quiet. Our goofy Italian guide continued to speak to us in a loud whisper through headphones, talking so rapidly as to be incomprehensible - half in English and half in Italian - until I had to turn him off. And then I just stared. Wonder. Astonishment. Inspiration. Reverence. Humility. All of these together equal awe.

Despite the fact that both of my grandfathers were Baptist preachers, I am not a particularly religious person per se; but I am spiritual and I believe in an all-powerful creative force. There has to be something. This whole deal did not just happen, randomly, in my belief system. The universe came into being somehow. So did our solar system, and the Planet Earth, and every single member of the animal kingdom, as well as of the human race. My God is that creative force. To the degree that I have religion I agree with Albert Einstein, who said, "Try and penetrate with our limited means the secrets of nature and you will find that, behind all the discernable laws and connections, there remains something subtle, intangible and inexplicable. Veneration for this force beyond anything that we can comprehend is my religion. To that extent I am, in fact, religious." One does not have to be religious at all in order to fully appreciate Michelangelo's gorgeous, powerful image of God, extending his finger in Adam's direction - the magical spark of life and divinity contained therein - with the entire long, beautiful, tumultuous and frequently terrible human story to follow. I was mesmerized. I felt small. Lump in the throat. Heart racing. Tears. It was a sight I shall never forget for as long as I live.

I witnessed my two daughters being born, 26 and 24 years ago. Two lives full of promise, just beginning. My wife and I were and remain responsible for both. We will be their parents, always. As I write this paragraph, my beloved mother passed away just about 48 hours ago, at the age of 90 and after three weeks in hospice. She had been in decline for the past four years, and was enjoying no quality of life; this formerly vivacious woman could no longer walk or feed herself, and her short-term memory was gone. She died quietly in her sleep, as far as we could tell comfortable and pain free, while my sister held her hand. She had a good long life, well-lived, and was a wonderful mother to me and my two siblings. We will miss her, but we are relieved that she is finally at peace. Her ordeal – and ours – is over. It was an incredibly hard thing to watch. If awe is reverence sometimes mixed with fear, then that is the awe I felt in my Mom's slow but inexorable decline. We are all human. There is a cycle of life; we come into this world humble and helpless, and many of us go out in the same way. We will all die, and that certainty causes at least trepidation, if not outright fear, for most of us. It sure does for me. Woody Allen once said, "I don't fear death. I just don't want to be there when it happens." But, unfortunately for Woody and all the rest of us, too, as the title of a biography of rocker Jim Morrison - who died at age 27 - reminds us, *No One Here Gets Out Alive.*

⬌

Dacher Keltner, a psychologist who heads the University of California Berkeley's Social Interaction Lab, says "Awe is the feeling of being in the presence of something vast or beyond human scale that transcends our current understanding of things." Dr. Keltner studies emotions, and in 2013 his lab began Project Awe, a three-year scholarly effort that generated significant research on this most fascinating of emotions. Interestingly, awe is not always about that which is massive or momentous in scale. Keltner observes: "People often talk about awe as seeing the Grand Canyon or meeting Nelson Mandela, but our studies show it also can be much more accessible – a friend so generous you're astounded, or you see a cool pattern of shadows on leaves."

Awe is a fundamental and universal aspect of the human condition; we are all wired to feel it. And, as studies are revealing, it is important for several beneficial reasons. First, awe causes us to act more collaboratively; it binds us together because it helps us to realize that, while we may be small, we are still a critical part of the larger whole. We all matter, and we are joined together as members of the human race. Awe also causes us to stop and to think and to see things in new ways. It makes us more attentive to detail and willing to open ourselves up to fresh possibilities and information. Unbelievably, research shows that awe makes us nicer; it makes us more fair and generous; and it makes us happier. Finally, awe may even alter our bodies and have healing potential. Awe is the emotion that researchers say can best predict reduced levels of inflammation that is linked to depression. Recent studies have also connected the experience of awe in nature to such beneficial health outcomes as reduced blood pressure and stronger immune systems.

Awe in nature: it is both exciting and humbling to think that so much of what has the potential to strike us as awe-inspiring is in the natural world, whether it be looking skyward at the grandeur of the highest Sequoia tree, or lowering our view to study the most intricate pattern in a fallen leaf on the forest floor. Yet we mostly remain indoors, generally seated, slaves to our devices and television and social media, thinking small thoughts, oblivious to the glory and even beneficence of the natural world that surrounds us, or is at least within our reach, if only we tried.

━━━━▶

Researchers recently analyzed the memoirs, interviews and oral histories associated with more than 50 astronauts, all of whom had traveled into outer space. When looking down from an enormous distance upon the miniscule, fragile blue dot that is the Planet Earth, the astronauts subsequently reported a feeling of intense attachment and oneness with their brethren, the billions of members of the human family. These adventurous souls expressed a heightened sense of both spirituality and universalism as a result of their unique opportunity to see the world from a different point of view. One of the scholars said that, from the perspective of the star voyagers, the earth "looks small against the vastness of space and yet represents all that we hold meaningful." In a unique and compelling way, they had experienced the special kind of awe that only the connection with the power and majesty of the natural world can bring about.

CHAPTER THIRTEEN

COWS, COLLEGES & CONTENTMENT

NORTHFIELD, MINNESOTA

"For Carleton College will be a cathedral, not of bricks and mortar, but of ideas, and with a spire so high, lighted by a beacon so bright, that it will be a guide through all the years of their lives to all who study here."

— LAURENCE MCKINLEY GOULD, PRESIDENT OF CARLETON, 1945-1962 —

O n the morning of September 7, 1876, eight sturdy, well-armed horsemen, clad in long linen dusters, casually rode toward the humble little prairie town of Northfield, Minnesota. Four of the men entered town, attracting attention and drawing stares as two of them briefly scoped out the First National Bank, which was fronted on Division Street, and one of several tenants of a two-story stone structure called the Scriver Building. Around 11 a.m., five of the men gathered in J.G. Jeft's restaurant on the western bank of the Cannon River. The cowboys were relaxed, talkative and enjoyed their bountiful meal of ham and four fried eggs each. They paid their bill, then reconvened as a gang of eight a couple of miles outside of town. They had done their reconnaissance, finalized their plans, and proceeded to canter back to Northfield in three tactical teams. The most famous personage among them was the notorious outlaw Jesse James. Accompanying Jesse were his brother Frank; the three Younger brothers, Coleman, Jim and Bob; and three more bandits named Charlie Pitts, Clell Miller and Bill Chadwell.

The historical record remains elusive on certain points, with contradictory eyewitness accounts, but the first grouping of men may have been comprised of the James brothers and Pitts, who rode into town in the lead echelon. Miller and Cole Younger came in just behind, with Bob and Jim Younger, along with Chadwell, bringing up the rear. Just prior to 2 p.m., the riders crossed the small iron bridge that spanned the Cannon River and passed through Mill Square. Jesse and his partners turned the corner onto Division Street, dismounted, and hitched their horses in front of the bank. Miller and Cole Younger soon followed and positioned themselves as lookouts outside the bank's door. At that moment, Jesse James and his two henchmen entered the bank, drew their pistols, and leapt over the counter. "Throw up your hands, for we intend to rob the bank," one of them screamed. They ordered the bank's three employees onto their knees.

The robbers had not reckoned on the stubbornness of Joseph Heywood, a 39-year-old Union army veteran, bookkeeper, treasurer of Carleton College, and the acting cashier at the bank that day. "Now open the safe you Goddamned son of a bitch," they shouted. "It's a time lock," responded Heywood, "and cannot be opened now." (The safe was actually, at that moment, unlocked.) Heywood broke free from his tormentors and yelled, "Murder!" at the top of his lungs, which earned him a crushing blow with a pistol to the side of his head. As Heywood lay dazed in a heap on the floor, the outlaws realized they had another problem. Gunfire had erupted on the street outside.

Alert townspeople had quickly surmised that these strangers had arrived in Northfield with bad intentions, and that the bank was their target. When chaos ensued, the outlaws outside the bank began to curse loudly and fire their guns in an effort to cow the citizens. That reaction served only to drive people inside, or under cover, where several plucky folk proceeded to set themselves up in protected positions with rifles, shotguns and pistols. The James Gang began to receive what ultimately became withering and deadly fire from many directions, delivered by the aroused and incensed citizenry of Northfield. Miller was hit in the face with birdshot, then finally shot dead out of his saddle. Cole Younger was wounded in the hip. Chadwell went down, also dead. The Younger brothers desperately gathered together in front of the bank, exposed, and returned fire as best they could. A townsman who was a Swedish immigrant and spoke no English was killed in the crossfire. Bob Younger's right elbow was shattered. Finally, Cole kicked open the bank's door and yelled inside: "The game is up. We are beaten." As the desperados left the bank, in a gesture of unpardonable savagery, one of them (some historians assert that it was Jesse James, others say it was his brother Frank) put his pistol next to Heywood's head and murdered him in cold blood. The outlaws had stolen next to nothing, a few coins at best. Thoroughly beaten and blasted to pieces, they raced south, out of town. Pitts would be killed and all three Younger brothers captured by a vengeful posse within two weeks. The James boys stuck together and made good their escape, but they and their nefarious outlaw days were as good as over.

Every year since World War II, on the second weekend in September, the town of Northfield celebrates "The Defeat of Jesse James Days." Thousands of people watch a reenactment of the failed robbery. Horses dash up and down Division Street, lots of noisy blank guns are fired, and everyone has a great time remembering the extraordinary event when a bunch of regular citizens kicked the butts of the great Jesse James and his band. Just prior to our graduation, a high-school classmate of mine told me that her great-grandmother had personally witnessed the whole bloody battle in 1876 – determined townsfolk versus the infamous James Gang - from the window of her boarding room on Division Street. At the time, the young woman was a student at the recently established Carleton College. This story fascinated me because I was about to matriculate to Carleton, set to begin classes in September of 1976, precisely 100 years after perhaps the most momentous event in the life of the town of Northfield.

I am one of the fortunate people who had a terrific experience as a college undergraduate. I loved Carleton then, and still do. I was a solid B+ student, with a political science major, who probably could have done more academically except that I was tremendously busy having a really good time. The classic movie comedy *Animal House* had come out during my sophomore year and it was, unfortunately, influential in my life. I recognized that college was supposed to be fun! We had wild toga parties, listened to loud music, spent hours devising and playing pranks on each other, streaked the St. Olaf library, not once but twice (St. Olaf is the other small liberal arts college in Northfield, established by a group of Norwegian Lutherans in 1874), and drank lots of cheap beer (*Wisconsin Premium, Leinenkugel's, Hauenstein,* etc.). I don't believe I missed a kegger during the entire four years; perfect attendance. I had a brief foray into politics, serving one year on the Carleton Student Association Senate. I made a bunch of great friends, several of whom are still close buddies to this day.

I was a good athlete. I played wide receiver on the varsity football team and caught a handful of passes, including three in the first (and only) NCAA-sanctioned metric game in college football history. On September 17, 1977, 9,000 spectators filled Laird Stadium on our campus to watch this unique game, which was the brainchild of a Carleton chemistry professor. We received national coverage, including a mention in *Sports Illustrated* magazine. The field was realigned with metric markings and, in the game program, player heights were given in centimeters and weights in kilograms. At the time, apparently, I was 175 centimeters tall and weighed 70 kilograms. Weird shit. Our cross-town nemesis, St. Olaf, beat the tar out of us that (un)pleasant fall afternoon, 43-0. All in all, an historic but also embarrassing moment in the annals of Carleton football. Over my college career, I scored three touchdowns. People laugh at that pathetic total, but I figure it is three more intercollegiate touchdowns than 99.992 percent of the general population has ever scored, so I am okay with those stats.

I also captained the track team as a sprinter. I finished second in the Midwest Conference 60-yard dash finals three years in a row. I lost to a different guy each year, including to my friend and teammate Danal Abrams, in our junior season. He had never beaten me before, nor did he ever do so subsequently at that distance, but he nipped me at the tape on that day. Again, I am okay with it. Danal and I have been lifelong friends, for 40+ years, and if we squared off in a footrace now, we would surely both end up hospitalized. The glory days are over, and we know it; but I will say it seems that the older we get, the better we were. In my senior year I received the *John Millen Award* as the outstanding individual contributor to track and field. This was, and remains, one of the great honors of my lifetime, because the award was conferred by a vote of my teammates. I loved those guys. I also played club rugby - a frickin' crazy game - and lots of intramurals. I easily learned as much in athletic competition as I ever did in the classroom (I recall the Duke of Wellington's probably apocryphal quote: "The Battle of Waterloo was won on the playing fields of Eton.")

I have sustained many injuries, primarily in sports and mostly at Carleton, but not always, over the years. Starting from the head and moving down to the toes, here is the listing: Three football concussions, nicely spread out, one each in junior high, high school and college. Here's how that goes down: you get smacked real hard in the head, you see a blind spot, only one eye is working, you feel nauseous, you have a massive headache, you can't remember much, and then you go back into the game. *He got his bell rung, but he's okay, we need him.* For the next day or two you are godawful sick. Also a Marine Corps concussion, in a training accident. This is of course concerning, with all the new data about football and debilitating head injuries. Apparently the condition is called "chronic traumatic encephalopathy." So far I seem to continue to be high-functioning, but I guess we shall see. I have had stiches next to my right eye after my head wacked a passenger-side window, as a kid, in an auto accident. The only time I have ever had other-than-surgical stiches, but no concussion there, as far as I know. I have broken teeth in both football and baseball. I have sprained my neck many times, which is literally a pain in the neck. I have had surgeries to repair both shoulders (torn labrum, biceps tendon out of place). A nasty, bluish-green sack of fluid on my elbow after it got banged, in football. A broken thumb and multiple dislocated fingers. A broken wrist. Busted ribs on both sides of my body. I had spinal surgery when I was in my mid-30s as a result of a bulging lower disk that was putting pressure on the nerves running down my right leg. I believe this was also a football-related injury, as I competed during the era when we were actively coached to use the head as a battering ram, which I enthusiastically did, and which I am guessing compressed the spine. Back strains. Numerous contusions, but the worst was one in my gluteus maximus. Yes, you guessed right, that was a pain in the ass. Torn hamstrings and quadriceps (both legs, track mishaps). Shin splints. Multiple sprained ankles - a badly sprained right ankle in my senior collegiate season of football was one of the most painful injuries of all. More recently, you know that I ripped several toenails off of my feet descending Kilimanjaro. I will say this though, and I am so thankful for this fact: my knees were never injured, not even a bruise or a sprain, which seems astounding given all the other unfortunate crap that happened. The knees are pristine and function extremely well to the present day, and I am grateful.

So that's the list. Not much to gripe about, really. I have never been shot; I am not missing a limb or an eye; I am not hideously scarred; I have never endured an extended hospital stay. Knock on wood. Every day that I get out of bed and feel pretty good - which is most days now that I put myself in harm's way less frequently - I am happy and consider myself a lucky man.

←————→

With its idyllic rural setting, two small but highly-rated liberal arts colleges, and generally laid-back atmosphere, the town of Northfield proudly proclaims itself a place of "cows, colleges & contentment." (Northfield is now technically a city but it has always seemed like a town to me, so that is what I call it.) The town was established in 1856 by John W. North. North was a native New Yorker, trained in the law, and a staunch Methodist evangelical and abolitionist. He moved to Minnesota for financial and health reasons, and to bring his anti-slavery crusade to the Midwest. North desired to establish a new community whose citizens were committed, like him, to education, religion, the abolition of slavery and, finally, temperance (glad he was long gone by the time we held our endless beer parties). North purchased lands near the Cannon River – in what is now northeastern Rice County, about 40 miles south of Minneapolis - with a vision of creating a township that would serve as an agricultural and cultural center. He built two sawmills and a gristmill on the river; attracted merchants, carpenters and blacksmiths; established the Northfield Lyceum Society; and worked to bring a railroad to town. When the trains finally arrived at the end of the Civil War in 1865, Northfield began to grow dramatically. The 1860 population of 867 had increased to 2,227 by 1870. The town demographic, in addition to New Yorkers and New Englanders, now consisted of Canadians and even some Norwegian immigrants. Over time, wheat and corn farms eventually gave way to dairy and beef operations. Today, the region also produces corn, soybeans and hogs. The local Malt-O-Meal plant still makes the famous cereal; it kicks up an all-pervasive and not entirely pleasant odor that, upon taking it in, no person's olfactory senses will ever forget. I just sniffed it the other day when I was in Northfield for a business lunch, which brought me down memory lane. Generations of Carleton and St. Olaf students know that lovely smell extremely well. Northfield - current (2018) population just over 20,000 - remains to this day a quaint and thriving town, in no small part because of its not-one-but-two highly regarded institutions of higher learning.

Members of the General Congregational Conference of Minnesota founded Northfield College in 1866. In 1870 the first president, James Strong, a Congregationalist minister, ventured to New England on a fundraising trip. Subsequent to hitting up a wealthy Massachusetts manufacturer named William Carleton for money, Strong was seriously injured when the carriage in which he was riding was struck by a train. Perhaps out of pity, or because he was impressed by Strong's near-miraculous survival of his injuries, Carleton donated, unconditionally, the princely sum of $50,000 to the fledgling school. The board of trustees promptly renamed the place Carleton College – they were no dummies, and I'm glad they did what they did; the name Carleton College has a much more distinguished ring to it, in my opinion, than Northfield College. Carleton was a secular, co-educational institution from the very beginning. The first two graduates, James Dow and Myra Brown, later married each other.

Carleton of course grew in size, reach and reputation over the years. Many accomplished and even famous faculty and alumni have passed through its hallowed halls. My favorite Carleton personality of all time is Laurence McKinley Gould. Gould was the very quintessence of the scholar-adventurer. He served in the U.S. Army during World War 1, then went on to earn a doctorate in geology from the University of Michigan, where he subsequently taught. He studied glaciers in Greenland and helped map the Canadian Arctic. He served as chief scientist and second-in-command for Richard E. Byrd's South Pole expedition in 1928-30, and came home a national celebrity. Gould arrived at Carleton in 1932 to head up the geology department. He became president in 1945 and served until 1962 - 30 years of service all together. Known for his charm, eloquence, and flashy red neckties, Gould was a remarkable leader who improved and expanded Carleton in countless ways. He frequently told students, "You are forever a part of Carleton, and Carleton is forever a part of you." Gould ended his career teaching at the University of Arizona, and as president of the American Association for the Advancement of Science. He lived until just shy of his 99th birthday. Larry Gould was a really cool guy.

Today, Carleton enrolls around 2,000 students from all 50 states and 35 foreign countries. More than half of students are female and nearly a quarter identify themselves as people of color. The school offers 1,000 courses in 32 majors (including Environmental Studies). The campus, with its incredibly striking and eclectic architecture, is just over 1,000 acres, which includes a gorgeous 880-acre arboretum. Carleton consistently ranks near the top in national surveys of small liberal arts institutions. The college's mission is "to provide an exceptional undergraduate liberal arts education," and it does. Please forgive me as I go on and on about my alma mater, but I am proud of Carleton and can't help myself. It is just a damn fine institution, and my experience there shaped my life in more important ways than I could ever possibly recount.

←———————→

I am also deeply proud of Carleton for the incredibly progressive and responsible stance that it has taken with respect to climate change. In the preface to its 2011 "Climate Action Plan," President Steven Poskanser says, "Carleton has a long-standing reputation for leadership in environmental initiatives, from the Cowling Arboretum in the 1920s to being the first college to construct a commercial-sized wind turbine in September 2004. Being a signatory to the American College and University Presidents' Climate Commitment furthers the dedication to environmental stewardship demonstrated by our predecessors and aligns Carleton with more than 670 other higher educational institutions."

In 2010, Carleton formed a Climate Action Plan Steering Committee consisting of a diverse group of faculty, staff, students and one trustee, along with outside expert advisors. Their collective goal was big and bold: to examine carbon reduction strategies that would enable the school to become climate neutral by the year 2050. The Action Plan begins with the frightening conclusion that if "Carleton does nothing to reduce its [greenhouse gas] emissions, current assumptions of campus square-footage and population growth are anticipated to result in a *45 percent increase* to Carleton's carbon footprint by the year 2050" (emphasis added). The steering committee's work was incredibly complex. They examined reduction strategies with an eye toward a cost/benefit analysis based upon two key measurements: average annual metric tons of carbon dioxide equivalent (MTCDE) reduced and the cost per average annual MTCDE reduced, including first cost plus net annual operating costs - or savings – from the start date to 2050. In addition to their study of energy supply and demand, the committee focused as well on possible opportunities in transportation, waste management, procurement and land management.

The Action Plan states unambiguously that beyond a 10-year timeframe, predictions regarding costs, paybacks, technological, economic and political considerations are difficult to make; so the plan would need to be updated regularly. But the overall objective is clear: "Although the steering committee acknowledges that this plan is only a starting point, it is intended to foster a focused awareness of campus-wide sustainability initiatives, inspire educational opportunities, and instill a widespread network of environmental best practices into our standard operating procedures. Carleton College is pleased to be among the growing number of American colleges and universities who are stepping forward as proactive leaders to create more sustainable campuses and actively address the threat of global climate change."

Pursuant to the Climate Action Plan, Carleton installed a second gigantic wind turbine in 2011. The school's first turbine is connected to the public electricity grid. Carleton sells the electricity to Xcel Energy at a wholesale rate, keeps all renewable energy credits, and also earns state incentives. The newer turbine connects directly to the campus electrical grid and meets 25-30 percent of Carleton's annual electricity demand. In the summer of 2017, the school began to implement a new utility master plan that seeks to locate three geothermal well fields on campus. The goal is to replace the current steam plant with a clean, low-temperature hot water system. Carleton is the first college campus in Minnesota to implement such a geothermal-based district energy system; the project will involve the drilling of more than 300 vertical wells (each of them 520 feet deep) along with the installation of 60 miles of new and replacement piping. The geothermal system will reduce annual central plant operating expenses by 35-40 percent, generating $40 million in savings over the next three decades. As a result, Carleton should reach the first interim milestone in the Action Plan, and continue on the path toward climate neutrality by 2050. In August of 2017 Martha Larsen, manager of campus energy and sustainability at Carleton, explained, "By transitioning to a system that requires far less heat input, we will have the flexibility to use a much more diverse portfolio of energy sources, including renewable energy technologies of today and the future.... Given the maintenance needs of our existing 100-year old steam system, the goals of our Climate Action Plan, and the plans to construct a new science building at the center of campus, we recognized this as an optimal time to modernize our campus infrastructure while permanently shifting the College to a more cost effective and less carbon intense mode of operation."

$\longleftrightarrow$

Almost 40 years ago, in 1969, the great Laurence McKinley Gould presciently observed: "Man is fouling his own nest, and for the first time in human history the chief danger to our survival comes from ourselves instead of the forces of nature." We are currently enduring a U.S. presidential administration that is openly hostile to the reality of climate change - and in many ways is actively working against those who are attempting to address the challenge. As a result, the efforts of individual actors, state and other units of government, private enterprise, and institutions like Carleton College to reduce our carbon footprint are all the more necessary and critical to the future of the Earth.

CHAPTER FOURTEEN

CAYO HUEUSA

KEY WEST, FLORIDA

"Come weal, come woe; come progress, come decay; come nature with her beauty, come man with his mistakes; nothing can mar the sky, the water, the sunrise and sunset, which makes the unchanging and unchangeable Key West."

— JEFFERSON BROWNE —

Key West is noisy: loud traffic; loud sirens; loud music; loud people, many of them – of all ages – completely inebriated, at every hour of the day and night. Roosters (yes, roosters) crowing, also seemingly at all hours of the day and night. Key West is commercialized: hundreds of shops, manned by aggressive, sometimes cranky shopkeepers, purveying t-shirts, hats and a million tchotchkes, not one of those shops distinguished in any meaningful way from any of the others. Street vendors, musicians, and myriad performers of various feats of derring-do (sword swallowing, etc.) abound, all trying to make a buck and scrape by. Key West is crowded: thousands of tourists on any given day, depending on the time of year, the problem exacerbated by the immense ocean liners that sit in a row at the dock and disgorge hordes of passengers on a regular basis. College students on spring break show up, and then do what college students on spring break do. Key West is not really a place for kids: Faith and I made the grave parental error in judgment of bringing our two young daughters there during the annual bacchanal known as Fantasy Fest. Not a good idea. We had to avoid Duval Street entirely.

Thomas McGuane, who spent lots of time both fishing and partying in Key West many decades ago, reflected: "Key West in the sixties and seventies. Good heavens, a great and corrupt gardenia of an island in a wilderness of shoals and mangroves where we sometimes went [fishing] from old wooden bars, shuddering with dance music and the heaving of like-minded characters." But then, "When I went back to Key West ten years later, I was astonished. The disreputable and rundown Duval Street had become a glut of T-shirt shops and tourist traps. The end of the street was frequently blocked to the height of several stories by cruise ships, while the city itself smelled of spring break barf twenty-four hours a day. Half the writers of the East Coast had moved here to immerse themselves in the sort of cannibalism they'd learned up north. Among the towering hotels and condominiums, the marina where I used to keep my skiff was encrusted with petrochemical grime and operated by the sort of surly rednecks with catfish mustaches who seem to have proliferated in the charter-boat trade around the world."

Oh come on, Tommy, I think you doth protest too much. Smelling of barf all the time? Half the writers of the East Coast? Towering hotels and condominiums? I know, I know, there was nothing like the good old days. As I've indicated, I'm readily willing to acknowledge that Key West ain't perfect; but it really is - and has been ever since I first visited in the early 2000s - one of the happiest of my happy places in all the world. Let's discuss. But first, as always, a bit of history.

⬤━━━━━▶

The island of Key West is a strange and wondrous place. It is the last island of the Florida Keys and the southernmost city in the continental United States. If a person started driving the original U.S. East Coast Route One in Fort Kent, Maine, and drove south for as far as she could go, she would arrive in Key West, which represents "Mile Zero" of Route One. Miami sits 154 miles to the north, the island of Cuba 90 miles to the south. The warm blue waters of the great river in the sea known as the Gulf Stream, flow in a relentless clockwise current of from two to four knots north between Key West and Cuba, hugging the northeast coast of the U.S., then turning east and sweeping across the vast

Atlantic all the way to Europe.

Legend has it that ages ago, the acquisitive Seminole Indians of Florida, forever in search of new territories to conquer, pursued the Calusa Indians in a southwesterly direction from key to key until the Calusas turned and fought in a last stand battle on the southernmost island. Those Calusas who were lucky enough to survive the desperate fight fled in their canoes to Cuba. The rest were wiped out and rotted where they fell. In the 16th century, Spanish explorers who were searching for a safe route from the Straits of Florida to the New World came upon the tragic scene: beaches littered with relics from the battle and the bleached skeletal remains of Calusa warriors, piled high. The Spaniards gave the place the haunting name "Cayo Hueso," or Island of Bones. Traffic in treasure-laden ships traveling the Gulf Stream between the New World and Europe gradually increased, generating interest from pirates who hid in the coves and channels of the Keys, waiting to strike. Frequent shipwrecks along the perilous coral reefs also attracted Bahamas-based wreckers who salvaged the sunken cargoes. In 1763, Spain ceded Florida to England, and when the English settlers arrived, they converted—or, the Spanish would say, corrupted—the name Cayo Hueso into Key West.

Control of Key West eventually reverted back to the Spanish, and in 1821 an American businessman named John Whitehead purchased the island for $2,000. Whitehead envisioned huge commercial possibilities in sea-driven industries for the island. In 1822, the U.S. Navy sent Commodore David Porter to Key West with the mission of ridding the Caribbean Ocean of piracy, which he more or less succeeded in doing. Key West was incorporated in 1828 and, within a decade, it was the largest and richest city in the territory of Florida, primarily as a result of a robust salvage industry. Other industries such as ship-fitting, turtling, sponging and cigar-making soon came to flourish. As a deep-water port at the juncture of two oceans, Key West served as an important naval base in both the American Civil War and the Spanish-American War, and beyond. The island could not be accessed other than by sea until 1912, when industrialist Henry Flagler completed his 150-mile-long Florida East Coast Rail Extension, linking Key West to the mainland.

But Key West succumbed to economic disaster in the ensuing years. Labor problems and destructive hurricanes drove the cigar industry away.

Tourism began to wane, and then the Great Depression struck with such calamitous effect that, by 1934, 80 percent of the population was on relief. There was talk of complete abandonment of the island as Key West spiraled from a city with the highest-per-capita income in America to among the lowest. Finally, on Labor Day in 1935, the most destructive recorded hurricane in history struck the Upper Keys. Winds of more than 200 miles per hour generated tidal waves that killed hundreds of people and destroyed the railroad.

A visionary man named Julius Stone, who was the director of the Florida Federal Emergency Relief Agency, stepped into the void and relentlessly promoted Key West as America's most amazing tropical tourist attraction. Soon, the Overseas Highway and the Seven-Mile Bridge replaced the railroad, so it was now possible to drive to Key West. Air service became a popular and convenient way to reach the island. With Key West's ravishing natural beauty and incredible climate—the average annual temperature is 77 degrees with only 39 inches of rain per year—over time, the population began to grow again. Key West became a haunt for significant numbers of artists and writers, some famous and most not-so-famous. The island came to be dotted with scores and eventually hundreds of bars, restaurants, hotels, and guest houses. Today, Key West continues to draw diverse and eclectic people, including a sizeable and openly gay population, both as residents and visitors.

◀━━━━▶

Faith and I have been to Key West many times over the years. She has come to love the place as much as I do, but with a caveat: "I will never move there, because I think it will be underwater at some point in the reasonable near future," she tells me. A pessimistic view, I must say, but in the event that she is right, we will just enjoy the island as visitors for now.

We love the year-round warm temperatures, the not-too frequent and short-in duration rainstorms, the Gulf and ocean breezes, the unforgettable sunsets, and the seeming lack of insects - natives tell us they exist, but I have yet to see a mosquito; in Minnesota, the mosquito, the scourge of our summertime, is known as the state bird. The food and wine scene is fantastic, with more first-rate restaurants per square mile - Key West is just over seven square miles in size - I think, than any place in America. Despite Duval Street's cheesy reputation, there are actually any number of fine art dealerships along the path. We also love the diversity and the accepting attitude; Faith says, "In Key West, I can walk around really looking like shit, grubby clothes, hair everywhere, and no one comments or even notices." There is a distinct 'live and let live' gestalt that permeates everything. Finally, there is a lot to do in Key West. There are all the touristy things: we visit Harry Truman's Southern White House at the Naval Annex; we have been to Fort Zachary Taylor and the various gardens and aquariums; we walk through the Hemingway House and marvel at the six-toed cats. We have been snorkeling. I have golfed and been scuba diving. But above all else, I and my lady love to come to Key West to fish.

A few years ago we met a fishing captain named Dexter Simmons. I saw his name mentioned in one of my guy magazines (*Esquire*? *Outside*? *Men's Journal*? I don't remember); he came highly recommended, and he has never disappointed. Dexter is a really interesting guy. He grew up in the Northeast where he became an accomplished skier. He ended up in Oregon, where he earned a master's degree in sports marketing. I once asked him how many Florida Keys fishing guides had master's degrees, and he answered, "More than you would think." He stayed out west and worked as a part-time ski instructor, eventually making his way into the business side of the skiing industry full-time. But, like a lot of people in the corporate game, he became jaded and decided that there had to be something more to life. He visited Key West and knew, then and there, that he needed to relocate to paradise and become a fishing guide. That was in 1990, and he has never looked back. Dexter is a great guide: knowledgeable, calm, conversational, fun. We enjoy his company enormously.

We have been out on the expansive, multi-hued waters with Dexter several times, mostly on the Gulf of Mexico side. We have known great days of fishing, and we have been skunked. One time, I hooked what Dexter estimated to be a 115-pound tarpon, and I stood in the brace at the center of the boat and fought with that bad boy for 90 minutes. An hour-and-a-half with that damned fish! It was a great battle, for the primary reason that he was exactly as strong as I was. We were like two very evenly matched wrestlers. Just as I would reel him in close to the boat, he would turn away and run. Dexter advised me to try to move his head back and forth as I pulled him in, to disorient and tire him. *Tire him? What about me?* Our goal was merely to bring him near enough to take a photo, then release him home, but I did not succeed. He finally moved around to the back of the boat and the line snapped when it became entangled with the engine. These days, one does not often have the opportunity for an epic fight where nobody really gets hurt, and so I was grateful despite the fact that I lost him. *He got away, but God bless him, he made my day.*

On another occasion, as we fished shallow, sandy-bottomed water for smaller species like amberjack, grouper and tuna, a long, lean, steel-gray barracuda parked himself right underneath Dexter's boat. We could see him clearly and he waited there, patiently, like an undersized German U-boat, to pounce on our prey as soon as we hooked it. Really smart technique. We would catch a fish, Dexter would yell, "Reel him in" and, despite our frantic efforts, Mr. Barracuda would devour his poor, helpless victim in a matter of seconds. Dexter later told us that he had caught this particular barracuda on at least two or three occasions (he recognized a unique tooth and mouth configuration on this fish), and that Dexter's young son had named the fish Philip. Well, Philip the Barracuda put a considerable damper on our angling adventure on that particular morning.

In early 2017, with my 60th birthday pending in January of 2018, I said to Faith, "You know what I'd really like to do on my next birthday? Go fishing with Dexter." We made the arrangements, but then became deeply concerned for all of our friends in the Keys when, in the fall of '17, Hurricane Irma – the most powerful Atlantic hurricane in recorded history - struck with thunderous fury. I will deal in more detail later in the book with the subject of hurricanes, but suffice to say that Irma devastated the Keys. It is said that one quarter of the buildings in the Keys were seriously damaged or destroyed. Seventy five people throughout Florida were killed. Even a month after Irma hit in September, the landscape remained littered with shattered structures, random junk and downed trees. Overall damage estimates for Irma were as high as $300 billion.

In the Keys, tourism is a $1.6 billion per year industry. The hospitality industry employs roughly half of the workforce. Key West alone entertained 3.8 million visitors in 2016. When countless hotels, restaurants, charter operations, dive shops and other small enterprises either went out of business altogether or closed for repairs, the regional economy suffered a massive set-back. But as we were to see, the people of the Keys are resilient. By October 1st, Highway One had reopened, permitting traffic to flow freely again all the way from Key Largo down to Key West. The utilities quickly restored electrical power in most places. Key West was actually fortunate: the damage suffered there was relatively minor compared to the near total destruction of property just a few miles up the line of the Keys to the northeast. The ubiquitous cruise ships returned to Key West by late September - unsightly though they may be - to the profound relief of strapped business owners throughout the island. But economic recovery has remained slow. When we arrived on January 26th, Faith and I could see that the place was not nearly as crowded as it had been on all of our previous visits. It was actually kind of nice to go at a slower pace, but we could truly sense the suffering that people had been through. We were glad to be back in this wonderful locale, doing what we could do by spending a couple of bucks to help out. We could not wait to talk to our friend Dexter to get his take on things.

My 60th birthday, January 29, 2018, dawned rainy in Key West. We even experienced lightning that morning. We called Dexter and agreed to stay on top of the forecast and meet him in the early afternoon, if things cleared up. We have learned that if you don't like the weather in Key West just hang around for an hour or two and it will change. After lunch the sun came out, the wind died down, and temperatures got up to 78 degrees. Perfect fishing weather. Dexter took us out to a spot called Cottrell Key, in the Gulf of Mexico, about 10 miles west of Key West; we saw a leaping school of bottlenose dolphins along the way. Dexter said we would start by searching for barracuda, but after an hour or so with spinning rods and a long, rubberized yellow lure that supposedly resembles barracuda prey as it speeds through the water, we had been shut out. We tried both casting from a stationary boat and trolling along reefs, but had no luck. So we changed lures, attached some live shrimp, and went after smaller species. We finally had a bit of activity as we caught a hand-ful of grey snappers. They are feisty little dudes. Faith actually out-fished me, as she has done on a number of occasions. But we generally don't keep score; we just have fun. Later in the afternoon we went hunting again after barracuda, fishing a shallow, sandy patch of water. This time we could actually see the buggers, and Dexter would call out where he wanted me to cast while Faith took a well-deserved break from the action. At one point, I hooked a 'cuda and fought him for a very exciting minute or so. He finally severed the line, we assume with his very impressive teeth, and he was off to freedom. I succeeded on several occasions in landing a well-aimed cast right in front of a fish, but by now they were wise to our ways and merely swam off, probably giving me the barracuda version of the finger as they went on their way. Such was our day on the water. We had a terrific time.

◄──────►

We asked Dexter about the storm. His was indeed a tale of woe. He and his wife live with their 15-year-old son in a single-family home on Sugar Loaf Key, about 17 miles north and east of Key West. They left the Keys prior to the hurricane and stayed at his in-laws' home in Mississippi. Thankfully, unlike others, they had a place to go. The storm struck Sugar Loaf on September 12. I said to Dexter, "You will always remember September 11 as a day of national disaster and September 12 as a day of personal disaster." He agreed. Damage to his home was estimated to be $200,000. His roof was wrecked, and his deck torn away. Eighty percent of the trees in his yard, mostly palms, were uprooted. The insurance company balked, and he had to hire a representative to attempt to negotiate a fair settlement for him. They were back in the house, but now mold problems had cropped up. He was coughing and hacking and having trouble breathing as a result. Dexter estimated it would be six months before all repairs would be complete. But he acknowledged that it could have been worse: his next-door neighbor's home was completely leveled. *So you count your blessings.*

Nevertheless, Faith and I were moved and saddened to hear this story of how a personal friend of ours, and his family, had had their lives completely upended as a result of a cataclysmic weather event. "What do you think of climate change?" Faith asked Dexter. He paused thoughtfully before answering:

"Climate change is a serious issue. I have seen it coming in my years in the Keys. Waters are rising and the islands are sinking. Temperatures are warmer. Storms are more severe. We are foolish to ignore it."

CHAPTER FIFTEEN

THE INCA TRAIL

MACHU PICCHU, PERU

"Solvitur ambulando: It is solved by walking."
— ST. AUGUSTINE —

He was a tall, skinny drink of water. He stood 6'4" and weighed in at a scant 170 pounds. He was a professor of Latin American History at his alma mater, Yale University, but the life of an academic bored him to tears. He was an adventurer, mightily ambitious, and fairly lusted for fame. In today's world, he would have kept close track of his number of followers, as well as likes and dislikes on social media. Hiram Bingham (1875-1956) lived a productive and fascinating life – marrying an heiress to the Tiffany's fortune, serving with distinction in World War One, and later becoming a U.S. senator. But no subsequent achievement could possibly top his "discovery" of one of the world's most significant and iconic archaeological sites, the mystical, long-abandoned mountaintop city of Machu Picchu, in the Andes Mountains of Peru.

Bingham had heard rumors of a "lost city." He was in South America to make a name for himself, exploring just such possibilities. A local resident named Melchor Arteaga confirmed that there were ruins worth seeing nearby. Bingham threw a silver dollar reward Arteaga's way if he would guide him to the site. On the rainy morning of July 24, 1911 - a day when every other member of Bingham's expedition conveniently found something else to do - the trek began. When Bingham inquired as to exactly where they were going, Arteaga pointed to the top of the mountain. At around noon, at an elevation of 2,500 feet, Bingham and his guide reached a small hut on a ridgetop, with a splendid view of the nearby peaks and cloud cover. The native farming family who lived there confirmed ruins nearby and offered the climbers cooked potatoes and cool, clear water to drink. Arteaga was tired and chose to stay and chat with his neighbors. A young boy was assigned to bring Bingham the rest of the way to the site.

Bingham later wrote, "Hardly had we left the hut and rounded the promontory, than we were confronted by an unexpected sight, a great flight of beautifully constructed stone-faced terraces, perhaps a hundred of them, each hundreds of feet long and ten feet high. Suddenly, I found myself confronted with the walls of ruined houses built of the finest quality Inca stonework... in the dense shadow, hiding in bamboo thickets and tangled vines, appeared here and there walls of white granite carefully cut and exquisitely fitted together." The boy was hard to follow as they climbed, as he was quicker than Bingham, nimble, and familiar with the terrain. Bingham realized that there were actually people living at the site, but that did not diminish his astonishment at what he was seeing: "I climbed a marvelous great stairway of large granite blocks, walked along a pampa where the Indians had a small vegetable garden, and came into a little clearing. Here were the ruins of two of the finest structures I have ever seen in Peru. Not only were they made of selected blocks of beautifully grained white granite; their walls contained ashlars of Cyclopean size, ten feet in length, and higher than a man. The sight held me spellbound.... I could scarcely believe my senses as I examined the larger blocks in the lower course, and estimated that they must weigh from ten to fifteen tons each. Would anyone believe what I had found?"

It was an existential moment in our marriage. Faith and I were confronting a serious challenge. We disagreed on the correct approach to solving the problem. We bickered, uncharacteristically. We were frustrated, and clearly at an impasse. We sulked. Finally, we sought help from an outside, expert resource. What was the crisis, you ask? We were trying to attach the fucking luggage tags to our duffels and backpacks prior to our trip to Peru. Our outfitter had sent them along with a request that we use them. You've seen those things. It's easy enough to attach the tab containing our contact information to the plastic, rubber-band-like loop, but then how to attach the loop to the bag itself was, frankly, throwing us for a loop. We finally went online and watched a demonstration of how to do it. Turns out you have to put the loop around the bag handle and then run the entire tab through the loop again. Takes three seconds and presto! The tag is secure. I commented to Faith, "If you don't tell anyone how stupid we are, I won't say anything either." She concurred. Our 33-year marriage, saved.

We had made a decision probably 18 months prior to try to walk the Inca Trail to Machu Picchu. The timing worked well for us to make the 12-day trip over the New Year holiday, from late December 2018 to early January 2019. We departed the day after Christmas and flew to Lima via Atlanta. This is a bit less exhausting than some of our other international travel – the flight from Atlanta only lasted just over six hours, and Lima is essentially in the Eastern Time Zone of the U.S. So making the adjustment in terms of jet lag was easy. The question was, how would we adapt to the altitude?

After a quick overnight in Lima, which sits at sea level, we were on a morning plane east to Cusco, which has an elevation of more than 11,000 feet. Quite a sudden and dramatic change. I had visited my doctor prior to our departure and he armed me with the altitude pills called Diamox (as well as antibiotics for diarrhea – more on that later). We checked into the Palacia Del Inca Hotel, and were greeted by our two wonderful Peruvian guides, Manuel (we called him Manny) and Hazel. Our group of a dozen assembled in the lobby, and we were soon off on a walking tour of Cusco. The idea was to get acclimated as soon as possible. This is a fascinating thing, because everyone reacts to altitude differently. An 85-year-old grandmother might be just fine while a 25-year-old triathlete struggles. Faith and I did well; we each had slight headaches and a little shortness of breath over the first couple of days, but soon felt better with just a dose of Advil – we never did need the Diamox. Other members of the group, however, were not as fortunate. One fellow never became accustomed to the altitude, no matter what he tried. He struggled during the hikes, felt nauseous, had no appetite, and did not feel better until the very end of our time together when we came down out of the thin air. He was a quiet, peaked dude for most of the trip.

Cusco was the Incan capital city. The Spanish arrived in Peru in 1532 and essentially sacked the Inca Empire over time, looting precious gold and silver while imposing their political and religious systems on the native population. In Cusco, the Spaniards deliberately built their own churches, monasteries and palaces directly on top of Inca sites. The Santo Domingo church, for example, sits on top of the Incan Temple of the Sun, known by the natives as Qorikancha. The intermingling of the two cultures was evident everywhere as we strolled the rough cobblestone streets. Spanish adobe construction fitted together with Inca foundations, exquisitely and precisely made by Inca craftsmen centuries ago. Some of the foundations looked like they had been laid in place just yesterday. There are ornate cathedrals, a busy central marketplace, mysterious alleyways and hidden courtyards. Faith and I commented that, with its obvious colonial Spanish influence, Cusco reminded us of a larger version of one of our favorite towns, Santa Fe in New Mexico. That night, we enjoyed dinner at an excellent restaurant on the plaza called the Inka Grill. I tasted alpaca (a slightly smaller relative of the llama, bred specifically for its luxuriant wool) meat for the first time. It was sliced thin, cooked medium rare, tender, lean, and absolutely delicious; we washed it down with a lush Chilean red.

The next morning, Friday, we took a bus on a westerly route toward Soraypampa. The ride involved numerous switchback turns back and forth along the steep mountainside, which were to me unnerving. You'll remember that I have a touch of the vertigo; I don't really like heights and especially when someone else, like a potentially psychopathic bus driver, is in control of whether I will live or die from a fatal fall, I am all the more uncomfortable. It certainly would have been a spectacular way to go for all of us, had we plummeted the thousands of feet to the valley below. Fortunately, he had taken his meds, drove carefully, and we made it. We visited ruins at a site called Quillarumiyoc. Here, Inca construction which was put in place many hundreds of years ago, probably in the early 1400s, looked in much better condition than a nearby Spanish adobe building which went up sometime in the 1700s. The adobe cracked and crumbled; the immaculately shaped and placed Inca brick walls looked as if they will survive another 500 years. The Inca architects and engineers generally did not use mortar, yet their stonework fits perfectly flush together; there are no open seams; and the bricks are not all rectangular – they are of many shapes and sizes. Exactly how they accomplished this intricate feat of design is something of a mystery.

We stopped at a small village called Millepata to refresh and buy snacks and other products that we would need on the trail. As we drove away, I saw a ghost – on this warm sunny afternoon, sitting quietly in a folding chair on a street corner, in her gorgeously colorful Peruvian garb, was an elderly woman who bore the exact likeness for my maternal grandmother, Hildur Engwall (she lived to be 100 years old but passed away way back in the mid-1990s; she was a pure Swede who nevertheless had dark eyes and a dark complexion and, incidentally, spoke Spanish). I laughed out loud, elbowed Faith, and was sorely tempted to ask the bus driver to stop so I could go give her a hug and say, "Gram Hildur, it's me, Jeff. What the heck are you doing living in Peru in 2018? It's been a long time! I still love you and think of you often. Well, everyone's waiting. Gotta go walk the Inca Trail. Bye." I guess everyone has a doppelganger somewhere.

We ultimately proceeded on by foot to the village of Marcoccasa. There is a humble little farmhouse there, a bit rundown but still occupied, way up on the hillside, called El Pedregal. The view from this place was stunning. We ate a simple lunch and then started trekking the Camino Real (Royal Path). Overall, this was a tough hike which ended up being about nine miles over more than seven hours for the day; we gained about 1200 feet in altitude. For the final four miles, we walked along an aqueduct that had been initially built by the Incas and improved and updated many times since then so as to be still highly functional as a source of clean, cold mountain water. The walk was dicey too: if you fell to the left toward the mountain you tumbled into the cement aqueduct, a drop of about six feet, and some kind of injury – but not death - would undoubtedly result. If you fell to the right, however, away from the side of the mountain, you were a goner after a drop of many thousands of feet. There is foliage along the right edge of the path which creates an optical illusion that gives the false impression that there are trees and other brush there that would cushion a fall. Not so, our guide Manny assured us: "There is nothing underneath that greenery that would prevent you from falling all the way to the bottom; we would likely never find you." Couple this knowledge with the fact that the trail narrows in certain places to shoulder-width or even less, and you have a potentially dangerous situation. We took note that the surefooted horses and mules that followed us carrying our duffels were not allowed to walk this portion of the trail. They took another route. So we were slow and careful in placing our steps. We knew we directly controlled our own destiny. I avoided vertigo (for the most part) by simply tricking my eyes into seeing only the left edge of the trail and the aqueduct beyond, or by focusing on Faith's footsteps in front of me; she had asked me to stay just behind her - she took comfort in knowing I was right there - which I did virtually the length of the Inca Trail. We were both highly focused but also engaged in an upbeat patter, encouraging each other. We arrived at our lodge – with incredible views of the snow peaked Humantay and Salkantay Mountains in the distance - at around 6 p.m. We all felt like we had accomplished something that day. We took a shower and unwound with a wonderful dinner of carrot soup, beef tips and chocolate mousse, accompanied by a Chilean cabernet (a vacation can't be all toil and peril, can it?)

←———→

The history of the Inca Empire unfolded gradually. At first, the small Inca tribe consisted of just one among many different ethnic groups. The Incas lived in the southern valley of Cusco. Beginning in the eleventh century and for 200 years thereafter the Incas had slowly – via military conquests and smart diplomacy – begun to expand their influence. But then, in the early 1400s, came explosive growth. Over just three generations the empire centered on the city of Cusco – the word translates as "naval of the world" – conquered tribes from the heart of the Andes Mountains to the coast and grew to rule over ten million subjects. The land mass controlled by the Incas, encompassing Peru, central Chile in the south and reaching north of the equator, eventually stretched for 2,500 miles. The domain known as Tawantinsuyu, meaning "four parts together," was in fact divided into four parts. From the main plaza of Cusco emanated four roads, one to each of the regions. The Incas were extremely talented and well-organized: they constructed impressive buildings, sacred shrines and monuments, recorded a population census, and spread their language, known as Quechua.

The emperor, whoever he may have been at any given time, ruled supreme. He was divine, the son of Inti, who was the sun god. He was considered to be immortal, so that when he died, his mummified body continued to occupy the palace where he had lived during life. Interpreters could conjure up advice and guidance from the dead emperor when necessary. The most important of the Inca emperors was called Pachacutec (the name means, "He who shakes the earth; when I asked Manny about Pachacutec, he got a faraway look in his eye and said simply, "He was a great man"); Pachacutec was an outstanding military hero and builder; under his reign the empire expanded rapidly, and it was he who began construction on the city of Machu Picchu, probably sometime between 1420 and 1450.

Spanish conquistadors, led by Francisco Pizarro, arrived in 1532. Pizarro and his small, armored band of military adventurers rode horses and possessed firearms. The Incans were frightened and intimidated by these strange, immense animals and a weapon which could cause death, seemingly invisibly, from a distance; they had no experience with either. The Spaniards confronted the Inca ruler Atahualpa in Cajamarca. This was truly a coming together of two cultures that did not understand each other. In effect, the Old World was meeting the New. The conquistadors defeated Atlahualpa's warriors, captured the king, and ruthlessly executed him. They arrived in Cusco the next year, and took control of the city for themselves. In addition to killing natives with their muskets and sabers, the Europeans also brought with them dread diseases such as smallpox, which devastated Inca populations over time. The next emperor, Manco Inca, mounted a futile resistance; by the late 1530s loyal Incas had gathered at Ollantaytambo, and eventually relocated to the forested confines of Vilcabamba (when Hiram Bingham arrived at Machu Picchu, he mistakenly believed he had discovered the fortress citadel of Vilcabamba, which was not in fact discovered until the 1960s.) From Vilcabamba the Incas launched a resistance movement against their dastardly Spanish oppressors which lasted 30 years. The Spanish established a viceroyalty, in Lima, in 1542; Lima was now the capital of Spanish-owned Peru. In 1572, the last of the Inca emperors, Tupa Amaru, was captured and publicly executed in Cusco. Thus ended the sad and tragic tale of the once glorious Inca Empire. But, I would suspect that Pachacutec laughs, because the Spaniards never did lay hands on him nor eyes on Machu Picchu.

⬅━━━━➡

Saturday morning, December 29, it had been one year to the day since my dearly-loved mother Doris had passed away. Faith and I noted the sad anniversary and agreed that we would hike in Doris's honor that day. We set out at 8:45 a.m., and it turned out to be an arduous trek; we needed every bit of inspiration we could muster. We started with a relatively gradual slope which eventually gave way to a much steeper grade. The effort was worth it, as we soon had a panoramic view of the amazing Vilcabamba Range. After a couple of hours, we had gained 1,100 feet in elevation and arrived at beautiful, fog-shrouded Lake Salkantay. We stopped for lunch. The promotional materials had suggested that "the more adventurous can take a dip in the cool glacial waters..." Were they nuts? We were all in our winter garb, down coats, hats, scarves, gloves, freezing our various body parts off. We hiked back down, which is easier than the ascent of course, but also very tricky. My experience has been that one is much more likely to lose footing on the way down than up, and conditions were wet and slippery.

It had become apparent that we had three or four group members, Faith included, who were utterly fascinated by the flora they were seeing all along our route. No tiny flower escaped their notice. These were our 'naturalists,' and it was a supreme pleasure to have them along. I asked Faith after the fact about what kinds of flowers she saw; she described white, red and plum-colored poppies, pinkish begonias, bright-yellow bidens (no relation to the former U.S. vice president), and a perennial purple flower called lupine.

There was a rawhide-tough cowboy named Felipe, a long-time member of Manny's team, who followed us the whole way leading his horse, carrying water and other additional supplies. He was our Peruvian "Marlboro Man." Our team member who was not adapting to the altitude actually had to ride the horse for a portion of the way. He looked awkward, but it beat wheezing and cramping up. His partner had stayed behind entirely, resting at the lodge with a head cold and not feeling well. We were accompanied both ways by two Peruvian brothers, Francisco and Santiago, who wore vivid traditional outfits and played the flute along the way. They were fun to interact with, Manny serving as our interpreter. They later set up shop at the lodge, where Faith and some of the other gals bought scarves and caps from them. Really nice, well-made stuff.

I need to preface this next little story by saying that I take no joy in any person's frightful situation or resulting injury. But sometimes people bring calamity down upon their own heads - in this case literally. Here's what happened. We were told by Manny and Hazel in no uncertain terms to ever walk anywhere, whether on the trail itself or even after hours around the relatively safe confines of the lodge, by ourselves. "There are pumas and bears and vipers and landslides and kicking horses and drunken cowboys and all kinds of dangerous poisonous things that can hurt or kill you in Peru," they warned. "Also, don't drink the water." Most of us were scared straight. But Murphy's Law says there is always one person in every group with wax in his – or in this case, her – ears. One of our members, a really nice, 67-year-old grandmother, a nurse from Iowa, decided to go exploring when she got back to the lodge. This woman was in terrific physical condition, but she had either not heard or ignored the very clear warnings of our guides. She set out alone on the short walk to a nearby river. In the distance, perhaps 50 feet away, she noticed a llama. Then she noticed that the llama was looking at her. Then she noticed a fire in the llama's eyes. Then she noticed that the llama was running in her direction. *Something startled him, or he is being chased*, she thought. Then she noticed, *That sumbitch is running straight at me, huffing and puffing. And he is bigger than me.* She now noticed that she was under attack, so she picked up a small stick to defend herself. The llama was not deterred, reared up on his hind legs and pushed her over with his front hooves (I think llamas have hooves.) She was now scared shitless. She got up and tumbled over a three-foot stone wall in hopes that he would not follow. No such luck. He hopped right over and bit her on the head. Yes, on the head. You heard me right: he took the top of her coconut into his choppers. He then reared up a second time, knocking her once again to the ground, and succeeded in breaking her wrist. He finally trotted off, satisfied that he had taught this unwanted intruder a lesson. I understand what you are probably thinking: *I know this author by now. He is making this shit up to embellish the story for cheap laughs.* My firm response is this: It's a fair point, but how could I possibly make this shit up? I mean honestly. It doesn't get any weirder than this. My kids used to caress llamas in the local petting zoo, for goodness sake. They are gentle, docile animals. Everyone knows that. A crazed, attack llama? Who would ever even think of it? Come on.

Anyhow, so she stumbled back into the lodge, blurted out her tale of woe, and got lots of sympathy amidst a stifled chuckle or two (one woman quietly lamented, "God, I wish I had captured it on video; it would have gone viral.") She was shaken, but okay, and we were all thankful for that. She could have been hurt much worse than she was. Manny diagnosed her with a broken wrist. She would need to be transported by emergency motor vehicle from this incredibly remote lodge (transport did not arrive until 11 p.m.) to Cusco, which is many hours distant. There, whatever lucky Peruvian orthopedic surgeon happened to be on call the next morning would operate on her wrist. They put her under a general anesthetic, reconnected her wrist bones, and put her in a cast. By all accounts, they did a fine job. I do give "Llama Woman" credit for guts. She was back with us 36 hours later, and completed the hike, all the way to Machu Picchu!

Sunday was a long day, and the official start of our Inca Trail adventure. We would hike eight miles from Soraypampa to our destination at the Wayra Lodge. We started early, just after 7 am, and did not arrive at the finish until after 3 pm. Our 2,500 foot ascent was steep, a challenging route up the Rio Blanco Valley, flanking Humantay Peak. This was a rigorous climb made all the more difficult by widely varying weather conditions. It was generally rainy and got colder as we climbed to the highest point we would reach during the entire trip, 15,200 feet. I remember on Kilimanjaro, despite days spent acclimatizing, that it was at exactly 15,000 feet that I started to feel stupid, like I had consumed several strong drinks. So one is indeed up in the thin air at that elevation. For some reason, I felt better in Peru at that altitude than I had in Africa. We were startled when, literally the moment we arrived at the peak, surrounded by the Vilcabamba Range, it began to snow. We had now seen everything during the last several days from hot, sweaty, shirtsleeve weather to gently falling snow. As we continued down the hill on our descent, several group members began to exhibit the beginning signs of hypothermia – people were wet and getting colder and a couple were a bit disoriented. We bundled up in as many layers as each of us had in our backpacks and tried to stay together; I gently rubbed the hands of one of our folks who was not feeling her fingers; she felt better and proceeded on. Manny and Hazel kept a close eye on us all. For Faith and me, it just felt like home in the wintertime. What goes up must come down, and over the next three hours we descended almost exactly as far as we had climbed, about 2,400 feet. We were very glad for a hot shower, a hearty dinner of beef and rice, and an Argentinian red. I told Faith that I felt like I did in college in the fall, the Sunday morning after I had played a football game on Saturday afternoon: very sore all over. She was too; in my journal I noted, "There is no true adventure without some pain." But a night's rest refreshes, thankfully.

You may be wondering about what happened on the trail when, ahem, nature called. We were questioning initially how that would work as well. Suffice to say there is not a single porta-potty on the Inca Trial: never was, ain't now and probably never will be. So we were to just go whenever we needed to, i.e., scoot behind a big rock, or a copse of trees, or right out in the open if you are not bashful. Guys admittedly have an easier time here: we just whip that thing out, hose down the area, shake and dance, then tuck 'er back in. The women, on the other hand, tended to work together as a team, helping and covering for each other. Toilet paper was gathered up in plastic bags and disposed of properly at the end of each day. None of us liked the idea of contributing to pollution along the trail, but when you saw a horse turd the size of a basketball just about every 25 paces on the path, and expended a great deal of energy trying to sidestep these steaming landmines, you realized that the Inca Trail had been a repository for animal and human waste for a damn long time – when I asked Manny when the trail had first been built, he said "No one knows for sure – maybe as long as 5,000 years ago." So that's five millennia of poopoo and pipi (as the Peruvians call it), all along the ancient pathway.

On New Year's Eve, we continued our descent as the temperature warmed and the landscape became increasingly more verdant. We had a shorter walk this day, around three or four hours, down to the Collpapampa

Valley. First, we would be in the cloud forest and then, finally, reach the rainforest, where flowers abounded and swarms of butterflies fluttered to and fro. The Collpa Lodge sits on a promontory at the confluence of three rivers. When we arrived, the cook and his staff were in the process of preparing a pachampa-style lunch. Basically, they threw a whole bunch of beef, pork, chicken, cuy (guinea pig), potatoes and more on to a pile of piping hot stones; they covered everything with wet cardboard and blankets, and then let it slow-cook all afternoon. The results were superb. The guinea pig was good – hard to pin down in terms of comparable flavor, tender but with not much meat on the little fella. Some of the group thought it tasted like a chicken/pork combo. I thought it was closer to beef-like. Peruvians raise guinea pigs like pets, but expressly for eating; my understanding is they don't get too attached to these animals ("kids, whatever you do, don't give the cuy a name.") For the first time, we drank a Peruvian wine, a 2016 cab and syrah blend called *Intipalka*. I had over the years come to the mistaken belief that, in South America, only the Argentinians and Chileans truly knew how to make high-quality wines. I was pleasantly proven a dumb ass, once again - the Peruvian wine was great.

⟵————⟶

That evening, before our dinner and New Year's Eve celebration, Manny and Hazel each delivered a brief, informal talk on certain aspects of Inca culture and history, and on Peru in general. When they were done, Manny opened it up to any questions we might have. I had heard him say earlier in the trip, "Our Mother Earth is ill." I asked him to talk about that comment, the effect of global warming on Peru and, specifically, about the status of the Peruvian rainforest, the lush green majesty of which we had just experienced earlier that day. His response was really interesting. Later on, several members of the group told me that they thought he was evading my question, and I thought so too at first. But I had decided, instead of interrupting and insisting that he get to the point like an obnoxious science- and data-driven American, to listen carefully to what he was saying. He is obviously a thoughtful guy who takes the long view of things. He talked about the fact that the Earth has always had problems; there have always been droughts, fires, floods. And the

Earth has always healed itself and survived, he said. He explained the very spiritual connection that most Peruvians have to the Earth, especially those who live in the country, in the mountains, in the rainforest. They are deeply connected to the Earth in a way that the typical American – myself included – does not well understand. They are deeply connected to the Earth because they have to be; their very survival depends upon it. And so, in taking the long view, the spiritual view, it seems that Manny believes that the Earth will survive. I did take note that he never asserted that the human race will survive. He didn't mention it, but there have been mass extinctions, too.

On the issue of the rainforest, he bluntly acknowledged that it is being dangerously and steadily depleted. He talked about seekers of gold, other mining interests, agriculture, and coca harvesting ("Cocaine is a huge business in Peru," he said, stating the obvious.) And the government is not doing much to help. This situation is serious not just for the Amazon rainforests of Peru and other South American countries, but for all of us. The Earth's tree canopy is essential to our global well-being. The very act of removing trees contributes to global warming. Trees extract carbon dioxide from the air and store it in their wood, and in the soil. When a tree is cut down or burned, that carbon dioxide is released back into the atmosphere, thus contributing to the greenhouse gas effect. Some experts believe that deforestation creates as much as ten percent per year of the total of harmful emissions. In 2017, 39 million acres – an area about the size of Bangladesh - of tropical forests were lost to deforestation, according to Global Forest Watch, a unit of the environmental organization called the World Resources Institute. The only year that has been worse for loss of acreage: 2016. To be sure, forests replenish themselves too, and that must be taken into account in evaluating the overall picture of tree health. But a number of studies have confirmed that tropical forests around the world are generally shrinking, with net losses exceeding new growth. As always, our problems are interconnected. With increasing drought comes greater risk of fires burning uncontrollably. In 2017, Brazilian farmers and ranchers who were attempting to clear rainforest for farmland set fires that raged out of control. Three million acres of trees were lost. And so it goes, and we do not learn.

Never have pancakes tasted so good, we all agreed. For the first and only time in 12 days, we were treated to light, thin, buttery, syrupy pancakes for breakfast. As many as we could eat; stacks of cakes. (The next day, at the next lodge, one of the women asked if they would be serving pancakes in the morning; when she was told no, she almost cried.) Our bellies full, we started out on the first day of the new year by continuing downhill – we would lose another 2,400 feet in elevation that day - into the Santa Teresa River Valley. We saw more signs of population there, and also lots of poverty. It was sad to see obviously hard-working families struggling just to get by day-to-day. We were deep in the rainforest now. A somewhat mangy, light-golden mutt named Ringo followed us the whole way, mostly looking for food scraps, I think. We passed abundant tropical fruit orchards, one of which Manny identified as featuring passion fruit. There were coffee plantations that smelled wonderful. It was all somehow indescribably invigorating. My wife the horticulturalist, who I argue playfully is trying to "save the world one tree at a time," has always told me that there are real human health benefits from spending time in the outdoors and, more specifically, in the forest. I asked her how that was so. She explained that trees emit airborne chemicals called phytoncides that protect them from insects. These are antibacterial and antifungal chemicals, and when humans breathe them in, our bodies respond by increasing white blood cells, which is of course a good thing. In addition to benefits for the immune system, studies have also shown that strolling through the forest can lower blood pressure, reduce stress, increase energy and improve sleep. Amazing! If only more people knew, they might get off their asses to take advantage of nature's free-of-charge, built-in health and fitness center in the woods.

After a five-hour hike and a 30-minute bus ride, we arrived at the Lucma Lodge early in the afternoon, got cleaned up, and took a tour of a nearby coffee plantation, called Café Viamonte. We had a fascinating interaction with the owners and learned a lot more than I ever knew about the elaborate process of producing a good cup of coffee, which we all take for granted. Man, those folks like their coffee strong. The weather was now temperate enough that Faith and some of the other women sat in the hot tub that evening before dinner.

The next morning she noticed several bug bites on her body, including an inflamed, painful bite right on her bottom (left cheek, to be specific). She actually suspected she may have sustained that bite not while hot-tubbing but rather out on the trail, when she was vulnerable as she relieved herself. In any event, this itchy, inflamed bite "bugged" her for the rest of the trip. It became a bit of a running joke. Before dinner the next evening, one the guys sat down with his cocktail and asked, "So Faith, how's your butt?" Instead of punching him in the face, I, like everyone else, just turned my head in her direction to await her response. *Yeah Faith, how is your butt?* Inquiring minds wanted to know. She was okay, she said, and we quickly moved on to the next topic.

Faith always tells me that I should live my life with "loving kindness," and give people the benefit of the doubt in all situations. Try to see things from another person's point of view, she tells me. Do unto others, she says. Be Zen, she recommends. I strive mightily to achieve this standard but, let's face it, when you meet a complete yahoo, and you have to spend 10 days with him (and it is virtually always a 'him'), well, it's tough. I mean, let's just call a spade a spade: he's a yahoo, okay? I don't want to dwell on this point or be mean-spirited, but there is always one in every group, isn't there? This is typically an older white male, perhaps affluent, bordering on narcissistic, might be educated but who is still not terribly bright, who always figures out a way to direct every piece of conversation back to some insanely boring anecdote about himself. Having absolutely no interest in others, and being slow on the uptake, he only knows one topic: "This happened to me..." or "I experienced that..." This guy frequently has a loud, grating voice to go with his other charms. Couple this trait with diarrhea of the mouth, i.e., the lack of any normal conversational sense of when to shut up, and it becomes problematic for the rest of the group. We had one on Kilimanjaro. We had one in Australia. And, by golly, we had one in Peru. Let's call him Gary. My mission simply became to avoid Gary; avoid Gary on the trail; avoid Gary during cocktail hour; good God, don't sit near Gary at dinner or lunch or breakfast, either. Gary reminded me of the guy on Kilimanjaro with the loose, windy bowels, "Sir Farts-a-Lot," who I similarly endeavored to avoid. Both men had lots of hot, stinky gas continually spewing from an orifice and they were, as I've said emphatically, to be avoided. So I avoided them, and everything worked out fine. 'Nuff said on this subject.

Next day was our final trek. We began with a steady, 1,900-foot ascent that lasted about five hours. We lunched on lentils, rice, and savory fresh trout at a place called Llactapata Pass, with spectacular views, finally, of the city of Machu Picchu in the far distance. We saw some ruins which, like Machu Picchu, had been found and brought to the attention of the world by Hiram Bingham. What followed was by far our steepest and most perilous descent. We would go down, down, down, 3,100 feet in three hours. The night before, in recalling the pain of my lost toenails on Kilimanjaro, both Faith and I filed our nails to the nub. In the morning, we put on an extra pair of socks and cinched up the bootlaces just a tad tighter than normal. This was a jarring, slippery hike with lots of switchbacks. It was torture on the quads and the knees. For the first and only time on the trek, I fell. I just sort of slowly lost my footing and keeled over to the right – fortunately not over the precipice - with no harm done (Faith never did fall once – she is a sure-footed lady.)

We had been warned by our guides in the later stages of the trek to be extremely wary of vipers. These are incredibly venomous snakes found in many parts of the world. In South America, the subfamily is known as Crotalinae, commonly called pit vipers or pit adders. Manny had actually hired some courageous local guys with machetes to move ahead of us on the march and keep an eye out for vipers. Manny had even seen them at Machu Picchu itself – he said that on one of the trips he guided, a woman leaned up against a wall at Machu Picchu and a viper, coiled and hidden in a gap in the granite, bit her on the arm. That story got our attention. We only saw one viper; he was dark golden in color with beautiful, staggered black stripes. He was probably not more than one foot in length, and was fairly recently dead. His head had been lopped off by some alert, machete-wielding cowboy on the trail. We proceeded on through bamboo forests and the usual diverse mountain terrain, all the way down to the brown, thunderously rushing Urabamba River. We had finished the hike, and felt a genuine sense of accomplishment. The Inca Trail itself is 26 miles; one of our group members calculated that we had probably walked a total of 40 miles over six days. High-fives were delivered all around. Now it was time to board a train for the half-hour ride to the village of Aguas Calientes, our final staging area prior to Machu Picchu.

My opening journal entry for Thursday the 3rd reads simply: "Machu Picchu!" The words translate as "old mountain" in Quechuan. It is surreal to actually be there. It is the iconic, mystical symbol of Peru, and undoubtedly one of the most significant archaeological sites in the world. It is a place made all the more intriguing because its history is so very much shrouded in mystery. Scholars believe that at its height, there were perhaps 200 dwellings with 1,000 residents. We know that the agricultural terraces were cultivated and abounded in the food the population needed to survive. We know that Machu Picchu's elevated position provided a commanding view and strategic defense, but was it constructed to be a military fortress or a warrior enclave? Probably not. Was it built during the time of the Emperor Pachacutec, in the 1400s? Probably. Was it a trading hub and transit station for agricultural or other products? Perhaps. Was it a religious center? Perhaps. Was it Pachacutec's country estate, a palace in effect serving as his "Camp David"? Perhaps. Was it occupied when the Spanish arrived in 1532? We don't know. Why was it abandoned? Was it a lack of water? Disease? The death of Pachacutec? We don't know for sure. And so on and so forth.

If you hate crowds, please don't go to Machu Picchu. The Inca Trail itself was not terribly crowded during our trek (there were several instances where I actually found myself quite alone, out of sight of any other person, for at least a few minutes on the Inca Trail – it was kind of neat) at least until we got closer to the end. But Manny told us that as many as 3,000-4,000 tourists a day jam into Machu Picchu during the high season. It's a big moneymaker for the Peruvian government. At about sixty American bucks a pop for admission, the Interior Ministry can make close to a quarter million dollars a day on this venture. So cram the people in they do.

But we made the best of it – we had come all this way, after all. We showed our passports and had our tickets stamped on the way in; on the way out, we stopped at a way station and stamped our passports with the "seal of Machu Picchu." As I think back on our visit, it is something of a jumble; the place is like a mosaic, and it is hard to get a handle on exactly where you are standing and what you are seeing at any given time. There are no explanatory plaques anywhere. The first buildings we saw as we came through the main gate were storage structures, designed to hold the crops that were produced on the endless terraces. These terraces were also designed to minimize erosion, and llamas gently graze there to this day. We meandered up to the Sun Gate, which was once the official – and only - entryway to the site, from the Inca Trail. Down below, there is a guardhouse, which I guess makes Machu Picchu the original gated community. The Temple of the Sun is a marvelous example of stone construction. Manny explained that in June, at the winter solstice in the Southern Hemisphere, the sunlight shines through a small window at the Temple of the Sun and precisely hits a flat granite stone that is presumed to be an Inca calendar. The Incas were keen astronomers, and highly in tune with the movements of the sun, the moon, and other heavenly bodies.

There are three primary sections to the city: the Sacred District, the Popular District, and the District of Priests and Nobility. We toured them all and marveled at the fountains, the palaces and the temples. There is an expansive, grassy common area. Once again, we stood in awe of the Incas as designers, architects and builders. As always, their stone construction fitted together perfectly. We noticed that the windows at Machu Picchu are not rectangular but rather trapezoidal – this gave the structures additional strength and allowed them to withstand the tremors of earthquakes, which these buildings have successfully done for 500 years. The historian in me tried to imagine in my mind's eye what the place looked like in its heyday. How was it built? How did the workers, without the benefit of the wheel or draft animals, move these enormous, heavy stones into position, perfectly placed? What did the people look like? What did they do all day? Were there children running about? What happened to them all, in the end? Fun questions to think about and speculate upon. But it's also nice to know that there are some answers that we shall never ascertain for sure; that fact keeps the study of history forever interesting.

Boy did we get sick when we got home. Holy cow. Faith had at the very end of the trip while still in Peru felt a touch of an upset stomach. She took the course of antibiotics my doctor had prescribed, Zithromax, and she felt better right away. We landed in the Twin Cities on a Sunday, felt tired but pretty good, and went about our business normally until late Thursday and into Friday. And then we both started feeling really weird; more specifically, we felt really bad. Flu symptoms: achy all over, chills, upset stomach, a spot of Montezuma's Revenge, no appetite, can't sleep, yada yada. On Saturday evening, we went to urgent care together. As we sat there in the examination room waiting for the doctor, wearing the surgical masks they had asked us to strap on at the front desk, I turned to her and said, "This is by far the most romantic Saturday evening we have ever spent together in almost 34 years." She agreed. The doc wasn't too worried. Said we picked up a nasty food or water-borne bug in Peru and brought it home. "These things typically take 4-14 days to gestate after you get home and then, Wham! You are sick." He was reluctant to prescribe more antibiotics, which kill the good gut bacteria as well as the bad. He told us that hydration was the most important key to recovery, so over the next few days we drank as much water as possible. He also recommended probiotics, which advice we ignored – Faith had read that probiotics really don't do much; better to just eat real, complex foods that contribute to a healthy biome. Bottom line was we were simply going to have to "gut" it out. For the next 48 hours, with Faith mostly on the mend, I was as sick as I'd been in a decade. Flat on my back. Could barely lift a bottle of water to my lips. Don't you hate when that happens?

This whole unpleasant final chapter did not diminish the epic magnitude of our adventure, or in any way taint our memory of Peru as a beautiful, mysterious place that we would always remember fondly. We want to go back to South America – maybe to trek Patagonia someday? We'll see. But the journey did, no doubt, cause us to appreciate all the more the simple things most of us do have here in America, and that we take so for granted: clean food and water; toilets that you can throw toilet paper into; generally sanitary conditions in most places, most of the time; excellent health care for those who can afford it; generally high standards of living. We are not perfect, but we are pretty lucky. One of the many reasons I love to travel is because I gain not only perspectives on new places, but a fresh point of view on familiar ones as well.

CHAPTER SIXTEEN

THE LAST BEST PLACE

MONTANA

"I'm in love with Montana. For other states I have admiration, respect, recognition, even some affection. But with Montana it is love. And it's difficult to analyze love when you are in it."

— JOHN STEINBECK, FROM
TRAVELS WITH CHARLIE: IN SEARCH OF AMERICA —

On June 27, 1805, Army Captain Meriwether Lewis – co-leader along with William Clark of the fabled Lewis and Clark Expedition – and the members of his Corps of Discovery paddled in their dugout canoes with great exertion against the powerful current of the Missouri River, in the western reaches of what is modern-day Montana. At around 9:00 a.m., the explorers rounded a bend and Lewis observed a junction with a river from the southeast. A short distance later two more rivers, a southwest fork and a middle fork, came together to form what was known as the Three Forks. Lewis named the southeast fork the Gallatin River, in honor of Secretary of the Treasury Albert Gallatin. The middle fork Lewis identified as the Madison River, after Secretary of State James Madison (more on the Madison River later.) The southwest fork, the river that Lewis and Clark knew they would need to take in continuation of their journey to the continental divide, Lewis called the Jefferson River, "... in honor of that illustrious personage Thomas Jefferson President of the United States."

It was Jefferson who had commissioned a mission of discovery across the unknown expanses of the newly acquired Louisiana Territory, with a goal of traveling all the way over the continental divide at the Rocky Mountains to the Pacific Ocean, and then back home again. Jefferson articulated his long-held vision when he wrote, "[I]t is impossible not to look forward to distant times, when our own rapid multiplication will expand itself beyond those limits and cover the whole... continent, with a people speaking the same language, governed in similar forms by similar laws." The president tasked Lewis and Clark with mapping the terrain they would cover, cataloguing the flora and fauna that they would see along the way, and initiating peaceful contact with any native tribes that they might encounter. More importantly, the expedition had a commercial purpose. It had been a common assumption for centuries, since the days of Christopher Columbus, that there must exist a great waterway across the North American continent that would connect the Atlantic to the Pacific Ocean. The discovery of the fabled Northwest Passage would enable commerce to flow unhindered from sea to sea. Control of this all-water route would confer great power and wealth; and so the 30-plus members of the Corps of Discovery embarked on an epic quest in the spring of 1804, knowing full well the import of their primary objective.

Two weeks after the Corps continued on its way from the Three Forks, came a momentous event. On the morning of August 12, Lewis and a small party arrived at the headwaters of the Missouri River, at that point just a meandering stream ascending a gentle slope at the eastern base of the Rocky Mountains. Lewis wrote in his journal, "Thus far I had accomplished one of those great objects on which my mind has been unalterably fixed for many years, judge then of the pleasure I felt in allying my thirst with this pure and ice cold water." The men rejoiced: "Two miles below McNeal had exultantly stood with a foot on each side of this little rivulet and thanked his god that he had lived to bestride the mighty & heretofore deemed endless Missouri." It remained only for Lewis to saunter up the short distance to the continental divide (a place now called Lehmi Pass, on today's Montana-Idaho border) and look down to see, if not the long-sought waterway directly to the Pacific Ocean, then at least an easy portage leading to that waterway, their conduit to the Pacific. Finally, intense curiosity about the nature of the Rocky Mountains and the location of the mystical Northwest Passage would be satisfied.

But when Lewis reached the crest and peered off into the distance, the only thing that he observed was more mountains, and more mountains, and more mountains, for as far as the eye could see. The dream of centuries, shattered in a single instant; the expedition had a long way yet to go to reach the Pacific. And then they would have to turn about and return all the way home. Lewis may have strongly considered curling up in the fetal position and sucking his thumb, discouraged to no end that his beloved and revered mentor, Thomas Jefferson, would be sorely disappointed with this outcome. If that is how Lewis felt, however, we will never know, for in his journal he simply and blandly reflected, "After refreshing ourselves we proceeded on to the top of the dividing ridge from which I discovered immence [sic] ranges of high mountains still to the west of us with their tips partially covered with snow..." Nevertheless, whether Lewis acknowledged it or not, it was at this precise moment that, to paraphrase historian John Logan Allen, "The geography of hope had given way to the geography of reality."

⬅━━━━➡

I believe that I can safely say I love Montana just as much as John Steinbeck did. It is truly one of my favorite places in the continental United States. My first recollections are from family auto trips that we took when I was a kid, driving across the seemingly never-ending length of Montana on our way from Minnesota to the west coast. Even then I recognized that this place looked like no other I had ever seen; it was spectacular – the sky really was big. When our own two girls were young, we drove to Montana and visited the Custer battlefield, among other places. Over the years, I was in the habit of trying to expose Anna and Lucia to historic venues. We had been to Gettysburg, of course, but also to George Washington's Mount Vernon, where Washington and his family members are buried there in a plot on the banks of the Potomac River, and Jefferson's Monticello, where there is also a small family cemetery; the great Jefferson lies in rest there. After all this, one year, I announced, "Girls, we're going on the road again as a family." To my great surprise, they practically wept as they responded, "Please, dad, not another dead-guy trip." They pleaded with me.

"Dead-guy trip? You mean you don't like the history vacations?"

"No dad. Everyone is dead, graves and cemeteries everywhere. They're all dead."

"Hmmm, I see. Well, where would you like to go instead?"

"Disney World, dad," they replied in unison, finally out of their funk and realizing they had a chance.

"Disney World?"

"Yes. Please dad."

"Well, you know darn well that Walt Disney is a dead guy. Has been for a long time."

"It's not the same, dad. It's just not the same. Please." Oh, the wailing and gnashing of teeth. They were pathetic.

So we went to Walt Disney World. Three years in a row. Hey, the Yacht and Beach Club is heavenly. So is the Grand Floridian. And the Animal Kingdom Lodge. Plus the food is good, and I like the rides just as much as the kids do. And believe it or not, both of my daughters, adults now and childhood trauma aside, have an interest in history. There you go. Compromise is the key. It all worked out in the end.

In the spirit of young daughters saying funny things, and related to the topic of fishing which I will cover in more detail in a bit, one of my favorite writers, Thomas McGuane, who is a Montana resident and avid fisherman, tells this story in his book, *The Longest Silence: A Life In Fishing*: "Recently, and among people we didn't know well, my eleven-year-old daughter said something that made jaws drop. Having heard the phrase 'the F-word,' possibly from a potty-mouthed sibling, and assuming in our house that it meant fishing, she told a group of guests, 'All my dad cares about is the F-word.' In the astonished silence that followed this showstopper, she added, 'When he's not doing it, he's reading about it.'"

Kids do say the darndest things.

←——————→

I have hunted, fished and otherwise recreated in Montana many times through the years, but this state that some refer to as The Last Best Place also became important to me professionally, in 2007. It was in that year that I led my first

Blue Knight seminar, at the former Custer Battlefield, site of the infamous Custer's Last Stand, and now known as the Little Bighorn Battlefield National Monument. The field is located on a massive Crow Indian reservation, about an hour southeast of Billings off of Interstate 90 and just a couple of miles south of the tiny town of Crow Agency. The basic storyline is familiar to most people: on June 25, 1876 Lieutenant Colonel George Armstrong Custer led his Seventh U.S. Cavalry, about 660 strong, in pursuit of a body of many thousands of Lakota Sioux and Northern Cheyenne Indians, under the leadership of the charismatic holy man, Sitting Bull. The Indians were encamped beside the Little Bighorn River, which they knew as the Greasy Grass. Custer's horsemen approached the village and he famously split his forces not one; not two; not three; but four ways, in an attempt to outflank and surround the village, capturing its inhabitants in the process. He felt he needed to accomplish this quickly, or else the Indians would escape and scatter as they had always done - in Custer's experience - in the past. What the one who the Indians knew as Son of the Morning Star did not reckon upon was that, this time, the angry Sioux and Cheyenne nations, about 1,500 warriors strong, would stand and fight him, and ferociously so. Custer and every single soldier in his immediate command, 210 troops, were wiped out to a man, many of them breathing their last on a spare, lonely knoll now called Last Stand Hill. Custer, two of his brothers, a brother-in-law and a nephew all lost their lives.

White America was shocked. How could the mighty Custer and his superb cavalry have been destroyed by an undisciplined band of savages? The reaction was akin to our own modern-day horror, revulsion and anger over the 9/11 attacks; as with the terrorist attacks, the response included a collective bloodlust for revenge. Ultimately, while the Battle of the Little Bighorn represented the greatest victory ever by Plains Indians over white soldiers, the event tragically foreshadowed the ultimate end of the Indian way of life. It is also deeply unfortunate that, until very recently, the battle has been interpreted in a skewed way at the actual site: the story mostly featured Custer the heroic and his beleaguered command versus merciless, faceless Indians who were determined to stop white progress, to deny western expansion, and to obstruct our realization of the dream of Manifest Destiny. The fact is that it was the Indians who were fighting to defend their homes and territory, as well as the way of life that they had known for thousands of years. In his superb and incredibly sad masterpiece, *Bury My Heart at Wounded Knee*, author Dee Brown says, "The Indians knew that life was equated with the earth and its resources, that America was a paradise, and they could not comprehend why the intruders from the East were determined to destroy all that was Indian as well as America itself." I always ask my teams at the end of our Little Bighorn experience: Who was fighting for freedom here?

It was only in this century, in 2003, that a monument acknowledging Indian bravery and resilience finally appeared on the battlefield. It is constructed in a circular form, cut deep into the earth, and open to the sky. An interpretive "living memorial" wall occupies the inner sanctum. The wall uses texts, quotations and pictographs to tell the Indian side of the story. A large bronze tracing of three Indian warriors on horseback and an Indian woman on foot stands forever silhouetted against the harsh Montana landscape and the awesome, endless horizon. It is called the Indian Memorial. It was designed to express a theme of "Peace Through Unity," and to celebrate and honor the memory of the Indian men, women and children who took part in the battle. Hopefully, on some level at least, this awe-inspiring monument serves to rectify the imbalance over the years in the portrayal of the Indian role and sacrifice on the banks of the Greasy Grass River.

I have taken many teams over this battleground since 2007. The event is structured in much the same way as the Gettysburg seminar, and we focus on many of the same leadership dimensions: common purpose, relationships and trust, communication, decision making, and so on; most of those principles were obviously lacking in Custer's command. The Little Bighorn experience is different from Gettysburg, however, in several key ways. First, while the Gettysburg National Battlefield Park is highly developed and commercialized, although the Park Service is hard at work trying to restore the field to its 1863 appearance, the Little Bighorn battle site remains quite pristine. There are many places on the field where, if one looks off into the distance, it could surely be 1876 again. No roads, no power lines, no KFC restaurants. One can much more easily go back in time, at least in the mind's eye, at the Little Bighorn. Second, at Gettysburg, all of the grave markers are contained within the National Cemetery. In contrast, at the Little Bighorn, there are white marble markers and red granite markers all over the field, to depict the approximate places where soldiers and Indians, respectively, fell in the battle. No one is actually buried beneath an individual marker; the dead on both sides were removed from the field, the Indians right away and the soldier bodies later, to be reinterred elsewhere. Most of the enlisted cavalrymen who died are buried in a mass grave underneath a monument on Last Stand Hill; Custer is buried at the U.S Military Academy, his alma mater, at West Point, New York. In the case of the white markers, one can see the chaotic disbursement and the frantic pattern of soldier movement from the southern end of the field to Last Stand Hill, where it all ended, to the north. Last Stand Hill is covered with markers, all of them white. Finally, although the Civil War certainly represented a clash of cultures to some extent, the Plains Indian Wars are much more concretely an example of the tragedy that can unfold when people of vastly different races and cultures fail to make any effort whatsoever to understand one another and, as a result, can only see their way to destroying each other. Out of irreconcilable conceptions of land ownership, broken promises, profound mutual lack of trust, and deep hatred and cruelty perpetrated by both races, the whole sad story could only come to a violent and heartbreaking conclusion. In the end, the overwhelming white onslaught from the East won out. Ironically, it was soldiers of the Seventh Cavalry Regiment, in December, 1890, shooting rapid-fire Hotchkiss guns, who murdered more than 150 Lakota Sioux Indian men, women and children, in South Dakota, at the notorious Wounded Knee Massacre. The Indian Wars were over, but the quiet desperation of many Native American people in the United States goes on.

◆——————▶

In the spring of 2009, I got a call from a fellow named Jack Uldrich. Jack is a futurist and a prolific author who makes his living primarily as a keynote speaker for corporate groups. He does not predict exactly what will happen in the future; he is the first one to acknowledge that no one knows the future. What he does do, very effectively, is explain to people that the pace of technological change is rapid, much more so than they think, and that their organizations need to adapt accordingly or be left hopelessly behind. His keynote – with lots of data and real-life examples to back up his arguments - frequently scares the shit out of his audiences. Sometimes, companies actually do change their policies, research and development focus, level of investment in technology, and so on, as a result of hearing his message. Jack had seen an article about Blue Knight in a local business publication and wanted to talk to me about possibly collaborating on a Lewis & Clark-themed historical seminar. Several years earlier, Jack had published a book on the leadership principles from the Corps of Discovery, called *Into the Unknown: Leadership Lessons from Lewis & Clark's Daring Westward Expedition*.

Jack and I have a lot in common: both Minnesota boys; both former military officers (he was in naval intelligence, which I tell him is an oxymoron, like "jumbo shrimp"); both with master's degrees in public administration; both fascinated by history and politics; both obsessive readers and writers; both like to have a cocktail or two, eat a steak dinner and, only occasionally, smoke a good cigar; both like to talk smack and tease each other endlessly: He makes fun of the Marine Corps, implies that Marines aren't very bright, but then I tell him the Navy exists only to give Marines a ride when we go off to fight and win America's wars somewhere far away. In short, Jack Uldrich is good people, and we immediately hit it off.

It took us a while, but we did finally develop a program which we launched in 2012, out of Great Falls, Montana, and have repeated many times since then. The saga of Lewis & Clark represents, to me, the American version of Homer's *Odyssey*. It really is an amazing story; if it were fiction it would not be believable. From 1804 to 1806, over the course of 863 days, the Corps of Discovery traveled 8,000 miles to the Pacific Ocean and back again. They mapped the unknown territory and documented everything they saw and did in a detailed, well-written set of journals that are still compelling, even riveting reading to this day. They encountered, peacefully and with the help of the young Shoshone woman, Sacajawea (Jack and I vehemently disagree on the correct pronunciation of her name; you should hear us go back and forth; I am quite sure that I am right and he is wrong), more than 70 Native American tribes. They had only one deadly run-in, when they killed two young Blackfeet warriors who were trying to steal weapons and horses, late in the journey on the way home. They lost just one man along the way, who died of what is believed to have been a burst appendix. The best doctor of the day could not have saved him. They returned home heroes, and would forever pass into legend as among the greatest of world explorers. The journey of Lewis & Clark was the 19th century equivalent of landing a man on the moon.

Our leadership experience focuses on important principles, so clearly demonstrated by Lewis & Clark, like having a higher calling and a common purpose; strategic preparation and venturing into the unknown; shared leadership; the importance of diversity; leading from the front; and leaving a lasting legacy, among many other lessons. Our teams respond well, and we have had a lot of fun. Jack is an esteemed professional colleague, a good friend, and one of the few truly brilliant people I've ever had the honor to work with in my long career. I can say all these nice things about him knowing that they won't go to his head, for the simple reason that I'm pretty sure he never reads my books, so I wouldn't expect that he'll be reading this one. I shouldn't be too critical; I think I have only read two of his current output of 11 books, and one of those, the one about Lewis & Clark, I had to read.

One other thing that Jack and I have in common is a love of fly fishing. On a number of occasions and in lots of different conditions, we have had the chance to troll the mighty Missouri River for trout.

⟵——————⟶

In July of 2016, Jack and I fished with a guide starting at a place called Holter's Dam, near the town of Cascade and just north of a winding stretch of the Missouri river that passes through majestic granite cliffs on either side. When Meriwether Lewis paddled through this place in the summer of 1805, he labeled it "The Gates of the Rocky Mountains." It was a tough day on the water for us, all in all. We settled in upstream at 8:30 a.m. and, over the course of probably five hours, floated seven miles with our guide manning the paddles as Jack and I stood up, braced in at the front and the back of the boat, and threw our lines in the river. The weather began cold - around 50 degrees - and rainy; we were bundled up in extra-warm, all-weather gear. But soon the rain stopped, the clouds dispersed, and the day got hot. We peeled off layers. The one constant was the wind, however, which made controlling the boat a challenge for our guide, and casting extremely difficult for the two fishermen, neither of whom is an expert caster. In addition, our guide was a bit of a hardass. He was sarcastic, not much of a teacher and, frankly, his approach made the experience quite a bit more stressful than it needed to be. We were ready to kill him by lunchtime. At one point, after I had snagged the man with my fishhook - inadvertently of course, but I'm not sure what Freud would say - for the second time in 10 minutes, he gave me a timeout and put me into what he called the "penalty box". I just had to sit there and was not allowed to cast again until I had gathered myself. No wonder he was crabby. While I sat in the penalty box with nothing to do, however, I asked him what he thought about climate change. After a long pause, he said quietly, "We are goofing up the earth." Despite it all, we reeled in four nice fish; we can prove that we caught at least two, because there are photos. One was a 19" brown trout, the other a 21" rainbow. Gorgeous creatures. We released them back into the river to live and fight another day.

In the fall of 2017, we had another guide and a better time, despite not catching a single fish. This guy was real mellow. He probably had smoked his fair share of doobies in his younger years; maybe even had one earlier that day. He was an excellent instructor, patient, and he encouraged rather than berated us. We practiced casting first, then got underway on another float down the Mighty Mo. But the day was especially cold and the fish just were not biting. So as we slowly drifted, the guide spent time simply talking to us about fly fishing, and the river. He knew a lot.

Here are a few of the things I have learned in the past several years about fly fishing, from books and magazines, guides, and many hours spent on the river: Fly rods come in a staggering array of types. They can be made from many kinds of materials such as hardwood, bamboo, graphite, carbon fiber, boron, and so forth. The fundamental purpose of any fly rod is to enable the fisherman to propel the attached fly forward with accuracy and touch. Rods range in length anywhere from four to 18 feet. A fly rod is essentially a lever, and a longer rod simply allows for greater mechanical advantage in casting. Typically, a nine-foot rod is a great choice.

Fishermen also talk about the 'action' of a rod, referring to where and how a rod bends under a load. A fast-action rod bends in the upper third, a moderate-action rod in the middle, and slow action bends the entire rod, from butt to tip. If one uses the wrong action, the ability to cast and present the fly properly, feel a strike, set the hook, and play a fish may be hindered. Given that, fast-action rods are typically preferable to slower action for most scenarios. Faster action provides greater sensitivity to vibrations and a quicker, more forcible strike. In short, power can be sent to the hook more rapidly. Finally, fast-action rods are more forgiving of casting mistakes. Beginners tend not to let the line fully extend on the back and the forward cast. A fast-action rod helps compensate for this flaw.

There is also the critical matter of the type of line to be used. Matching the wrong line with the wrong rod is a fly-fishing sin. Fly lines used to be made of braided silk, but these days are made of extruded, or shaped, plastic. Most fly lines are tapered to be wider at some points and narrower at others. The leader is a length - usually nine to 12 feet for river fishing - of tapered monofilament attached to the end of the fly line which transmits the energy of the cast from line to fly. The tippet is a shorter piece of level monofilament, one end attached to the thin end of the leader and the other end, finally, to the fly. This setup allows for the greatest ease and effectiveness in casting. The first 30 feet of a fly line is weighed and a number assigned to it; the greater the numeric designation, the heavier the line. This standardization of ratings allows the correct line to be used with the right rod. Fly rods are marked with a number stating the precise weight line to be used. In the end, exact configuration depends on the type of fishing one intends to do. Lines also come in different colors. Experts argue whether brightly colored and highly visible is best, or if dark and drab works better. Some people assert they know what colors a trout sees. Probably doubtful. Whatever the trout sees, for surface fishing with a long leader, color doesn't matter so much because only the leader and the fly hover over the fish. For fishing beneath the surface, with shorter leaders and the line closer to the fish, a drab color is probably preferred.

As for the all-important fly, there are four basic types. Dry flies float on the water and entice fish that are feeding at the surface. Streamers come in a variety of sizes, shapes, and colors. They are made to imitate creatures like minnows, frogs, crayfish, etc. Nymphs look like the insects and other small creatures that inhabit lakes and rivers. Some, like caddis flies, midges or mayflies, imitate the undeveloped forms of flying insects that hatch underwater. Other tiny crustaceans such as scuds, sow bugs, and crayfish never leave the water at all, and they are a favorite food of trout. Finally, terrestrials look like the insects that sometimes fall into a river such as grasshoppers, ants and crickets.

Fly casting is one of those physical activities, like tennis or golf, where the basic motion looks easy, and in fact is easy. It can be learned quickly, but the technique required to be a truly accomplished, accurate and deft fly-caster can take years to develop. The most frequently used cast, the overhead, involves using the forearm as a lever, lifting the rod just past vertical as the line leaves the water. Then begins the so-called power stroke, where the fisherman accelerates the upward movement of the rod, applies a little wrist snap, then stops and waits for the line to straighten out behind him. The forward cast then commences, with a similar kind of acceleration and stop, allowing the line to travel forward. The tip of the rod is lowered and additional line can be released by hand to achieve better distance as the line unfurls into the water ahead.

I have a business client who tells a hilarious story about fishing the Bighorn River with his wife, a novice; she made the backward power stroke and her fly landed in the water behind her; before she could begin her forward motion, a fish took the fly; she threw the whole thing forward, awkwardly, with a trout attached; she turned to her husband and said, "Well, I don't know what all the fuss is about, that wasn't hard at all." Remember Brad Pitt - or, more likely, his stand-in – fly casting in the movie, *A River Runs Through It*? It was a thing of beauty to behold. Poetry in motion.

At the end of our time on the water that day, we had been shut out, but that was of no consequence. The scenery was exquisite, the river peaceful, the company congenial, and we had learned a lot. I was reminded of a quote by Robert Traver, from his book *Trout Madness*: "Trout do not lie or cheat and cannot be bought or bribed or impressed by power, but respond only to quietude and humility and endless patience." I also love a quote I came upon by a Montana fishing guide named Miles Nolte. He said, "Rivers have histories, and histories are stories, and we create stories to weave the chaos of existence into some semblance of order. Rivers, like the stories we make of them, aren't static. No matter how often we return to our favorite bends or boulders, it's always different water."

◄————————►

There are many stories associated with the Madison River. In some ways, these stories about the efforts of mostly concerned and well-meaning agencies and citizens to manage the Madison over the past several decades serve as a microcosm of the even longer, sometimes not very successful history of ongoing human attempts to manipulate aquatic systems in Montana. In the end, it seems, the lesson is simply that Mother Nature is frequently best left alone.

In the late 1800s and into the 20th century, recreational fly fishing became increasingly more popular throughout Montana and other locations in the American West. A movement came into being that promoted what were perceived to be more attractive, albeit non-native trout species - rainbow, brown and brook - over uglier, native species that some people called "coarse" fish, such as cutthroat trout, bull trout and fluvial Arctic grayling. As author Jen Corrine Brown explains in her book, *Trout Culture: How Fly Fishing Forever Changed the Rocky Mountain West*: "Creating and maintaining trout fisheries required a striking amount of human control over nature. Fish culturalists, state agencies, and federal hatcheries planted billions of trout, devastating native ecosystems. In the trout aesthetic developed by the mid-twentieth century, many native fish became regarded as 'trash fish' to be discarded and ignored in this new regional culture."

In addition to growing millions of non-native fish in hatcheries and then dumping them by the truckload into rivers where they became, in essence, an invasive species, state agencies and fisheries managers also attempted to manipulate environments to produce more fish. In the interest of catering to the burgeoning population of fly fishermen, beginning in the 1930s, managers "improved" rivers with plantings designed to limit erosion, stabilize river banks and make shade. Headwater dams were installed on numerous rivers to create reservoirs which would control water flow and lessen the severity of floods. Other man made materials were used to impact the depth and size of trout pools. Officials undertook all of this activity with the belief that nature, left to its own devices, simply could not cope with the influx of fishermen. The result was generally disastrous for biodiversity in Montana's rivers.

Fortunately, this story has a mostly happy - if cautionary – ending, and it involves the Madison River. The Madison is today an iconic fly fishing destination in Montana, but few people understand why it is famous: the Madison has suffered and recovered from several near-death experiences over the past 50 years. In the late 1960s, the Madison experienced dramatically decreasing fish numbers, despite the Montana Fish, Wildlife and Parks Department (FWP) infusing the river with hundreds of thousands of hatchery fish each year. From 1967 to 1971, a FWP biologist named Dick Vincent made a study of the troubled waterway, and he started with a hugely counterintuitive and controversial premise. Vincent believed that heavily stocking rivers where trout were already reproducing successfully might actually decrease rather than improve the quality of the fisheries. People scoffed and were angry, and Vincent was not a very popular guy for a period of time. But then his thesis proved to be correct; with the cessation of stocking programs, the river came back to life and fish populations, particularly of the big specimens that fly fishermen love to land, rebounded dramatically. The impact of this finding was profound. As Jen Corrine Brown explains, "The most important factor in Montana's shift to wild trout management ... was [Vincent's] now-infamous study on the Madison River that led to a wholesale shift to wild trout management on all Montana rivers starting in 1972.... The study concluded that catchable-sized fish adversely affected wild trout populations, making hatchery stocking an expensive way to yield even worse fishing... Vincent's study definitively demonstrated the environmental tolls of the reliance on hatcheries." By 1975, the practice of hatchery stocking of rivers had ended in Montana. The result was a healthy, thriving wild trout population and a boon to the state's tourist economy.

But the Madison's trials and tribulations had not ended. From 1991 to 1997, as many as 90 percent of young rainbow trout died in the Madison as a result of a parasite that causes a malady known as whirling disease. Biologists assessed the situation as dire and predicted the nearly complete annihilation of the rainbow population. Again, nature prevailed. It seems that the 10 percent of juvenile fish that had survived the disaster of the mid-1990s had developed a resistance to the spores that caused whirling disease. With each succeeding generation, more and more genetically resistant fish survived. A recovery for the Madison which many experts had anticipated might take centuries, took a mere decade. Populations are still not at their peak, and growth rates are slower than they once were, but the situation has stabilized. With the beginning of this century, more guides and anglers than ever have flocked to the Madison, causing some consternation and occasional conflict.

The Madison weathered one more challenge when, in August of 2008, the intake structure failed in the dam farthest upstream from the Madison, known as Hebgen. Flows increased by four times and the reservoir drained rapidly during the three weeks that it took to stanch the rush of water. The accident resulted in fluctuating but mostly warmer surface water temperatures downriver, sometimes reaching 70 degrees or more, which is potentially fatal for trout. The Hebgen Dam remained under construction for many years, and the ecosystem had suffered a serious blow, but the Madison still continues to be a heavily fished river. Those who love the Madison are amazed at its resilience, but still concerned for its long-term health, and only cautiously optimistic at best.

Fishing guide Miles Nolte summarizes the feelings of many people in a 2016 article from *Gray's Sporting Journal*: "The story of the Madison stretches much further than its geographical scope. It's a research hub, a power supply, an economic driver, an agricultural teat, a driftboat highway, a trout mecca, an office, an escape from the office, an essential ecosystem. It's a place I go often, with and without clients, to disappear into a labyrinth of shallow, swift water. I fret for this river like the many people who have loved and depended on it before me, and those I assume will come after. I curse the summertime crowds, fully aware that I am one of them. I obsess over water temps and wring my hands when they crack that deadly 70-degree mark. I suppose something as rare and fragile as a healthy trout river in the 21st century should always seem in peril. If it weren't, we might get complacent."

Thomas McGuane, who cherishes Montana's rivers too, but has also spent a lifetime fishing the world over, similarly warns against complacency. The battle is nowhere close to being won. He says, "We have reached the time in the life of the planet, and humanity's demands upon it, when every fisherman will have to be a riverkeeper, a steward of marine shallows, a watchman on the high seas. We are beyond having to put back what we have taken out. We must put back more than we take out. We must make holy war on the enemies of aquatic life as we have against gillnetters, polluters, and drainers of wetlands. Otherwise... these creatures will continue to disappear at an accelerating rate. We will lose as much as we have lost already and there will be next to nothing, remnant populations, put-and-take, dim bulbs following the tank truck."

I would humbly add one more bit of advice. As the story of the Madison so poignantly reminds us, sometimes, those who love rivers must stop assuming that human beings always know best, resist the urge to intervene, and simply let nature, in all its wondrous ability to heal and perpetuate itself, take its own course.

CHAPTER SEVENTEEN

HIGH COTTON

THE ATLANTIC OCEAN

"There is nothing – absolutely nothing – half so much worth doing as simply messing about in boats."

— WATER RAT TO MOLE, IN KENNETH GRAHAME'S
THE WIND IN THE WILLOWS —

My ancestors were the Scandinavian Vikings, to be quite differentiated from my favorite NFL football team, the Minnesota Vikings, who are not nearly as tough as the Scandinavian Vikings were. My ancestors were extremely skilled seamen – oh sure, they were acquisitive and did more than their fair share of rampaging, pillaging and general war-making too, but they were great explorers and damn fine sailors. Their impressive nautical capabilities started with superb ships. Viking shipbuilders used heavy, sturdy woods such as oak or, in the parts of Scandinavia where oak did not grow, pine. They created a watertight shell of overlapping planks, which was then secured at the overlaps. Ribs inserted inside the planking gave the shells additional stability and stiffness. Prior to the introduction of sails, ships were simply rowed along the coastline. When hulls became strong and seaworthy enough, around the year 800, sails were added which allowed the Vikings to become true ocean voyagers. This was the beginning of the Viking Age, which lasted another 300 years.

We know a great deal about the construction of these ships because some noble Vikings were buried in their vessels, and these archaeological treasures have in a few cases been unearthed in modern times, sometimes with only iron nails and rivets in place, but with the clear outline of the dissolved wood of the ship imprinted upon the soil. Some ships, embedded in moist bogs, have also been found at least partially intact. There are, in addition, poems and sagas that describe the great Viking longships, as well as artistic depictions of them carved into wood or bone. Modern replicas of these ships have demonstrated that they were fast, stable and could sail within 70 degrees of the wind in a maneuver called tacking, which means they were able to make headway – albeit slowly - even when the wind blew against them. They could as a result travel in any direction on the high seas, not just with the wind at their backs. No one knows for sure when this capability became common among sailors, but that the Vikings could do it was significant. This ability to sail, anywhere and everywhere, over hundreds of years, enabled far-ranging Viking expeditions to reach the Caspian Sea in the east, Jerusalem in the south, the great forests of Russia in the north, and to the very edge of the known world, the Americas in the west, five centuries before Christopher Columbus.

My wife talks about my "Viking blood." Unlike many sailors, I did not come to the sport early in my childhood, but the fascination with boats and the sea has run in my veins throughout my life. I have done a lot of reading and taken sailing lessons and was, therefore, thrilled when my friend, John Youngblood, a lifelong and inveterate sailor, entered into a partnership with another gentleman and co-purchased a boat. John (who also has some Scandinavian ancestry and like me, unfortunately, is a long-suffering Minnesota Vikings fan) invited me to sail with him in the Atlantic Ocean off the coast of New England in the fall of 2017. I enthusiastically accepted. John and I have been close friends for more than 40 years, were mischievous college boys together way back when, and have always enjoyed each other's company. I talked on the phone prior to our trip with John's wife, Jennifer. I thanked her for letting John and I pal around together just the two of us, and reminded her that on a number of occasions in the past, as she well knew, John and I had found trouble when we were without "adult supervision." Or trouble had somehow found us. I can't say any more than that. She laughed and said she was confident that we would have nothing but smooth sailing, so to speak, on our adventure. Little did any of us know just how wrong her prediction would prove to be.

⬅━━━━━➡

I took introductory sailing lessons from a fine and highly professional organization called the American Sailing Association (ASA) back in 2012, with my then 21-year-old daughter, Anna. The course was called ASA 101, "Basic Keelboat," we learned a lot and we both passed with flying colors. We had our lessons over four days on Lake Minnetonka, in the western suburbs of the Twin Cities, sailing a simple 23-foot boat called the Ensign. Anna admitted to me afterward, somewhat sheepishly, that she actually hated when we "heeled," which is the action of a boat when it leans sideways as the wind hits its sails. A boat will sometimes heel so dramatically that even under quite normal conditions the leeward (away from the wind) side of the boat will be practically underwater, and sailors need to gather together on the windward edge, balance themselves, and hold on tight. In Anna's defense, when this happens, it would seem to any logical person who is without sailing experience that the damn thing is indeed going to tip right over. But it does not, because the force of the keel - a usually fin-shaped, weighted structural member beneath the hull of the boat - against the water offsets the pressure from the wind in the sails, and the boat stays upright. But it will heel, by golly, and lots of people besides Anna don't like the sensation one bit. This is not to say that sailboats do not occasionally capsize; they do. As a result, even though I thought I might have had a sailing buddy in Anna, now I did not, for very understandable reasons. And so it would be several years – five, to be exact - before I took to the water again.

In anticipation of my trip with John, I knew I needed more education and experience, and so I signed up for two more courses: ASA 103: "Coastal Cruising"; and ASA 104: "Bareboat Chartering." These condensed classes would take place over a long weekend just prior to my trip out east. We would sail out of Bayfield, Wisconsin, in a spectacular part of Lake Superior known as the Apostle Islands. Prior to the class, I spent many hours reading the two assigned textbooks; watching a cheesy-but-helpful-video, produced some time in the mid-1980s when everyone had long hair and short shorts, and provided as recommended viewing by the ASA; and practicing my sailor's knots. Faith thought I was daft as I sat for extended periods at the desk in my study, wrestling with a three-foot-long piece of rope, practicing those goddamned knots. I tried to do it based on the diagrams in the book, but I am not that smart, so I had to go to the internet and review a YouTube video called "The Nine Most Essential Sailor's Knots." Once I watched someone else go through the process step-by-step, I was good to go. My favorite knots are the "figure eight" and the "cleat hitch," for the simple reason that they are the two easiest to tie.

The Apostle Islands National Lakeshore, administered by the National Park Service, comprises 21 islands in Lake Superior and 12 miles of mainland along the Bayfield Peninsula in northern Wisconsin. The largest and best known island in the area, Madeline Island, is not technically a part of the national park but it is the only one of the islands that is inhabited year-round and it lures plenty of tourists. The islands are simply ravishing and contain abundant flora and fauna, wilderness areas, cultural amenities and a number of scenic historic lighthouses. I had heard all about this very special place but had never traveled there. On Wednesday, September 20th I hopped in the car and headed north from the suburban Twin Cities on Highway 35W to Duluth, then drove east through Superior, Wisconsin. I laughed while traveling the commercial stretch of Superior when I spied a joint called Julie's Family Restaurant. The small billboard outside Julie's said, "Now Hiring" on the top line and then, just below that, "Hot Turkey." I thought, *Now why would Julie be wanting to hire hot turkeys*? I love small town America.

I proceeded north on Highway 13, stopped for a fresh trout dinner, then arrived after dark at the Pike's Bay Marina just south of Bayfield. I made my way to Slip 322, where sat docked a 34-foot Hunter sailboat named *Jolly* Swagman. We learned later that 'swagman' is an Australian term referring to an itinerant worker who travels from farm to farm carrying his belongings in a bedroll called a swag; the 'jolly swagman' was a folk hero immortalized in the famous poem, "Waltzing Matilda." There was a light on inside the boat so I called out "Hello!" I was greeted by my ASA classmate, Wayne, who shook my hand in vigorous welcome and asked, "Do you want a beer?" I thought, *I'm gonna like this guy*. We got to know each other for a couple of hours but then, even after a long day, I slept poorly in the aft berth. I was comfortable in a sleeping bag, but the strange environment and lack of headspace threw me off.

We arose to a beautiful, sunny, 53-degree morning and then got in the car to meet our fellow sailing buddy, Terry, and our instructor, Bob, for breakfast at a place called Café Coco, in the tiny community of Washburn. As we savored Coco's special ham-and-cheddar-frittata, Bob told us a little bit about himself. Like me, he was former military with a business background. Bob had gotten fed up with the corporate routine and so decided to cast his lot as a sailing instructor, and an excellent one he was: knowledgeable, experienced, articulate, funny and patient. We spent the morning repeatedly docking *Jolly Swagman* under engine power, until we had the routine down. We sailed in the afternoon, with the wind at a healthy 13 knots, and practiced handling the sails, tacking (sailing into the wind) and jibing (sailing with the wind at our backs). We then came back to the Pike's Bay Marina and spent an hour reviewing for our ASA 103 test, which would be administered the next morning. A late dinner together at one of Bob's favorites, Ethel's, in Bayfield, capped off another busy day. The three students succeeded in passing our exam the following morning. We were officially 'Coastal Cruising' certified.

Friday morning's weather was extremely unsettled, with dark clouds and even lightning visible in the distance to the north. We passed the time inside the marina reviewing for our next test and going over coastal navigation techniques. Bob spread out a map and we took turns plotting positions and charting a course. The weather cleared after lunch and we were able to sail with winds at about 15 knots to a stunning spot called Frog's Bay, along the coastline. We practiced anchoring over and over – we would stay in this location for the night – and then rowed our dinghy ashore to explore. We came upon a long-abandoned cabin, joked uncomfortably about not wanting to find duct tape, shackles, and a banjo inside - all we could see was a filthy, well-worn mattress and other sundry items of junk - then followed a faint trail through the dense foliage. Bob and I commented that this must be what it was like to be on patrol in the jungles of 'Nam, but without the Viet Cong, thankfully. We decided we were thirsty for a beer and rowed back to the *Jolly Swagman*. Dinner that evening was Bob's outstanding recipe for grilled chicken, pasta and Spanish rice, with a Caesar salad. Oreo cookies and Fig Newtons for dessert. We told tall tales into the night and, eventually, saw more stars in the sky than I had witnessed since my time on Mount Kilimanjaro in Africa. Those of us who could do so (Bob) identified individual stars and planets and named several of the constellations. It was a breathtaking sight to behold, and made us all feel very tiny and unimportant. We rocked to sleep in the gentle waves of Frog's Bay.

Saturday dawned warm and dead calm, so we took to motoring our way about until the wind picked up in the late morning. We hoisted our mainsail and jib (a smaller sail forward of the mainsail) and finished our skills training, with several hours spent on man overboard drills (you gotta know that one), reefing (bringing in the sails gradually when winds become too strong), and heaving to (a technique for stopping the boat with the sails still up). We were glad we were able to practice when we did, as the wind died again. We decided to motor to the famous Madeline Island. Bob is a veteran of this unique destination, and insisted that our first stop be Tom's Burned Down Café.

"What the heck is Tom's Burned Down Café?" we inquired.

"Remember the bar from *Star Wars*, with all the various alien life forms and such?"

"Yes," we said.

"That's Tom's Burned Down Café."

And he was right. Apparently, what became Tom's was once an old tavern that, as you may have guessed, burned to the ground. Tom decided not to rebuild, but began to serve beer from the back of a truck near the ashes of the original structure. People showed up, Tom built some decks, then a bigger bar, then kind of enclosed everything, but not quite, underneath a gigantic tent. It is an airy venue, to say the least. Tom lives in a sort of ramshackle home right next door. At one point, *Maxim* magazine voted Tom's one of America's six best beach bars, even though it is not really on a beach. That's high praise. We loved Tom's. The staff and clientele were interesting, heavily tattooed and friendly, there were kids and dogs running around everywhere, and the beer was cold. We got ogled and whistled at by a band of rowdy, semi-inebriated 60-something women. Good stuff. Then it was off to a beach-side dinner of fish and chips, with a final stop at an ice cream parlor across the street. We motored back to Pikes' Bay, had a nightcap at the Portside Bar & Restaurant, and then slept like dead men.

Sunday morning the students got up early to study for our test, but I still just barely passed that sucker, with a score of 84 out of 100 (80 was a passing grade). I had received a 93 on the first test. Clearly, I had somehow gotten dumber as the training went on. Bob said, "Congratulations, but I think you over-studied." He was probably right – I should have just slept in and winged it, like I used to do in college. Oh well, we all now had our 'Bareboat Chartering" certification meaning, technically, we could go to a marina anywhere in the world and were supposed to be qualified to captain a charter. I damn well knew I was still a long way from confident enough to have the balls to try to charter a boat on my own anytime soon, or to subject a crew to my incompetence. I needed more experience. Which I was about to get in spades on the Atlantic Ocean, starting on Wednesday, September 27.

⬅━━━➡

I flew into Hartford, Connecticut in the early afternoon, and John picked me up for the drive to Bristol, Rhode Island, where his boat was docked. We stopped at a Burger King in Willimantic and enjoyed a salty, greasy Whopper meal. John solemnly placed one of those colorful cardboard crowns that the kids get to wear at Burger King upon my head, as if it were a coronation – not surprisingly, it did not quite fit - and we had our first photo op of the trip. We are both little boys at heart, like to mess around, and neither one of us has ever been particularly effective in acting as a buffer on the other one's behavior.

The boat is called *High Cotton*. John's partner, who named the boat, is a southern boy, originally from northeast Arkansas. According to Wiktionary. org: "The term 'high cotton' or 'tall cotton' originates from the rural farming community in the antebellum (pre-Civil War) South when 'high cotton' meant that the crops were good and the prices, were, too. The term has generalized to mean one is doing well or is successful." I guess guys who can buy expensive sailboats are, at least in the financial sense, doing well compared to most of the rest of us. They are, indeed, in high cotton. I have always lived by the maxim that instead of buying expensive shit yourself, just meet and befriend people who can afford expensive shit such as, for example, fine restaurant meals, wine cellars, season tickets, backyard pools, nice cars, lake homes, sailboats, and so forth. Spend time hanging around with them. I say, glom onto those folks. It is really fun and way cheaper, I have found.

The boat that eventually became *High Cotton* has lived a fascinating life. She was commissioned in 1993 as a bespoke design, the meticulous construction of which would take two full years. She was built at a shipyard in Taiwan and launched as the *Canvasback*, in 1995. The first owner was a wealthy restaurateur who had *Canvasback* transported via container ship to the United States, where she spent a number of years as a freshwater boat on Lake Erie. The first owner sold *Canvasback* to a buyer from Germany, in 2010, who renamed the vessel *Nijinski* and proceeded to sail her across the Atlantic to her new home port of Venice, Italy. The German owner eventually had her again transported across the Atlantic in a container ship, to Annapolis, Maryland. John's partner purchased the boat in the summer of 2015, and rechristened her *High Cotton*. John chartered the boat shortly thereafter just to see what she was about, fell in love, and entered into a co-ownership deal in July of 2016.

She is a gorgeous girl; I'm sorry, out of respect I should say lady, and she is incredibly sexy. *High Cotton* is a 52-foot sailboat, called a Little Harbor, and built by a well-known boat designer and sailor named Ted Hood. *High Cotton* was the seventh and final Little Harbor 52 ever constructed. So she is truly the last of a rare breed. Frederick Emmart "Ted" Hood (1927-2013) had an enormous influence on the world of yachting. He founded Hood Sailmakers which, during the '60s and '70s, became the world's largest sailmaker. He was equally successful as a sailor, skippering the boat *Courageous* to victory in the 1974 America's Cup. Hood opened Little Harbor Yachts, based in Portsmouth, Rhode Island but moved construction operations to northern Taiwan, near Taipei, in 1979. Ted Hood enjoyed a long and notable career as a marine inventor and yacht designer.

When I first laid eyes on *High Cotton*, I *oohed* and *aahed*. I had of course seen pictures, but it was really neat to finally meet her in person. Per long-standing nautical etiquette, I requested of John, "Permission to come aboard *High Cotton*, Captain Youngblood." He laughed: "Sure, come on board and check her out." The key to the boat's unique configuration, among many other things, is what is known as the "delta form hull." Hood's concept was that a shallow-draft, wide-beam, deep centerboard hull would not only be competitive from a racing standpoint, but also provide excellent load-carrying capability, interior comfort, and an easy, stable motion on high seas. The delta hull has no keel extension, but relies instead on a deeper-shaped hull with internal lead ballast - as opposed to a keel boat with ballast contained deep in the keel - and a centerboard which can be raised or lowered manually, using a winch, at any time. The adjustable centerboard allows even a large, heavy boat – *High Cotton* weighs an astonishing 65,000 pounds; that's more than thirty tons – to have a shallow draft, which is less than five feet for *High Cotton* when the centerboard and rudder are both up. She is therefore able to operate in considerably shallower waters than many keelboats. The delta hull's superior stability also means that these boats can support a larger, more powerful set of sails. The spacious interior hull volume of *High Cotton* accommodates more living space, and she is a comfortable, even luxurious boat indeed. Wood paneling abounds, and interior design features are highly functional yet aesthetically pleasing.

We hauled our gear aboard and then relaxed with a cocktail, a big gin & tonic - first things first. We noticed two young women at an adjacent dock getting ready to set sail for somewhere. I was out taking pictures of our boat when one of the gals struck up a conversation with me. She turned out to be a bit of a lunatic, slightly reminiscent of Glenn Close in *Fatal* Attraction, a movie that scared the crap out of every man who ever saw it, John and me included. Let's call our new friend "Alex." Alex claimed to be a boat electrician for a large, well known company called Garmin that, among other things, provides products and services for the sailing industry - she probably was - and she proceeded to tell John that his radar system was out. John already knew this, but how Alex knew it was somewhat perplexing. Even scary. She then somehow, without permission, came physically aboard *High Cotton* under the guise of inspecting the electricals; John is much nicer about these things than I am; after about five minutes of awkward technical conversation between the two of them I turned to John and said, "Let's not forget our dinner plans."

"Oh yeah," he responded.

"Well, nice talking to you, Alex," said I. And then she was on her way, but only reluctantly.

"Whew. Thanks for thinking of that, Jeff."

We drove into town and savored a plate of oysters, the bouillabaisse and a bottle of red at the Bristol Oyster Bar. As we made our way home to the marina, John queried quietly, "What will we do if Alex is aboard *High Cotton* when we get back?" "Shit our pants and prepare to die," I responded.

⬌

She was not there. We breathed easy. Then it was lights out. My journal entry for the next day, Thursday, September 28, begins simply, "Eventful day." We awoke to complete quiet and calm at the Bristol Marina. John's boatkeeper stopped by and the two of them discussed weather conditions and *High Cotton's* radar and compass situation. On the boatkeeper's recommendation, we ate breakfast at the Bristol Family Restaurant in town, a dive in the Youngblood/Appelquist tradition, where we had hash and eggs – I pointed out that this was the third meal in a row where we had both eaten the exact same thing. We have probably been hanging out together too long. Back on the boat, John gave me a thorough tour and briefing on everything: engine, bilges, batteries, electronics, safety features, fire extinguishers, lines, sails, etc. Like most females, she is complicated. Conditions had proceeded from dead to quite windy, about 20 knots out of the north, so we made our way without sails under engine power south to *High Cotton's* home port, Newport, Rhode Island, about 10 nautical miles away.

Our mission in Newport was to recover *High Cotton's* dinghy. Seems simple enough but the scenario was complicated by gusty winds and the fact that *High Cotton* sits at a dock when she is in Newport, but the dock is essentially a moor, i.e., it floats independently out in the water, not as part of a docking system that would allow us to disembark and walk ashore. There were many other boats similarly docked nearby. Oh, and John had a rookie crew member. John was as nervous as I've ever seen him as we had to take several passes at the dock before we could bring the boat in upwind; when he finally succeeded in edging her close, I jumped off and tied a quick cleat hitch with a spring line to secure her; thank goodness for all the knot practice. We then had to fasten the dinghy to the bow of the boat to avoid smashing her between us and the dock. As John gunned the engine to get us underway, I walked the dinghy's line – with great difficulty – from the bow to the stern, pulled it in tight and cinched it up so that it would trail comfortably behind us as we sailed. We motored out of Narragansett Bay to our next destination, Block Island, 25 miles to the south.

We were finally able to raise the jib, called a Genoa on *High Cotton* because it is large enough to extend aft of the main sail. We were sailing at last. The weather was warm and we wore shorts, but the sea was up and down, with swells that we estimated to be 8-10 feet. It was a smooth yet rolling ride on *High Cotton*, and we were even able to eat a ham and cheese sandwich - four meals in a row now - while riding the roller coaster. They say there are two kinds of sailors: those who have been seasick and those who will get seasick; apparently everyone has a breaking point. John said he had gotten sick only once, when he was eight years old, but never since then. I have always done well on boats in raucous waters, thanks to the Viking constitution, I guess. I've never felt nauseous, and even with the excitement we had coming on Saturday, I have not been sick to date. But I'm sure my turn will come.

We had been sailing for about six hours when we finally arrived at Block Island. We called the harbor master as we approached to receive our mooring assignment, but got no answer. The place was basically dead and seemingly done for the season. There were only a handful of boats in view. We picked a ball mooring and tied in. John has what I consider to be an outstanding personal sailing tradition, which is that every time he safely moors, docks or anchors, he opens a can of beer to celebrate, and he insists that his crew do the same. We downed a crisp, cold Yuengling.

"Would you crack a beer if you docked at 8 a.m.?" I asked.

"Why yes, I believe I would. So would you, on my orders."

"You are a good captain, and this is a most excellent tradition," I observed.

Block Island is part of a coastal archipelago called the Outer Lands region. It sits in the Atlantic Ocean 13 miles south of the shore of Rhode Island and 14 miles east of Montauk Point on Long Island. There are something like 1,000 people living year round on just under 10 square miles, but the population can swell to 20,000 on a busy, touristy summer day. We were glad, therefore, to be there during the off season. A significant part of the island is set aside for conservation, and it is a lovely place. We admired as much of the scenery as we could take in from our mooring, then proceeded to attach the outboard motor to the dinghy, which is also kind of a pain in the ass. I got into the dinghy while just maintaining my balance, sat in the back, John passed the 110- pound motor down to me with a lift, and I attached and secured it. We would need it to get to dinner later that evening. Our chosen venue was a well-known place called The Oar. It is famous for the hundreds of personalized oars which don the walls. We called to make sure they were open, then watched from our deck as another dinghy made its way to shore. Although we did not see exactly where those folks tied in, we were pretty sure we knew where to go. It mattered, because we were not ready to leave until after dark, around 1930.

We set out in choppy waters. Only with great luck were we both able to make it off the transom into the dinghy and stay dry. We untied and motored off. It was very dark, so we both had headlamps on to avoid a collision with a mooring ball. We wore jackets but did not wear life vests – why would we need them? We were only traveling about 400 yards. But damn if we didn't get soaking wet, both of us from head to toe, in the chop, and the water was cold. The low temperature would be in the mid-50s overnight, but the weather always seems more frigid on the water. *Shit*. We next had to maneuver around a minefield of pylons which had not looked that intimidating from a distance. We could not see any logical place to dock and so assumed we should just head for shore. *Bad idea*. We got into shallow, extremely rocky conditions, only to have the engine cut out. One of my favorite quotes from Hunter S. Thompson came to mind: "Call on God, but row away from the rocks." John got out in shin-deep water and attempted to pull us over to the dock. He slipped on the rocks and fell into the water, but was unhurt; this is good because he has a gimp knee from long-ago athletics, which has required multiple surgeries over the years. I had visions of him twisting it all out of shape.

We were swearing – not at each other, just at the situation. *Where was everyone tied in?* We finally got to the dock right at the shoreline and did a quick wraparound with our line. John said, "Hold onto this while I walk back out over the dock to see where we are supposed to be." I continued to sit in the dinghy and held on. He came back and said, "We need to move about 20 yards further out, so let's untie." In the process of doing that, while John stood on the dock above, my right hand became violently sandwiched between the rocking dinghy and the large, wooden, unforgiving pier. Please keep in mind, all we wanted to do here was eat some fucking dinner. I have been injured so many times in my life that I was able to automatically do a quick damage assessment. I was hurt, but knew the hand wasn't broken. I could flex my fingers, but I was bleeding. And when I say bleeding, I mean profusely. It was a gusher of crimson. We labored to tie in with everyone else, then proceeded to limp to the restroom situated underneath the restaurant. We were wet, freezing, dirty, tired and pissed off. I washed the hand, observed that I had a good scrape, bruising, and one deeper puncture wound, and then wrapped it up in tissue paper. I stuffed additional sheets in my pocket for later use to staunch the squirting flow of blood. Even though The Oar is an informal place, we did receive a few sideways glances as we made our way to the table. We must have looked as if we had been in a war zone. Finally, we each ordered something different from the other dude. John had the Mahi Mahi and I had the crab cakes. After all of that, the food was for shit (sorry Oar, I don't like to run around acting like a restaurant critic, but it's true.) Overcooked. Not good. Maybe the lead chef goes home to the mainland during the off-season.

We got the engine started again but still had almost as much trouble getting back to *High Cotton* as we had had in leaving her. We finally made it aboard. We got out of wet clothes and warmed up. I washed and smeared disinfectant on the hand, then covered it with a large bandage. It was time for bed. We acknowledged that our wives would have killed us if they had known what transpired that evening. So, bottom line, it's a very good thing that they did not know.

What had we learned? *Probably not enough.*

⬅━━━━➡

The weather was sublime on Friday. Since we were not sailing that day, we had some time to relax. We ate a light breakfast, sipped Starbucks instant coffee, lolled about the boat's cockpit, and read spy novels. John was into Alan Furst - also one of my favorites - and I was finishing up John le Carre's *Tinker Tailor*

Soldier Spy, which I had for some inexplicable reason never read. John commented that Alan Furst's male protagonist almost always get laid in the first few pages of the book. This was, I noted, in contrast with le Carre's cerebral, bespectacled, cherubic hero, George Smiley, who never does. Not in the first pages or, apparently, ever. Perhaps Smiley's dedication, purposefulness, and lack of distractions of the sensual kind explain his great success as a spy. Or not. What would Ian Fleming and his rogue, James Bond, say? These are the questions that philosophers ponder.

John had arranged for us to fish that afternoon and so, after a little-boy lunch – but with big-boy portions - of macaroni and weenies, at around 1400, our fishing guide, Craig, stopped by *High Cotton* to pick us up in his compact, center-console rig. We would be hunting for a favorite in this part of the Atlantic coastal area, striped bass, called "stripers," which would, hopefully, provide our supper. Stripers are said to taste wonderful; I have never had the pleasure. We would fish with spinning rods and a mix of colorful hard and soft plastic lures. The wind had picked up to about 10 knots, again out of the north; winds in this part of the Atlantic are usually out of the south/southwest. So conditions were less than smooth. Craig indicated he had been having a devil of a time in the past few days locating fish, primarily because of the effects of recent hurricane activity. The atypical high, northerly winds had pushed the fish from their familiar stomping grounds, and Craig was not sure where they had gone. Indeed, our first two hours were a complete bust, as we methodically explored the exterior of Block Island. We would fish for a bit, get skunked, then quickly pick up and move rapidly to the next spot. Craig was quiet during this time; he was a man of few words anyway, but we could tell that he was concentrating, trying to read the waters. The fish whisperer.

Finally, during the course of basically circumnavigating the entire island, we began to get some bites, but mainly teasers. Then suddenly, by golly, the fish were feeding and we reeled in one after the other. 'Twas a frenzy. We were so busy that, at one point, all three of us had a fish on the line. But they were all blue fish, porgies or sea bass; Craig told us the sea bass are excellent eating, but they were out of season and so we had to throw them all back. We never did land a striper. Eventually, as the afternoon wore on, we determined to keep the next big blue fish, and have him as our evening meal. Craig said blues are tasty when they have been feeding primarily on squid, which these blues had, and when they are bled immediately with a quick slash beneath the gills that drains the blood rapidly. We pulled in a healthy specimen who fought the good fight. Craig cleaned him up for us before we departed his company, and we now had two giant fillets for our grill. John's daughter, Eleanor (Ellie for short), manages the Fairfield Farm at the Hotchkiss School in Connecticut, her alma mater, and she had supplied us with a stash of potatoes and tomatoes, fresh from the earth. The meal was superb - all the more fun because we knew from whence all of our bounty had come - and capped a great day on the water. The next day, Saturday, would not be such a great day on the water.

Our guide had mentioned the effects of recent hurricanes. Indeed, John had been concerned that we might need to cancel our sailing plans entirely depending, specifically, on the whims of Hurricanes Maria and Jose. He watched the weather closely day-by-day and told me to just enjoy my time in the Apostle Islands. When decision-time came, he believed we were good to go with our sail.

Earlier in September, Hurricane Irma, clearly gaining strength from warmer-than-usual Atlantic waters, hit from the west like a massive locomotive as it devastated Barbuda, St. Martin, St. Barth's, Anguilla, and the British and U.S. Virgin Islands. Irma is one of only five hurricanes on record to achieve wind speeds of 185 miles per hour, which were sustained for an amazing 37 hours. Irma continued in its deadly path, grazing Puerto Rico, causing flooding in Cuba, and then barreling into the Turks and Caicos Islands and the southern Bahamas. Finally, the storm rolled its way through the Keys and then up the western coast of Florida, causing destruction as far north as Georgia. The tally of damage for Irma alone has been estimated at $50 billion.

But as of November, Irma was only one of 10 consecutive Atlantic storms to reach hurricane strength. They were: Franklin; Gert; Harvey (which submerged much of Houston and caused $125 billion in damage); Irma; Jose; Katia; Lee; Maria; Nate; and Ophelia. This phenomenon of 10 hurricanes in a row has not happened for better than a century, and in only three previous years since records have been kept (1878, 1886 and 1893). On the heels of Irma, Maria, also a Category 5 storm, caused damage to St. Lucia, Martinique, Guadeloupe, Dominica, St. Croix, and the British and U.S. Virgin Islands, before violently battering Puerto Rico, knocking out the power grid and other infrastructure. Tens of thousands of Puerto Ricans were left homeless. The Trump administration sat on its incompetent ass while Puerto Rico, in desperate need of help, fought for its figurative life.

All of this turbulent and ruinous hurricane activity begs the question: What is happening here? The fact is, the link between climate change and increasing numbers of hurricanes is not as solid as the connection between warmer temperatures and the resulting severe droughts, raging fires and melting polar ice, for example. One of the reasons this is true is that the sample size of hurricanes is simply too small. But there is no argument that warmer waters, at the very least, may provide additional fuel for hurricanes. Hurricanes have a chance to develop when the water temperature beneath them is at 26 degrees Celsius, or around 79 degrees Fahrenheit, or warmer. Scientists note that, as a result of climate change, both the number of days when ocean waters will reach those temperatures and the extent of ocean areas that will achieve that level of warmth, are increasing. Thus, whatever the frequency of individual hurricanes themselves, these days, the conditions for bigger, longer and more destructive storms are clearly present. In August of 2017, a climate scientist from Texas Tech University named Dr. Katharine Hayhoe told the *New York Times* that, with respect to hurricanes, "We care about a changing climate because it exacerbates the natural risks and hazards that we already face."

We slept till 0800 on Saturday. The morning was sunny, but it had rained hard overnight and we left a hatch open. Woops. Not the last mistake we would make that day. The water pump had activated periodically during the night; it sounded to me like a brief burst of machine gun fire. Sometime mid-morning, the automatic bilge pump went on and stayed on. "What's up?" I inquired.

"We have a leak," came the reply. Not words that any boat owner ever wants to speak. John began to troubleshoot the problem, attempting to locate the leak. He called his boatkeeper, for advice. As they conversed, John located the issue, which was a plastic tube next to the diesel engine. The tube had come loose from its connection, and was actually gushing water. We turned off the system and John reconnected the tube. John surmised that the source of the water was the starboard fresh water tank. It seems we had already lost three quarters of a 110-gallon tank, but *High Cotton* has two gigantic tanks, and we were fortunately not out in the middle of the ocean. The tube came loose again, and continued to leak, but it was just emitting residual liquid. John re-attached it. We flipped over to the port tank for the remainder of the trip, hoping that it was not also part of the same faulty connection. And we only used that tank when we absolutely needed it. I said she was complicated, and she is. John's observation at the end of it all: "Every time I sail on this boat, some shit breaks or something goes wrong. Oh well, I guess that's just boating..."

Our objective for the day was to eat lunch and then sail around 1400 to a spot called St. Judith's Point of Refuge, about 12 nautical miles away (one nautical mile is equal to 1.1508 statute miles), to the north. It was apparently an interesting place, and we would anchor in that harbor overnight. We planned everything carefully, examining our maps meticulously to determine how we would time the tide to maximize our approach to the entry into a very narrow, shallow and potentially crowded harbor. If we could not negotiate the harbor, we would anchor in the open just outside of it. We checked our weather reports and learned that winds would be out of the north at around 15 knots (a knot is a unit of speed equal to one nautical mile per hour), with a possibility of rain. We discussed whether we should remove the outboard engine from the dinghy and secure it to the main boat before getting underway, but because we thought it would be an easy sail, we did not take that step.

We motored out of Block Island Harbor and proceeded under power without deploying our sails. It would turn out to be a very good thing that we did not. I have a picture of John at the wheel of *High Cotton* at that moment. He is wearing wet weather gear, but he looks dry and confident. He wears a determined captain's visage. I then pointed my phone forward and took a picture of what we were traveling into. Skies were cloudy and quite grey, and it looked as if there would be rain ahead, but that was not unexpected. The sea state was relatively calm. We moved ahead without hesitation. This would be the last photo that either of us would take on that day.

Within short order, we noticed the wind picking up speed. We sat tight in the cockpit, John continuing to steer manually, and monitored the situation closely with all of our electronics. We did not don life vests, or strap ourselves to the boat. Probably should have done that, but we did not. Didn't even talk about it. I'm sure the gurus at ASA would be saying, "This isn't any sailor that we have trained – did we give this guy certifications?" Suddenly, the sustained wind increased from about 10 knots to over 30, in a period of just about 10 seconds. John and I looked at each other, dumbfounded. *What's going on?* I asked and John told me that in a lifetime of sailing, the stiffest wind he had ever experienced was 31 knots. We hit that figure and then some, and the rain began. A deluge. By now, *High Cotton*, she was a rockin' and rollin'. I guessed that this is what they call a sudden squall.

Why do people laugh in a situation like this? Once, years ago, I was on a commercial airliner that lost altitude rapidly and unexpectedly in the middle of the flight. It was in the old days when they actually served meals in economy class, and they had just served up a meal. The food went flying, and people screamed in terror as their hands and even hair flew straight up into the air, while we dropped from the sky, precipitously. We learned later that a flight attendant had been seriously injured, and that as a result of the jolt there was structural damage to the airplane. After probably eight seconds of agony and terror, the plane finally leveled off. What did we passengers do then? After a brief silence, we laughed. Uproariously. Commenting on this strange phenomenon during wartime, Winston Churchill once said, "But who in war will not have his laugh amid the skulls?" I don't know the answer. But John and I laughed. Not uproariously – because we were not yet out of danger – but not nervously, either. Just a good, hearty belly laugh. *What the fuck is this fine mess we've gotten ourselves into now? Why does this always happen to us? What is this shit? Let's live to tell the story, okay?*

In 1805, the year that Britain's Horatio Nelson decisively defeated Napoleon's combined French and Spanish fleet at the Battle of Trafalgar, a British admiral named Sir Francis Beaufort published a table that has famously and forever since been known as the Beaufort Scale. Beaufort compiled observable signs such as sea state and the behavior of smoke and flags that would serve as indicators of varying levels of wind speed. The Beaufort Scale is still widely used by sailors today, because it is accurate. Beaufort described 12 distinct forces reflecting wind speed, and how to recognize them.

At 31 knots, John had experienced what the Beaufort Scale would characterize as a Force 7, or near gale. John and I knew that 34 knots was officially a gale. When we hit that, which we soon did, we fist bumped. *Hey, now we can say we were in a gale together. If we get out of this. But even if we don't, people will certainly know that we went down in a gale together.* Again, strange human behavior. But our storm was not done. Admiral Beaufort would have been proud, as we finally tapped out at just over 44 knots: Beaufort Force 9, a severe gale. This was sustained wind speeds at more than 50 standard miles per hour (44 x 1.1508 = 50.63). My friends, I can tell you, that is one wild-assed wind. It was like riding a 65,000-pound bucking bronco, but a fat one that moved in slow motion. We were completely soaked as high frequency waves that we estimated at 10-15 feet battered and splashed the entire length of the boat. John would call out, "Big wave!" as *High Cotton* nosed her way violently into the surf. But she always somehow came out again, God bless her courageous soul.

John was becoming hypothermic. He needed to go below to dry off and put on warmer gear. I took over the wheel and promptly got us all turned around. John fell down while he was in the cabin. What if he had knocked himself out? *Oh, brother.* But he did not hurt himself and he took over steering again. Or what if we had lost engine power? *Not good.* But we did not, and so were able to maintain a semblance of slow but steady forward propulsion. Or what if the dinghy engine had been ruined or lost when the dinghy flipped over, and it did, which absolutely infuriated John? Yes, we should have secured the engine earlier, but it miraculously started again a few days later. Or what if I had fallen overboard when John asked me to go forward ("Hang on for your life!" he shouted by way of encouragement – he needn't have bothered to remind me of this imperative) to pull up the fenders from the side of the boat, which we had also neglected to do? This was a dumb order, but I was even dumber to follow it - the former Marine in me coming out. I proceeded forward, crouched low, held onto the wooden handrails for all I was worth, completed the task, and got safely back to the cockpit. I did not go into the drink. At this point, the ASA brass would be shouting, with justification, "Strip this guy of every certification we have ever given him!" Desperate times, desperate measures.

My journal for that day, filled out on Sunday, says, "Neptune was furious." Yes he was. We had, early in the journey, agreed that we would never get to St. Judith's safely and should turn around with the intent of trying to get back into Block Island Harbor, to the east. We were able to turn about without mishap. But John was understandably concerned that if we put ourselves at anything other than nose into the north wind under moderate engine power, i.e., if we became positioned sideways to the wind, that we might be knocked down or run aground because of the sheer size, frequency and force of the waves and the wind. Remember, I said earlier, boats do occasionally capsize. Also, visibility was terrible, and Block Island's entry is narrow and relatively shallow. It would have been exceedingly tricky. We therefore sat more or less in place, treading water, outside the entrance to Block Island, tantalizingly close to our goal, facing our nemesis, the blistering, wet north wind, and we just gutted it out. For a couple of hours. We listened intently to the Coast Guard on the radio as several vessels which had also been caught in the gale called in distress signals, meaning those poor folks feared imminent disaster. In one case, it sounded like a sailor was all by himself on a smaller vessel. We understand that the Coast Guard did a wonderful job that day and was able to get to every boat that was in trouble. We did not call in a distress signal, because we still controlled our destiny, even if just barely. Ironically, we were never out of sight of land during the whole experience. But as John reminded me, the vast majority of boating accidents happen close to shore rather than out on the high seas. We were stuck for the time being.

We clearly made a number of mistakes during the course of this ordeal, which I have recounted. As any professional athlete who is worth his salt would say, "That is all on us, no excuses." But we were also just plain unlucky. We did not exhibit bad judgment in going forward in what we assumed would only be rainy, mildly windy conditions. People sail in that stuff all the time. Nor could we have anticipated that the weather would turn on a dime; that in one moment it would be somewhat blustery, but in short order a severe gale would be upon us. We did our research; we looked at the weather; we considered the tides; we were careful - and yet we could not have predicted what happened. We were jinxed. The suddenness with which the weather changed – no doubt it has ever been thus on the world's oceans – was utterly frightening. What if we had been in the middle of the Atlantic, hundreds of miles from landfall? What then? *I guess you just ride it out.*

But we also did a number of things right: first and foremost, we both stayed calm, maintained our composure, kept in control of our faculties. No panic. This is perhaps the most important advice I could ever give anyone faced with a similar, potentially life-threatening circumstance: stay calm, people. We communicated. We never stopped talking. We gabbed the whole time. We laughed, bantered, swore, bitched, looked at our electronics, tried to research the weather, listened to the radio, made absurd observations, and stayed friends. We never exchanged a harsh word. There were urgent, but never harsh, words ("Big wave!" "Hang on for your life!" Etc.) We were in it together, no matter how it might turn out. We agreed at every point along the way on the primary decisions that needed to be made. We agreed the weather was turning bad and, therefore, we needed to make some decisions - a no brainer; we agreed we would not make St. Judith's Point; we agreed on the timing for turning back; we agreed to face into the wind and sustain a minimum of forward momentum, just enough to allow us to maintain our position; we agreed during the gale's most violent phase that an attempt to reenter Block Island was not smart; we agreed when conditions had moderated slightly that we should make a run for the harbor; we helped each other negotiate the passage through the narrow channel; we moored ourselves securely, together, John driving with me managing the lines, in waves that were quite boisterous even within the protection of the harbor; we were still rocking a bit but agreed we were okay, finally, and that it was time to breathe a sigh of relief; we agreed that we deserved to crack open a beer, per captain's well-established protocol; we agreed that a bottle or two of red wine (it might have ended up being three; I don't rightly recall) and porterhouse steaks on the grill would be a good end to this most eventful, tumultuous day; we agreed that we needed to talk everything through, to process exactly what had happened, and so we spent several hours doing that; we agreed that we loved life, loved our families, and appreciated our friendship; lastly, although we never said it out loud, I believe we both agreed that we were happy to be safe and sound.

◄──────►

We awakened around 0630 on Sunday after a hard sleep. We had our cup of morning java, and then attempted to right the dinghy. As we struggled to attach the dinghy to the lift at the rear of *High Cotton*, a very nice couple from the next boat over got into their dinghy, motored on over, and helped us get that thing flipped over. We had lost the oars, a gas can, a wooden bench, and a water scoop, but not the engine which, fortunately, was not ruined. We ate our favorite hash and eggs again and got underway to our destination of Newport, Rhode Island, at 0845. With a headwind out of the north at around 10-12 knots, we were for the first time able to be completely under sail, with both the mainsail and the Genoa fully deployed. We tacked back and forth and I got some good practice driving *High Cotton*. We covered 25 miles and arrived in Newport at 1330. Then there was a pause to listen to the radio for a couple of hours as our beleaguered but beloved Minnesota Vikings lost to the Detroit Lions, 14-7. We shouldn't have bothered. *If they win a Super Bowl in our lifetime we will consider ourselves blessed.* We wanted to spend some time bumming around town, but couldn't make it the 75 yards or so to shore because the dang oars to the dinghy were at the bottom of the Atlantic somewhere. So we called the launch service and spent the rest of a bright, splendid day exploring the "Sailing Capital of the World." Bustling, quaint, with endless rows of sailboats, lots of spectacular mansions and vintage historical buildings, Newport is a treat. Our final seafood dinner at a spot on the water called The Mooring was delectable, even despite the $3.50 price tag per oyster. Then it was back to the boat for one final opportunity to be gently rocked to sleep on the water.

Monday's mission was to get home. To begin the day, winds were out of the north (what a surprise) at a sturdy 15 knots or so. We decided to motor to Bristol, in the interest of getting there sooner rather than later. The wind tailed off a bit to 8-10, our ride was uneventful, and while I manned the helm - actually, autopilot manned the helm while I just watched - John attempted to fix the fishing line on one of his reels that had become hopelessly tangled. We arrived, docked, got her all cleaned up and secured, and said our final farewells to that magnificent lady, *High Cotton*.

———————▶

As we drove to the Hartford airport for my flight home, I examined my right hand. The scrape I received when the hand got caught between the dinghy and the pier was healing nicely, but it was still ugly, bruised and scabbed over. The puncture wound – I have experience in these matters – looked deep enough that it would make at least a small forever mark. I turned to John and said, "When you go on a trip and come home with both a permanent scar and a great, death-defying story to tell, as a general rule, in my way of thinking, you've had success." We both laughed and John agreed with the sentiment.

We also both agreed with a quote we came upon from a book by H. Jackson Browne, called *P.S. I Love You*. In it, Brown relates what his mother once wrote to him in a letter: "Twenty years from now you will be more disappointed by the things you didn't do than the ones you did do. So throw off the bowlines. Sail away from the safe harbor. Catch the trade winds in your sails. Explore. Dream. Discover."

CHAPTER EIGHTEEN

QUATTOUR AMICUS

THE FOUR FRIENDS FELLOWSHIP

"We make a living by what we get, we make a life by what we give."
— WINSTON CHURCHILL —

In the spring of 1526, the legendary Turkish ruler Suleiman I, known as the "Magnificent," set out from Constantinople at the head of his 100,000-man army. His objective: Hungary. The Hungarian king, Louis II, was said to be a nice young man but a bit indolent, far more interested in having a good time and sleeping late than in leading his soldiers against the great Ottoman sultan. Eventually, and too late, Louis recognized the seriousness of the situation. He cajoled and begged his noblemen to support him in raising troops to counter the threat, but he was met with a decided lack of action. Finally, in a move that was either brave, foolhardy, or both, Louis took the field himself, alone, in an effort to shame his nobles into following his example. The tactic worked, and Louis marched to a soggy plain south of the tiny village of Mohacs with a force that eventually reached 25,000. It was there that the youthful king and his noblemen set up camp and awaited the Turkish onslaught.

The Battle of Mohacs, fought ferociously on August 29, 1526, ended badly for the Hungarians. The Turks tricked Louis into a frontal assault, then attacked his flanks and raked his depleted formations with cannon fire. His army and, in effect, his country were destroyed. The casualties included 20,000 Hungarians killed in combat or executed when they surrendered themselves, three archbishops, five bishops, 500 nobles, and King Louis himself, who was trampled in the frantic retreat and drowned as he tried escape over marshy ground. His body was discovered a month later. Hungary ultimately came under Ottoman rule and, to this day, Hungarians regard Mohacs as a traumatic disaster and a tragic turning point in the history of their nation. Today, when a Hungarian experiences bad luck, it is a common expression to say, "More was lost at Mohacs."

←————→

"Just like King Louis II at Mohacs, I will be the first to take action, shaming my three noblemen into following me." Our friend Pete Ross is a great amateur military historian. Pete is a Stanford Law School graduate who has become a successful California litigator. Along with his partner Eric George, Pete runs his own boutique law firm with offices in Beverly Hills, San Francisco and New York City. Pete was speaking to Christian Hakala, Director of Major Gifts at our alma mater, Carleton College. Fortunately for Pete, Christian was a 1994 Carleton history major, also fascinated by all things military, and probably one of only a handful of people on the planet who would have understood the obscure reference to Louis II and Mohacs (without having to Google it). "Oh right," said Christian, "I see what you mean."

In late 2007, Pete had approached Christian about the possibility of endowing some kind of a scholarship or fellowship at Carleton. Unfortunately, a recession (the wicked one known as The Great Recession) and generally tough economic times put the project on hold for a number of years. It was not until January of 2012 that Pete and Christian got together again. In that meeting, Pete made his declaration about the Battle of Mohacs. The "three noblemen" that he referenced were John Youngblood (John is a Northwestern University Kellogg Business School graduate who has had a career in financial services; he is the founder and president of Gallatin Capital LLC, based in New York City); Danal Abrams (Danal is a Columbia Law School grad who has had a long legal career in both private practice and, for the past 18 years, in the general counsel's office at Moore Capital Management, also in New York City); and yours truly (you know me.) We have all four been the beneficiaries of wonderful families, educational opportunities and just generally fortunate circumstances. We have worked very hard, but we have been fortunate, too. And we know it. So it was time to 'pay it forward.'

We had met and befriended each other ages ago at Carleton. We had played sports together. We had drunk beer together. We had a hell of a good time together. Don't get me wrong, we were good boys. In particular, we were all four the sons of loving mothers, have become the husbands of strong wives (who would give us 'what for' on a moment's notice) and the fathers of daughters, six of them among the four of us – as a result, we have always treated women with respect. In fact, you might even say we have become champions for women. We had gone our separate ways after college, but the friendship has lasted for more than 40 years. And Pete was now determined to coerce his buddies into opening up their wallets to do something worthwhile and everlasting for our beloved Carleton College. The four of us had a conference call with Christian (Danal and Pete are Jewish; Danal once asked, "Should Pete and I be concerned that our primary liaison for this very important undertaking is named Christian?") in August of 2012, then another in November. In those calls, we hashed out the details of what would become the "Four Friends Fellowship." So the boys sucked it up, whipped out their checkbooks, and the game was afoot.

Perhaps the best way to describe the fellowship is to simply quote from the current link on Carleton's website:

"The Four Friends Fellowship was established in 2012 by grants to Carleton from John Youngblood '81, Peter Ross '80, Danal Abrams '80, and Jeff Appelquist ‹80 (collectively, 'Four Friends') in thanks for all the experiences they have had together since meeting at Carleton in the late '70s. In establishing the fellowship, The Four Friends seek to express their fondness for Carleton College and appreciation for the abiding friendships which often begin during college and grow throughout a lifetime. The Fellowship will be awarded annually to that group of two or more Carleton students proposing the most compelling experience.

'Road trips' are often the first thing that come to mind when college students think about shared experiences that deepen friendship. While a trip or journey of some kind might be entirely appropriate and travel has been

funded in previous years, we also strongly encourage proposals for collabora-
tive projects as well. Use your imagination and consider such options as an
art or science project right here at Carleton; the creation and performance of a
musical and/or dramatic work; or a volunteer project in the local community.

"... Projects must include a 'bring-back' component designed to share the
experience with the Carleton community and generate ongoing enthusiasm
for the Four Friends Fellowship... Successful Four Friends Fellowship applicants will collaborate on the development of a group experience that is creative, but feasible. Selection will be based on the following criteria: original-
ity of the idea (including its spirit of adventure and discovery); viability of
the plan and budget; evidence of extensive collaboration in the proposal and
the plan itself (including the potential for bonding among the participants);
the overall quality of the proposal; and the quality of the proposed 'bring-
back' component of the project.

Do not feel constrained when imagining possible experiences that
could be funded, and do not assume that you must already be very close
friends in order to apply for this award. You might wish to explore a friendship or common interest that is just emerging! Think collaboration, creativity
and camaraderie..."

◀━━━━▶

Over the years we have had a lot of fun reviewing, debating and supporting
some really cool projects and experiences. We have typically chosen to fund a
couple of projects per year. In the fellowship's first full year, 2013, we were able
to finance two amazing trips – and two of my all-time favorite Four Friends
adventures. These kids set the bar high for subsequent classes.

Jonathan Kagan-Kans (Carleton class of 2014) and his buddy Marcus
Rider (also '14) ventured to Nassau in the Bahamas, became SCUBA-certified,
and dove with reef sharks. Their cause was to learn more about sharks as "en-
dangered animals with a dangerous reputation." They called their project:
"Sharks Are Friends, Not Food." Jonathan wrote to us before the trip, "I can't
tell you how excited I am by this opportunity. Marcus and I are so thrilled that
you decided to fund our project and we are confident that it will be an experi-

ence that will bring us closer together, but also will bring something valuable back to Carleton. Oh, and we're only a little tiny bit scared of sharks. Thanks again, I can't tell you how much we appreciate you giving us this chance." The guys described what it was like to dive with sharks: "The first moment when you're standing on the edge of the boat looking down, and you see the familiar, sinister, dark forms of sharks cruising by, is disorienting. But once you jump in and submerge, you realize that the sharks are not interested in you. They are simply being. And it is a beautiful thing to understand that something you have been taught to fear your whole life is actually quite majestic. It was exhilarating seeing the sharks up so close with what seemed to be a shared sense of curiosity regarding one another." Jonathan and Marcus went on to produce a wonderful video in conjunction with their efforts, and I loved it (so did the other three friends) – especially with its environmental and endangered-species angle.

Also in the fellowship's first year, we helped two young women take an extraordinary journey. Ellie Schmidt ('14) wrote to us beforehand: "I am incredibly grateful for this chance to use this amazing fellowship! I would love to be able to help this kind of fellowship continue into the future; it is one of a kind and I think helps foster maybe the most important thing in the world – connections with other people! I can't wait to take on this adventure with my best friend." Ellie and her friend, Grace Zahrah ('14), traveled across the American West late in 2013 to create an experimental, loose-narrative film in tribute to their favorite American artists, including Ansel Adams, Georgia O'Keefe, and the Beat poets. They described their journey: "We spent all of our time in parts of the U.S. we'd never seen before. We have both traveled extensively abroad, and so experiencing the strange and beautiful American West was a surprising adventure. One memorable experience was taking a tour through Antelope Canyon, a narrow, beautiful slot canyon shaped by lightning floods. Our tour guide was a Navajo woman named Lulu, who told us about her experience as a tour guide and had stories that were hilarious, sad, and thought-provoking... The canyon itself felt like a cathedral; it was awe-inspiring and felt a bit holy." Ellie and Grace submitted their film to several experimental film festivals, in addition to sharing it with the Carleton community. We were incredibly proud of all four students, and lived vicariously through them as they ventured forth, living their young lives to the fullest, and then giving something back in return. They had gotten us off to a great start.

In 2014, Gina Kabasakalis ('17) and Cassandra Prenn-Vasilakas ('17) back-packed along the traditional route of El Camino de Santiago in Spain in an incredible journey of self-discovery. That same year, Mia Orans ('17) and Sarah Goldman ('17) biked all the way from Connecticut to Nova Scotia and then back again (with a couple of ferry rides along the way.) Their mission was to stay and work at four different farms along the way, in 40-days. I had a chance to meet these four amazing young women at an alumni dinner at Carleton. We all sat together, ate the rubber chicken and soggy peas, and they regaled me with hilarious stories about the reality of extended periods of living in close quarters together. We laughed really hard. *It can get stinky, let's just say that*. Friendships are indeed tested, but they all came out of their experiences with a deeper bond than ever. Mia and Sarah wrote me a thank-you note later. They said, "It was great meeting you this fall, and we wanted to thank you again for supporting our 'four-wheel' bike adventure this past summer. We will truly remember this trip for the rest of our lives and had a great time learning how to milk sheep, harvest garlic and other veggies, fix-a-flat, and bike 50 (!) miles in a day. We also look forward to teaching other Carls how to plan their own bike trip."

Sarah Abdel-Jelil ('16), Gabriela Olvera ('16) and Khuaten Maaneb de Macedo ('16) submitted a really interesting proposal for the 2015 school year, which we funded. They traveled to New Orleans 10 years after the devastation of Hurricane Katrina, with the objective of exploring music as a mode of community healing. Through observation of performances and discussions with musicians, audience members and citizens in the wider community, the students gained a sense of the incredibly important role that music plays in people's lives. But they learned so much more, and were struck by the ongoing racial divisions in New Orleans (and in our country as a whole). Gabby said, "Seeing how federal aid money was given so disproportionately was hard, and that's always in the back of my mind now in classroom discussion. I'm a po-litical science major, and this experience has definitely shaped what I want to do... I want to work in the public sector, hopefully with people who can't afford housing. And after a year or two of working, I'd like to go to graduate school for urban planning." Sarah was similarly inspired: "This experience has just seeped into my unconscious. Seeing the stark divide made me realize I want to work on social justice issues... It has allowed us to be more creative, and to see all these intersections that don't happen in the classroom. On campus, you are in a 'political science' class, or then you go to an 'art' class – in life those things aren't really separate, though. I don't think I would be seeing all of these connections if it weren't for this fellowship."

When asked how she and her friends heard about the Four Friends Fellowship, Mabel Frank ('19) chuckled: "We heard some people talking about it and thought it was too good to be true. The four of us [she and her pals Maya Kassahun ('19), Lynn Barbera ('19) and Brynne Diggins ('19)] formed naturally as a group, and we just started brainstorming ridiculous ideas, talking about everything we could possibly do. From there, we knew we had to take advantage of such an incredible opportunity." These tight friends quickly agreed that "food and feminism have been integral in creating valuable relationships between the four of us," and that they also shared a sense of disdain and frustration toward the overwhelmingly male-dominated food and restaurant industry (and it is). They decided that their "goal is to explore the intersection of food and feminism by interviewing women who own restaurants. We want to hear their stories: What drew them into the food business? What is their relationship with food as both restaurant owners and women? Having these conversations will challenge the notion that women are supposed to *make* you a sandwich, not eat it." And so that is what these four friends did. Along the way, they created a blog that captured their experiences and they made a documentary film. Brava and well done!

Perhaps the most poignant and heart-rending of the Four Friends adventures came in 2016, when Will Hardt ('18), Bonnie Lindgren ('18), Soren Schlassa ('18) and Tina Sieben ('18) embarked on journey to Scotland. They had lost their dear friend and classmate, Zach Brokaw, who was killed in an automobile accident during their sophomore year. They were devastated. They vividly recalled a conversation they had had with Zach when they were freshman. He had suggested that, when the timing was right, the five of them should "set out to see the world." Zach never got the chance, but Will, Bonnie,

Soren and Tina determined that they would honor his memory in a way that he would have loved – they would journey to Scotland and backpack together for 300 miles. Bonnie said, "After Zach died, I watched the movie *The Way*, about a man whose son dies while hiking the El Camino de Santiago in Spain, and the father finishes it for him. I thought a hike like that would be a way for us to memorialize Zach – and planning it together was actually really therapeutic. It gave us something to look forward to and plan for." The students reported after their trek, "We talked a lot about Zach... We did most of our grieving while we planned the trip, so on the trail it was more fun. It was more remembering when he did certain things, funny things we remembered. We had talked to his mom before and carried some of his ashes with us. Most of them we scattered. It was much more of a journey than a vacation..."

Pete Ross had the original vision for the fellowship. When I asked him what was in his mind at that time, he said, "For me, the friendships we cemented at Carleton have deepened and become more meaningful over time. They are to be celebrated. The idea of the fellowship was conceived in that spirit: celebration of good things that have come to pass, while at the same time giving back to the institution that brought us together." When I asked Danal what he remembered about the beginnings of the fellowship, he responded, "No recollection. Too old. However, the basis for it was the four of us had done a zillion things together over the years, but all of these were 'inward' looking in a way that only we and those closest to us could appreciate. The Four Friends was a way to provide an outward expression of the benefits of lifelong friendships, while also acknowledging that Carleton was the wellspring of the whole thing. In addition, it gave us a mid-life initiative that we could all do together. Naming it initially was a particular hoot for us." (We had batted around a number of possible names for the fellowship, some good, others not so good.) John concurred, when asked what he enjoys most about the fellowship: "It has been a really fun thing for us to do together as friends and pretty rewarding to meet the recipients and realize that we have been able to both deepen their friendships and impact their lives in a positive way."

I have always loved the quote from Pierre Teilhard Chardin (whoever the heck that guy was): "The world is round so that friendship may encircle it."

CONCLUSION

"Here is your country. Cherish these natural wonders, cherish the natural resources, cherish the history and romance as a sacred heritage, for your children and your children's children."

— THEODORE ROOSEVELT —

The World Economic Forum is an annual gathering in Davos, Switzerland of movers and shakers in politics, business, science, academe and entertainment. During a luncheon at the January, 2019 meeting, a 16-year-old Swedish climate activist named Greta Thunberg – who gained fame as the organizer of a school strike for climate action outside of the Swedish Parliament building – told the gathered elite of global thought and leadership: "I don't want your hope... I want you to panic... I want you to act as you would in a crisis. I want you to act as if the house is on fire, because it is."

In the United States, a group of teenagers has formed an organization called Zero Hour, which is described as "an environmentally focused, creatively minded and technologically savvy nationwide coalition." The group commenced their campaign with a protest march in July, 2018 at the National Mall in Washington D.C., conducted in concert with sister demonstrations across the nation. Zero Hour's leadership team met with nearly 40 federal lawmakers to explain their platform. Their objective is to inspire other young people to step up, get organized and demand radical action on climate change.

Zero Hour has received financial support and sponsorship offers from dozens of established environmental and advocacy groups. Jamie Margolin, 16, had the original idea for Zero Hour. As the movement grew in strength and momentum she said, "We flipped the scenario as the underdog. We've proven ourselves. We are on the verge of something amazing. We're going to change history."

"... and a little child shall lead them," the book of Isaiah tells us.

◄—————►

Imagine that you are very sick. You feel really poorly, and you have for some time. You hate to admit it, but you know you have mostly brought it upon yourself. You are only 40 years old, but for decades you have smoked a pack of cigarettes a day. Marlboros. You drink too much – Scotch, and lots of it, is your go-to beverage. You eat shitty food in vast quantities. Fast food is your favorite: KFC? Check. Taco Bell? Check. Mac & Don's? Super-sized check. You are overweight; no, correct that, you have become obese. You sleep poorly at night, when you sleep at all. You have that apnea thing going. You are stressed out with a job that you hate and a boss who is a jackass. You are lonely and just generally frustrated with life. The list goes on. But, fortunately, you have the time and the luxury of consulting with 100 doctors about your condition. Of those 100 doctors, 97 of them tell you that your situation is desperate. Unless you make profound changes in your lifestyle, now and with urgency, the outcome is a certainty: you will die (and soon). Now, having received that advice from 97 competent medical professionals, would you listen to the three that told you, "Don't worry – be happy - you'll be just fine."?

The late New York Senator Daniel Patrick Moynihan is supposed to have said: "You are entitled to your own opinion. You are not entitled to your own facts." Second American president and relentless, ever-logical litigating attorney John Adams once observed, "Facts are stubborn things; and whatever may be our wishes, our inclinations, or the dictates of our passions, they cannot alter the state of facts and evidence."

It is a fact that almost unanimously, scientists who have researched and written peer-reviewed articles on the climate crisis agree that it is a crisis; it is mostly man-made; that our situation is dire; and that immediate and dramatic action must take place in order for us to avert the worst outcomes. Here are some additional facts:

- In October of 2018, the United Nations Intergovernmental Panel on Climate Change (the panel was created in 1988 and tasked with synthesizing the conclusions of leading climate scientists, for which it won the 2007 Nobel Peace Prize) delivered a report with input from 91 scientists representing 40 countries. Several small island nations that had participated in the 2015 Paris talks - in which 195 countries agreed to limit increases in global warming to 2 degrees Celsius below preindustrial levels – asked that the intergovernmental panel consider an even lower threshold of 1.5 degrees Celsius. Concern over rising seas prompted the island nations to request that the issue be studied further. The panel agreed that the lower standard should become the new target. Absent a stricter threshold, the study concluded, the world will experience catastrophic environmental and social consequences: vanishing coral reefs (I have seen it with my own eyes in the Great Barrier Reef of Australia), increased drought, larger and more intense wildfires (my own family and many others were tragically impacted by the raging 2018 infernos in California), famine, and human conflict over scarce land, food and water resources. The bottom line, the report concludes, is that we have about a decade to drastically cut greenhouse gases and increase renewable energy sources.

- The congressionally-mandated Fourth National Climate Assessment was issued in November 2018. Representing the work of 13 federal agencies and some 300 scientists, the report runs to more than 1,000 pages and breaks down the impacts of climate change across America. David Easterling, a scientist at the National Oceanic and Atmospheric Administrations and one of the report's authors, states that global warming will "threaten the health and well-being of the American people" and "disrupt many areas of life, exacerbating existing challenges and revealing new risks." Absent immediate and dramatic action to reduce global greenhouse-gas emissions, infrastructure and ecosystems will be damaged across the U.S. (as outlined in the book, bird species in Hawaii and pheasant populations in South Dakota, among many other members of the animal kingdom, are seriously affected by environmental factors); extreme weather events will become much more commonplace; disease will spread; agricultural output will be reduced; trade will be disrupted; and the U.S. economy will lose hundreds of billions of dollars by the end of this century. President Trump's response to his own scientists? "I don't believe it."

- An analysis published in the journal *Science* in January 2019 concludes that the world's oceans are heating up much more rapidly than previously estimated. Among the places that I have covered in this book, warming and rising seas are happening in the Indian Ocean, the Atlantic, the Pacific, and in iconic cities like Venice. It is happening all around us. The melting Arctic icecap alone dumps approximately 14,000 tons of water every second into the Earth's oceans which has, more than any other factor, contributed to rising waters. Over time, the oceans have been an amazing buffer, and have slowed the effects of global warming by absorbing more than one quarter of greenhouse gases that are pumped into the atmosphere. But the resulting surging water temperatures create havoc by decimating marine ecosystems, creating longer-lasting and more powerful hurricanes, and raising sea levels.

- In September of 2016, in a comprehensive analysis of outdoor air quality around the globe, the World Health Organization concluded that 92 percent of human beings breathe what is classified as unhealthy air (defined as air with concentrations of fine particulate matter above 10 micrograms per 35.3 cubic feet). Dozens of scientists participated in the study over 18 months; they gathered data from satellites, air-transport models, and ground monitors in more than 3,000 worldwide locations. Approximately three million deaths per year – as a result of cardiovascular, pulmonary and other diseases – are linked to poor air quality; one-third of those deaths are in Europe and the Americas, the rest in the Western Pacific and Southeast Asia.

- The Global Carbon Project, a group of 100 scientists from more than 50 academic and research institutions, reported in December 2018 that global greenhouse emissions accelerated in 2018. In the U.S., carbon dioxide emissions increased by an estimated 3.4 percent. Scientists attributed the surge to an unexpected and significant uptick in oil usage around the world. People are buying more cars and driving them farther. The resulting emissions spike is jarring, and makes it highly unlikely the U.S. will meet its pre-Paris, Obama-era commitment to reduce greenhouse gases by 26 to 28 percent below 2005 levels by 2025. The report compared the spike in emissions to a "speeding freight train."

- In February 2019 the National Oceanic and Atmospheric Administration reported that the number of billion-dollar weather events has more than doubled in the U.S. in recent years. Over the last 40 years, the U.S. has experienced 241 billion-dollar (adjusted for inflation) weather and climate events. Up until 2013, those disasters took place an average of six times per year. In the last five years, however, there has been an average of more than 12 catastrophic events annually. In 2018, there were 14 separate billion-dollar weather and climate events, which cost a total of $91 billion and took almost 250 lives. Three 2018 events alone cost a combined $73 billion: Hurricanes Michael and Florence, and the raging Western wildfires. But the worst year on record was not 2018. In 2017, Hurricanes Harvey, Irma and Maria, along with wildfires and other disasters, cost the United States $306 billion in total damages. My friend and I took a wild sailboat ride in a Force Nine gale in the wake of Hurricanes Maria and Jose in the fall of '17.

- NASA scientists announced in February 2019 that the Earth's unmistakable warming trend continues. The average surface temperature in 2018 represented the fourth highest in 140 years of record-keeping. The five hottest years on record have been the last five. Since 2001, 18 of the 19 warmest years on record have occurred. NASA scientist Gavin A. Schmidt, director of the Goddard Institute for Space Studies, said, "We're no longer taking about a situation where global warming is something in the future. It's here. It's now."

In my introduction, I said that climate-change deniers give me heartburn, and they do – they frustrate me (I'm quite sure I frustrate them, too.) On the other hand, I have always appreciated people who take a skeptical view of life; I myself have always been one to question conventional wisdom. I have acknowledged that climate science is complex, and it is. I am certainly no expert. There are many moving parts, and it is very appropriate that we all ask lots of questions. Recent polling by Yale University shows that 73 percent – the highest number in a decade of polling - of the American population now accepts that climate change is real and needs to be addressed. That's great, lots of people have come around, but it also means that more than one person in five is still not convinced. So how do we convince those people? I suspect that it is not by dismissing or condescending to them. Nor is it by questioning their intelligence, or their integrity, or their patriotism, or by attempting to browbeat them into submission with the power or our argument, or with scare tactics. None of those approaches are fair, nor do they represent the right way to treat anyone, even those with whom we may vehemently disagree. When you do those things, folks tend to just dig in their heels deeper. They feel personally attacked; they can't help but see the problem as partisan or political.

In their book, *The Way Forward: How Cities, Businesses, and Citizens can Save the Planet*, authors Michael Bloomberg and Carl Pope address this issue, and in a way that resonates with me. They say, "One of the most important [actions each of us can take] is also one of the simplest: doing a better job of communicating with friends, family, and neighbors – not only about the nature of the problem, but also about the benefits of the solutions.... The best way to reach skeptics is for more people to tell climate success stories. How taking action improves our lives in the here and now. How it makes us healthier. How it improves our life span. How is saves us money... How it helps those in poverty connect with job opportunities. How it helps us compete in the world. How it strengthens the economy... We will never win hearts and minds simply by trying to convince people to stop eating meat or give up their cars, but we can win them by demonstrating how fighting climate change is good for them, for their families, for their communities." Hear hear. I have always believed that the world can be changed through the power of telling positive stories. Let's have a civil conversation and see if we can't win over some more hearts and minds.

I am a hypocrite. I have written an entire book that in significant part concerns the perils of climate change, and yet there is so much more that I could and should be doing in my own life. I don't drive much, primarily because I work out of a home office, but my vehicle is bigger and less fuel efficient than it should be. I am fascinated by the potential for electric vehicles, am following developments closely, and would very much like to get into an electric car at some point. I fly all over creation in connection with my work. Jetliners are incredible polluters, and I feel complicit. That's a hard one for me and anyone else who needs to travel to do their job. Oh, but for a bullet train powered by the sun. I have learned in the course of researching this book about how the elaborate process of putting red meat on the table negatively impacts the planet. Red-meat production requires huge tracts of land to raise cattle, and it emits significant greenhouse gases. The World Economic Forum published a report in January 2019 that estimated global greenhouse-gas emissions would be reduced by one quarter, and deaths from overconsumption of red and processed meats would fall by five percent in more affluent countries, if people simply switched to other sources of protein besides red meat. Tucking into that delicious, medium-rare porterhouse, or that sizzling, crispy bacon too often can cause a whole range of health issues, from diabetes to heart disease to cancer. The stuff just isn't good for you, but I have always loved it so. This was a tough one, but here I have made a significant change, drastically reducing my consumption of steak, bacon and other processed meats. I used to eat steak probably twice a week; now, perhaps once or twice a month. But I am still guilty in other ways. I spend too much time letting the hot shower pound on my back. I stand for excessive periods of time in front of an open refrigerator. When it gets cold in Minnesota during the winter, which it does (remember the three standards: cold, really cold, and fucking cold), we turn up the thermostat. Not too high, but probably higher than it should be. I don't always turn out the lights, or recycle every recyclable. I am a hypocrite. But awareness that one has a problem is the first step in dealing with the problem. And so I am, as I suspect most of my readers are too, a continuing work in progress.

Some people despair that the actions of one individual can't possibly make a difference when it comes to climate change. In theory, that is no doubt true. But if everyone had that attitude, we would all be screwed. If, on the other hand, we all decide that each of us can make a difference, then that is powerful stuff. All of us collectively can indeed change history. What are some things that we should be doing? For most people, our biggest carbon footprint comes from transportation emissions. Passenger vehicles account for 60 percent of the carbon pollution caused by transportation. Airplanes account for 9 percent. Getting everyone into an electric vehicle would be a huge deal. Better yet, how about foregoing a vehicle entirely? (My daughter Luci is determined to never own a car in her lifetime.) How about walking or biking to work? Or taking public transportation? Around the house, do you have the choice of a utility company that generates power through wind or solar? If so, hire those guys. Or install solar panels in your home. Seal air leaks to cut your heating and air conditioning bills. Buy energy-efficient appliances. Do the wash only when necessary. Use cold water in the washing machine and dry your clothes on low heat. Light-emitting diode (LED) bulbs are putting incandescent bulbs out of business. Let the yard go native; mowing pollutes the air. Cut back on meat consumption. Go local and organic; eat your fruits and vegetables; buy in bulk. All of these steps will help.

But I would submit that the most important thing we can be doing as individuals is to just make sure we participate actively in the discussion. Communicate your views on climate change, in a civil, respectful way. Read and study. Learn all you can. Write a letter to the editor, or to your senator or representative. Blog. Heck, write a book about it, for crying out loud. Contribute to the Sierra Club, or the Nature Conservancy, or any other organization you know of that is doing good work around environmental causes. Register to vote. Cast your ballot. Vote for candidates at the local, regional, state and, especially, at the national level, who take this issue seriously and are prepared to use their power for the good. Just be a thinking, caring, involved citizen – that's the best advice I can give.

I said at the end of the first chapter that perhaps there is reason to hope. I do believe there is reason to hope, and here's why. Martin Luther King Jr. once said (in a quote that was not original to him), "The arc of the moral universe is long, but it bends toward justice." My deep study and sense of the 'long arc of history' tell me that we may just come around in time to avert the worst of climate change outcomes. We have overcome enormous odds before. In America, our nation was humbly born in a bloody revolution against a seemingly invincible foe, the British Empire. Our country was torn apart by a terrible civil war, but the union was preserved and the evil that was the institution of slavery was destroyed. A little later in our history, women finally won the right to vote. My own parents lived through the Great Depression. We fought one world war, and then another, when freedom-loving nations around the globe united as allies against the mighty scourge of totalitarianism. We are still fighting for civil rights in America, but we have made progress. Just a few years ago, it would have been inconceivable that gay marriage would ever be legal and accepted by a majority of Americans, but now it is. And in a climate-specific example, when scientists identified a dangerously thinning ozone layer in the 1980s, the nations of the world took action. In 1987, a group of countries agreed in the Montreal Protocol to eliminate damaging chlorofluorocarbons that were releasing chlorine and bromine into the atmosphere and destroying the ozone layer. The United States had taken the lead in the process, drafting the treaty that was ultimately adopted. As an outcome, experts say the upper ozone layer over the Northern Hemisphere will have repaired itself by the 2030s; the Antarctic ozone should be fully healthy in the 2060s. This is extremely good news, because it proves that we can come together and act globally to address climate-related issues. All of these challenges, in some cases for extended periods of time, seemed insurmountable. But as the economist Rudi Dornbusch once astutely observed, "Things take longer to happen than you think they will, and then they happen faster than you thought they could."

There is much that is happening that is good. I mentioned that young people around the world are engaged and mobilizing. Primatologist and conservationist Jane Goodall said in a *Time* magazine essay in early 2019, "My greatest reason for hope for our future is the passion of young people. When we listen to them and empower them, the next generation is desperate to protect nature. Unfortunately so many children are unable to spend time in nature because of education systems rooted in technology and geared only to the demands of a materialistic world... Today in some 80 countries, groups are taking action to heal the harms we have inflicted.... The challenges we face are daunting, but nature is resilient, the human intellect incredible. So now, as our youth join forces to tackle problems we have created, let us give them the support they need and help them in their fight to save the natural world – on which we ourselves depend."

Many experts agree that the most important step that can be taken globally is for governments to put a price on pollution, thereby incentivizing polluters to pollute less and move to cleaner forms of energy. This is of course controversial and a very tough sell politically, especially in the United States (voters in Washington State rejected a November 2018 ballot initiative that would have imposed America's first tax on carbon-dioxide pollution.) But other countries are leading the way. Canadian Prime Minister Justin Trudeau, also quoted in *Time*, says, "Pricing pollution is the single most powerful way to cut emissions while driving economic growth. Since doing so in 1991, Sweden has grown its economy and cut its emissions by 60 percent and 25 percent, respectively. Here at home, the four provinces with a price on pollution in 2017 led the country in economic growth, while Canada led the G-7. As of 2019, it is no longer free to pollute anywhere in Canada. Lower emissions, cleaner air, a stronger economy. The science and economics behind pollution pricing are settled. In the international fight against climate change, a national price on pollution should be the norm. Indeed, it is already a necessity."

If some national governments are lacking the courage and political will to act, hundreds of units of government, businesses, communities (such as the seaside towns in Mexico's Baja California Peninsula), philanthropies and other institutions (such as Carleton College) are stepping into the breach. After President Trump vowed to pull the U.S. out of the Paris climate accord, 16 states and Puerto Rico committed to uphold the terms of the agreement anyway. New Democratic governors in seven states that are not a part of this climate alliance have identified climate change as a major problem. Several state governors have pledged to move their states to 100 percent carbon-free electricity. In California, which if it were an independent nation would have the sixth-largest economy in the world, under the leadership of Governor Jerry Brown (since retired), a broad effort is underway to cut emissions across the board and from all sources by 40 percent from 1990 levels by 2030. Brown has been a key impetus behind the Under2 Coalition, which is an alliance of 175 cities, states and other entities representing 35 nations and more than one billion people. The Under2 Coalition is committed to reducing carbon emissions, whether the U.S. participates in the Paris accords or not. Governor Brown has said, "In California, facts and science still matter."

Businesses are stepping up. Corporate investments in wind and solar power grew 13 percent in 2018 from the year before to a total of $16 billion. That number should double again in 2019. Dozens of Fortune 500 companies (among them, AT&T, Apple, General Motors, Google, Microsoft, Nestle and Walmart) have invested billions of dollars in wind and solar to power their own operations. The further good news here is that in just the last five years, the average cost of solar power worldwide has decreased by 65 percent; the cost of onshore wind is down by 15 percent. Microsoft now deploys wind and solar power that is equal to half the demand of its global data centers. Brian Janous, Microsoft's general manager of energy, was quoted in the *New York Times* in the summer of 2018: "We didn't intend to do this as a statement about Paris, though it has become a statement that we're definitely still in... But with how fast wind and solar prices have fallen, we see this as something that makes financial sense." More than twenty Fortune 500 companies have said that in the next few years they will power 100 percent of their electrical requirements with wind and solar. Even oil companies, believe it or not, are going green – if you can't beat 'em, join 'em. In September 2018, ExxonMobil, Chevron and Occidental Petroleum became part of the Oil and Gas Climate Initiative (OGCI), a coalition of large energy companies which is providing $1 billion to fund research and reduce emissions. The companies of OGCI have collectively committed to reducing their own methane emissions by one-third over the next six years. Whether I fully trust these guys, I am unsure, but at least it's a start.

On the macro scale, the news is not all bad, either. In December of 2018, representatives from close to 200 countries - including a reluctant U.S. eager to protect its own interests - met in Katowice, Poland to hammer out a deal that keeps the Paris climate accord alive. The diplomats agreed to terms that require every country to adhere to a uniform set of standards to measure emissions. Each nation will also use a detailed, standard set of rules to track the success or failure of its own climate policies. The agreement calls on countries to voluntarily accelerate plans to reduce emissions before a further round of talks in 2020. The meeting in Katowice was contentious, but in the end an agreement was struck. Even the U.S. signed on the dotted line. Many attendees believe the deal does not go far enough, that it is too little, too late. Will that be the case, or will the long arc of history finally bend our way and good things happen faster than we ever thought they could?

Perhaps there is reason to hope.

ACKNOWLEDGMENTS

To the Fab Four Wonder Women of the literary and design world, who have been with me on all five books: Anne Hodgson, my editor; Dawn Carlson, my proofreader; Emily Rodvold, of Lift Creative, my designer; and Dara Beevas, of Wise Ink, my publisher: you are all four beautiful inside and out, and talented in ways that I am not. This book is so much better for your efforts (and patience). It takes a village, doesn't it? Thankyou.

To the three members of the Four Friends Fellowship team who are not me, and their amazing spouses: John and Jennifer Youngblood; Pete and Nancy Ross; and Danal and Wendy Abrams. What a journey it's been. I love you guys, till death do us part.

To the memory of my dear mother Doris, to my father Carl, my brother Tom and my sister Joan, thanks for being my wonderful first immediate family. To daughters Anna, Lucia and, especially, the woman who (profoundly lacking in judgment, some might say) accompanied me on many of these death-defying adventures, and to whom I dedicated this book, my wife Faith, thanks for being my wonderful second immediate family. I love you all with all my heart.

PHOTO CREDITS, ET CETERA

Front cover photo: the author at the Gates of the Rocky Mountains, near Mann Gulch, between Great Falls and Helena, Montana, July 2015. Photo by Jack Uldrich.

Front flap: the author fishing in the Gulf of Mexico, near Cottrell Key, off of Key West, Florida, on his 60th birthday, January 29, 2018. Photo by Faith Appelquist.

Back flap: the author sailing *High Cotton* in the Atlantic Ocean, off of Newport, Rhode Island, October 2017. Photo by John Youngblood.

Back cover photos, starting top left and moving left to right: the author as a 24-year-old Marine infantry officer, near Pohang, South Korea, December 1982. Photo by First Lieutenant James Westenhoff; the author on Mount Kilimanjaro, Tanzania, Africa, at 15,000 feet, January 2017. Photo by a fellow climber; the author and wife Faith at the city of Machu Picchu, Peru, January 2019. Photo by Rebecca Elliott; the author (left), daughter Lucia, wife Faith, and daughter Anna at the Great Barrier Reef, Australia, November 2018. Photo by Joe Giles; the author (far left) with Carleton College sophomores on Cemetery Hill, Gettysburg, Pennsylvania, March 2015. Photo by Rachel Leatham; Tom Appelquist (left) Abigail Rethwisch, Denise Paulson, Richard Paulson, Faith Appelquist and the author at the Santa Fe Opera, Santa Fe, New Mexico,

August 2016. Photo by a friendly stranger; the author and Jack Uldrich on the banks of the Missouri River, near Great Falls, Montana, July 2016. Photo by a friendly stranger; the author and John Magnusson, on the western shores of Iceland, August 2018. Photo by John's iPhone, perched on a rock; John Young-blood (left), Faith Appelquist, the author, and Danal Abrams, hunting pheasants near Estelline, South Dakota, October 2016. Photo by Andy Hansen; the Four Friends, left to right, John Youngblood, the author, Pete Ross, and Danal Abrams at the Darioush Winery, Napa Valley, California, April 2016. Photo by Nancy Hochman Ross.

In a few places in the book, I have borrowed slightly revised passages from three of my previous books, *Sacred Ground, Wisdom Is Not Enough,* and *The Great Wild West.* In other words, I have more or less plagiarized myself, but at least I'm admitting it and not trying to pull a fast one. If the previous books had been bestsellers I would have thought twice, but they weren't so I didn't. I hope the reader will not mind. In addition, for a variety of reasons but, most importantly, because I am lazy, I have also Americanized the spellings throughout. This will be particularly noticeable to those people who are reading the Icelandic chapter and who happen to be fluent in Old Norse or Icelandic. Those folks will curse me. On the other side of the coin, most of my readers, I believe, will neither notice nor care. Any factual errors or other mistakes in the book are my responsibility alone.